**WITHDRAWN
UTSA LIBRARIES**

STORY UNUSED

STORY UNUSED

A Correspondent in the Far East
1963-67

by Arthur Cook

London . George Allen & Unwin Ltd
Ruskin House   Museum Street

FIRST PUBLISHED IN 1971

This book is copyright under the Berne Convention. All rights reserved. Apart from any fair dealing for the purpose of private study, research, criticism or review, as permitted under the Copyright Act, 1956, no part of this publication may be reproduced, stored in retrieval system, or transmitted, in any form or by any means, electronic, electrical, chemical, mechanical, optical, photocopying, recording or otherwise, without the prior permission of the copyright owner. Enquiries should be addressed to the Publishers.

© Arthur Cook 1971

ISBN 0 04 950013 9

PRINTED IN GREAT BRITAIN
in 11 point Baskerville
BY UNWIN BROTHERS LIMITED
WOKING AND LONDON

Contents

		page	
	PROLOGUE		11
1.	INDIAN MYTH		20
	The Indo-Pakistani War – September 1965		20
2.	THE CALM BEFORE		56
	Return to the Far East and the foundation of the Malaysian Federation – September 1963		58
	Vietnam, the first visit – September 1963		63
	American 'advisers' in action – October 1963		67
	Burning of the Buddhist monks – October 1963		78
3.	ROUND TRIP		83
	Fight with British officialdom – Singapore, June 1964		89
	Strange meeting with President Sukarno – Tokyo, January 1964		94
	Robert Kennedy fails as 'peace' envoy – Tokyo, Manila and Kuala Lumpur – January 1964		105
4.	LAOTIAN MEETING		122
	War on the Plain of Jars – Laos, May 1964		141
5.	UNPEACEFUL TEMPLES		148
	Indonesian-Malaysian 'peace' talks – Bangkok, February 1964		152
6.	THE INNOCENTS		158
	Vietnam's struggle for peace. Military crisis. The farce of American-backed 'democracy' – Vietnam, 1964		160
	The bombing of North Vietnam – February 1965		163
	Landing of the Leathernecks – March 1965		166
	Refugees from American bombing. With the Vietcong in the Delta. Aboard an aircraft carrier in the Gulf of Tonkin – April 1965		173
	The battle for food. The River War. Night attack over the Delta – May 1965		183
	American dollars for the Vietcong. Death whilst dining		190
	In an American bombing raid – June 1965		197
7.	JUNGLE WAR		209
	Indonesian 'invasion' of Malaya – Malaysia, 1964–1965		209
	In a jet-fighter strike against the invaders – Singapore and Malaya, December 26th 1964		210
	The jungle war – Borneo, January 1965		214

STORY UNUSED

8. MEETINGS IN CEYLON — 225
Mrs Bandaranaike; a woman's craving for power – Ceylon, March 1965 — 227
Emil Savundra; a bizarre encounter – Colombo, July 1966 — 235

9. THE BREAKUP — 239
Warning Malaysia, trouble on horizon – July 16th 1965 — 241
Attacked by Tunku Abdul Rahman as 'enemy of Malaysia' – July 21st 1965 — 242
The trouble arrives; Singapore expelled from federation – August 9th 1965 — 244

10. END OF A DREAM — 248
Revolution in Indonesia; a break into Jakarta – October 1965 — 250
The ruins of Sukarno's empire. Facing the British army in Indonesian Borneo. Bali. Sukarno's Japanese wife – Indonesia, 1966 — 252
Sukarno's final downfall – Jakarta, February–March 1967 — 270

11. HONG KONG — 275
The world of Suzie Wong. British ships to North Vietnam – Hong Kong, February 1966 — 280

12. THE LAST PLEA — 283
Buddhist rebellion in Vietnam. Nuns burn with the monks — 285
War comes to Hue – Vietnam, May–June 1966 — 292

13. POLITICIANS, RIGHT AND LEFT — 296
Edward Heath, January 1966 — 296
Denis Healey, April 1967 — 303

EPILOGUE — 308
INDEX — 310

Illustrations

1.	The Indo-Pakistan war of 1965. *facing page*	64
2.	Pakistani airmen	65
	Pakistani family in the ruins of a house	65
3.	A Buddhist monk commits ritual suicide	96
4.	Ngo Dinh Diem, President of South Vietnam	97
	Robert Kennedy with President Sukarno	97
5.	Soldiers of the Pathet Lao forces	128
	Evacuees from the Plain of Jars	128
6.	Vietnamese girl during the battle for Dong Xoai	129
7.	Vietnamese mother with dead child	160
8.	Body of a girl killed during an airstrike	161
	Two Vietnamese farmers during a South Vietnamese attack	161
9.	Civilians caught in a jungle battle	192
10.	South Vietnamese searching for Vietcong guerillas	193
	Two guerillas flushed from a flooded paddy	193
11.	A Long line of US helicopters	224
	A US supply helicopter unloading	224
12.	Mrs Sirimavo Bandaranaika	225
13.	Tunku Abdul Rahman, Malaysian Prime Minister	256
	Lee Kuan Yew, Prime Minister of Singapore	256
14.	Corporal Michael O'Donaghue in Borneo	257
15.	Arthur Cook in Borneo	288
16.	Buddhist leader Thich Tri Quang in Hue	289
	Nguyan Cao Ky, and wife	289

Prologue

I could hear the sound of heavy breathing. Gradually it became louder, but my dazed mind was not registering what it was. My body was numb; my brain might not have been there. Only the sound of the deep sucking in and blowing out of air existed, floating somewhere around me, cloudlike.

Was it seconds or minutes before my eyes opened? Certainly, at first, nothing distinguishable came through the fog, nothing connected. Nothing existed but the breathing sounds and the vague, cloudlike floating.

Slowly – but again the process was timeless – the shape in front of my eyes began to take on form: a massive bush of grey whiskers stood out from a face I dimly remembered. Surmounting the shock of hair which practically hid the features was a lace skullcap, white and beautifully worked. The heavy breathing became more real and it came from somewhere among the whiskers. My brain was struggling. I knew this, but I could do nothing to help it. That part where the memory lay was pounding in an effort to help me. But what was 'me'? A dream would have been more tangible.

Then memory responded: this was the face into which I had looked as the needle was plunged into my arm. A second, a minute, an hour or a year before? I had no way of knowing. But my eyes were focusing. They turned sideways to see a syringe poised over my arm again; I watched the needle enter the flesh, but there was no feeling; my brain was crying out words, but they would not come to my lips. A second syringe appeared in the hand I looked at with horror and the needle penetrated yet again before I was conscious of a voice, my own, saying, 'Please, no more, no more!'

'It's all right now, it's all right now.' From among the whiskers came the words, but they sounded frightened, not reassuring. The whiskers were closer to me now and I could feel the breathing on my face; a hand covered my forehead and I felt it hot as the voice said once more, 'Yes, it's all right now'.

The whiskers and skullcap moved from my line of vision and

my eyes began to focus on what was beyond. There were shapes and, as when a camera lens is turned, the picture cleared. A dozen faces were peering at me, but not a word was spoken; some mouths hung open and from dark skins, patched with grey, eyes stared at me as though watching a ghost. I stared back as they stood motionless. The clouds began to disperse and I felt the first tingles of blood pulsing through my limbs. Slowly my head turned as I took in the scene: to my right someone was kneeling, holding my wrist, and to the left knelt another dusky-faced man holding the other wrist. Somehow, among the crush of bodies, was a third, bending over with a stethoscope at my heart and the bewhiskered man was kneeling with still another syringe poised at the ready.

Yes, feeling was returning. I could sense it in my arms, my legs, my body, but it was one of intense cold. For minutes more the faces and bodies obscured the sight of anything else, but then the man with the stethoscope spoke, the two holding my pulses stood up and the dreaded syringe was taken away. I was lying on my back on a tiled floor, stripped of all my clothes except my brief nylon underpants. The tiled floor! It was coming back: that was the last thing I had seen, hurtling towards me as the world had blacked out within three seconds of the bewhiskered medical orderly jabbing the needle into me – an inoculation against cholera.

I tried to move but my limbs were powerless. Another man bent over me: 'Don't try to move,' he was saying. 'You must rest'. I looked at the face to see an almost black skin which was now ashen pale. It was the doctor who had smiled disbelievingly when I had told him of a reaction from a previous cholera inoculation. Now he was shaking like a leaf.

For perhaps fifteen minutes I lay on the cold floor, trying to raise myself, but sinking back as the doctor said time and again, 'You must rest'. The frightened faces had disappeared from the room one by one; now only the doctor, sitting at his desk smoking and stubbing out cigarettes with trembling fingers, and the bewhiskered orderly who stood forever watching me, remained. My eyes travelled around the room and found the clock on the wall which my memory was now telling me should be there; from the upside-down view I made out the hands as pointing to five minutes past three. It had been just after two o'clock when I had walked into that room, I was remembering; perhaps ten minutes had been taken up with my explanations and the doctor's assurances that no harm could come to me. It could only be in my imagination that I would react to the vaccine, he had said, and I was remembering my final words as I capitulated to the senior and expert knowledge of a member of the medical profession: 'Well, so long as you know what you are doing'. Then had come the needle, the realization that I was pitching forward from the chair – oblivion. What had happened in all this time?

I was to find out, but now the Pakistani doctor was in no state to hold a clinical discussion and even more loathe to admit that some small but dangerous chink or lapse in his training had all but left a corpse on his hands. To me at that particular time the greatest lapse was that, lying on the tiled floor, I was perished from the cold. I am sure I could have stayed there for another hour whilst the doctor contemplated the near disaster and the orderly stood by speechless. After all, it had been his hand which had plunged that first needle in.

Somehow, I lifted myself into a sitting position and the orderly hurriedly helped me, half crawling, to the chair and up into it. 'My clothes,' I said, pointing to the slacks and shirt on the other side of the room, and the orderly, now out of his apparent semi-coma, brought them. He helped me into them but I was still frozen. 'Blanket,' I said. I could not command, my voice like my body was still not fully alive. The blanket was brought and for another half hour I sat with the chain smoking and twitching doctor occasionally watching me and saying, 'You must rest'.

In time the urge came, 'Cigarette', I said and the orderly jumped into action once again. Smilingly, as if in wonderment, he lit it for me; twice I drew on it but hated the taste and let it burn away between my fingers. The clock's hands were showing four o'clock and I was feeling strong enough to speak. 'Doctor,' I said, 'I came here for a cholera certificate, may I please have it? I wish to leave.'

Startled, the doctor turned to me. 'Leave,' he said, 'You cannot leave. The ambulance is waiting to take you to hospital, where we will keep you under observation for a few days.'

Hospital. Observation. The words were anathema to me. It is just as much a part of a foreign correspondent's life to stay out of such places as it is to find himself in situations which might lead to such an eventuality. But hospital and observation in a Pakistani hospital in Rawalpindi, even the mere suggestion horrified me. I'd seen the insides of countless hospitals in Asia, the Middle East and Africa but only as a visitor. Grubby bed linen, horrible smells and the most unhygienic operating theatres, from which bloody swabs and bandages were thrown out of windows to the delight of millions of flies. No, not for me! I was weak, I knew, but not so weak that I should stay in the clutches of the medical system in Rawalpindi. It had done a lot of damage already, although I knew not quite what. My only and urgent thought at this moment was to create a vast distance between me and this room in the shortest possible time.

My mind was flashing back to Singapore, eighteen or so months before. An essential part of a correspondent's equipment are his medical documents, more important than his air travel credit card or the store of travellers cheques and foreign currency, mostly dollars, for their colour was magic everywhere, and just as important as the visas which could fill a passport in six months. Inoculations against typhoid, typhus, yellow fever, cholera and a few more of the hazards which might beset a globetrotter: I had certificates for them all. I even had one announcing the fact that I had been immunized against the plague in Vietnam. Periodical checks had to be made to see that the validity of the certificates had not expired; just one out of date could easily lead to two weeks quarantine – as has happened to colleagues of mine – in countries one would not choose for a holiday, and to unenthusiastic cables from ones editor in London. Vaccinations against smallpox last for three years, other inoculations for periods of from five years down to one. Only one was any real nuisance: cholera, inoculations and certificates had to be renewed every six months.

Over the years so many pints of different vaccines had been pumped into me that I had become immune even to the immediate effects which make so many uncomfortable. But the cholera shots had begun to hurt. Perhaps I had had between twenty and thirty of them and one, whose effects I had put down to a dirty needle in Borneo two years earlier, had left me with a vastly swollen and painful arm for a week. The shot in Singapore was disastrous. Within hours I was twisted into shapes which would have made a film hunchback look attractive; for days I was propped on a bed with twenty or more cushions and pillows supporting every tiny part of me that might move, and every move, however slight, was agony.

Of course, my doctor was alarmed. Dear John, huge and teddybearlike and great fun at a party, no doubt a brilliant medico too, appeared whitefaced at my bedside. He repeated the visits every few hours until I finally straightened myself out and the excruciating pain subsided. But like so many doctors, John did not deem it necessary to tell the patient the details of what had, or might have caused such an unusual and unpretty occurrence. Over a brandy, when the crisis was well in the background, John announced, 'Spasms, old man, I don't think I'll give you any more cholera shots. Just let me know when you need them and I'll keep you supplied with certificates.' Then John did let me into his confidence. As a civilian doctor he was attached to the British forces in Singapore and he said, 'Do you know, old man, the cholera vaccine we have here is the wrong type for the local cholera, it's just a waste of time giving it to the troops.'

'Spasms' was the only explanation with which I was equipped when I walked into the clinic of the doctor in Rawalpindi that Saturday morning, September 25th, 1965. Pakistan's war with India was over and I wanted to get back to my base, and home, in Singapore. As always I had checked my medical documents, they were all in order except the one for cholera, which had expired two days before, and John was not near to supply me with another; he was back in Singapore and I knew there was no way through that airport with an out-of-date cholera certificate. I had thought back on the dingy clinic I went to once in Dar es Salaam when it was in Tanganyika: a yellow fever shot was my requirement then and the medical orderly, quite straightfaced, had pointed to a handwritten notice on the wall. 'Yellow fever inoculations,' it read, 'With vaccine, £1.

Without vaccine £1½'. I paid my one pound and had the shot. Amusing as the notice had been at first glance, it was shattering to realize how, in a government clinic, all the efforts and money spent by the World Health Organization could be frittered away.

Fear of the needle is, of course, widespread across the world and false medical certificates have done much to spread diseases from one country to another. But it was not with any thought that I would be spreading cholera that I entered the clinic in Rawalpindi. I didn't expect to find such a notice on the wall as had been presented to me in Dar es Salaam. I just wanted to get home to Singapore and felt it would be wise to explain the effects of a previous cholera shot and the fact that my own doctor would give me no more.

'What type of spasms?' asked the doctor and I twisted myself into some sort of incongruous shape until I felt ridiculous. 'Hmmm,' said the doctor and it was obvious he was trying to hide a smile. 'I will have to consult the superintendent, but I'm sure you are worrying about nothing. Would you please come back after lunch.'

It was a smiling and confident man who greeted me as I walked into his office later, but I had been thinking over lunch that if John had decided to give me no more inoculations there must be good reason, and anyway, I did not want a few more days of those spasms or whatever they were called. The doctor, however, was adamant, even when I explained the previous symptoms yet again. 'The superintendent says we cannot issue a certificate unless we administer the vaccine,' he told me in his lilting, Welsh-like accent. 'You have nothing to fear. We will take all precautions.' He called the medical orderly and the magnificently bearded figure in its white skullcap and flowing, embroidered gown hurried into the room. He nicked the skin of my arm and rubbed it violently, gazed at it for at least four seconds and looked at me gleefully. 'Test dose,' he announced. 'You see, no effects.' It was then that I capitulated: 'Well,' I said, 'as long as you know what you are doing. . . .'

Now I sat in the chair, shrouded in a blanket, and my mind was made up. 'Doctor,' I said. 'I came here for a certificate and have had the inoculation. I don't know what you've done, but

I have no intention of going to your hospital. I need your ambulance, but to take me to my hotel. Please let me have the certificate.'

The doctor began: 'But you must be under observation; we need to keep you . . .' and I cut him short with, 'Please, the certificate.' He began again: 'It is very dangerous, you . . .', and I interrupted again. 'What has happened to me?' I demanded, and his figures drummed on the desk nervously. It took him seconds to reply and he did not look at me. 'You have had a reaction,' he said.

Despite my weak state I was becoming furious. Like John, here was another doctor refusing to explain what had obviously, in my language, been something drastic enough to be more than a 'reaction'. It may have been good medical explanation but not good enough for me. 'Would you please give me a letter explaining it,' I asked.

In their own tongue the doctor and the orderly had a short and agitated conversation. The orderly left to return five minutes later and handed the doctor a badly typed letter on paper obviously torn from a school-type exercise book. With the certificate it was passed to me and I read quickly the words: 'He experienced reaction . . . six injections of adrenalin, three of coramine . . .'. There followed the names of other stimulants, but I had read enough.

'What was the reaction, in plain language please,' I demanded. 'What has happened?' The doctor's hands were shaking again and his face was turning that strange shade of grey on an almost negroid colouring. He lit another cigarette with difficulty and turned to me; he inhaled deeply three times and spoke. 'Your heart stopped,' he said. 'We had great difficulty in restarting it.'

I lay on my bed back in Flashmans Hotel. There had been more protests, but that is where the ambulance took me. God, I thought, what a stupid way to die! Over the previous three weeks hundreds of Indian heavy guns, mortar shells, strafing Indian jet planes and the blasting of Indian Centurion tanks, not to mention the ever-present snipers, had failed to bring about my death, and yet here was one stupid doctor, through his inability – or was it just plain refusal – to listen to a mere non-medico's fears, who had nearly seen me into the next world with a syringe full of cholera vaccine. But was there a next world? I had certainly not been to one, but then, would I have been classified as dead just because my heart had stopped? My only sensation, and it had been in seconds, was of a grey turning black into nothingness, absolute nothingness. If that was dying from a heart attack I envy those who can get it over so quickly and hope my eventual end comes the same way again.

The Germans in the Second World War had attempted many times to kill me when I was flying fighter planes and I thought of the day when my Spitfire hurtled towards the ground out of control after an operation over France. Uncomfortable for a while, a cracked head takes time to mend and my eyes were never back to normal again, but I survived. A Persian mob in Abadan, 1951, screamed for my blood in a sacrificial frenzy, but I had stayed just that one jump ahead of them. My car was blown up later that year, seconds after I left it in the Canal Zone of Egypt, when fanatics took on the whole British forces in the area. A second car was riddled with bullets only days later as I drove along the deserted road from Ismailia to Suez. Lumumba's rabble of troops, tried to winkle me out of my hotel in the Congo in 1960, and the next president, Mobutu, planned my sticky end the following year, when he sent his para-commandos after me. Riots, revolutions, war in Vietnam and Middle Eastern jails, I had seen them all and kept my head ducked on many occasions.

I was used to that sort of life. It was my life and my way of life. Editors sitting in their plush chairs thousands of miles away in London have always been fond of sending their correspondents cables saying 'don't take any risks' when expecting them to stick their necks right into any world cauldron which is boiling. But paramount on my mind through everything was the importance of getting the story and getting it into the newspaper. A dead correspondent is of no use to anyone; he only brings a large sum in insurance money to his newspaper. The main idea is to survive one difficult assignment and be ready for the next; needles and vaccines had never been in my well-worked-out calculations.

PROLOGUE

My mind was working at full speed, but my body was still not abreast of it. I rang the bell and waited the customary Flashmans Hotel fifteen minutes for the small, turbanned and dirty-white skirted boy to arrive. 'Get me three large brandies,' I ordered and the boy withdrew wide-eyed. I had no idea what a doctor would have prescribed under the circumstances, but I was in no frame of mind to consult one. I drank the three brandies within half an hour and with each one I felt stronger. Later that evening I felt fit enough to walk to a Pakistani Information Service reception to be met with a colleague's words, 'My God, what's wrong with you? You look as though you've seen a ghost.'

It was days later, home in Singapore, that the full significance of that 'ghost' was explained to me and it set off an entirely new set of calculations by which I have had to live ever since and to which I shall have to adhere for whatever is to be the future. I am now a member of the reluctant élite, maybe one in a million – two million, it really does not matter – known as anaphylactics. My heart refuses to accept most of the ingredients of vaccines or antibiotics which are so commonplace today. A shot of penicillin, an anti-tetanus injection which is regarded in most places in the world as the immediate need of any badly injured person, even an injection of novacain in the gum before a dental extraction, as I discovered in a near miss a year later, any of them can kill me in seconds. I was lucky to have recovered in Rawalpindi, I was told; the possibility of recovering again was practically nil.

So the decision had to be made: I must give up my life as a foreign correspondent or make other arrangements. I chose the latter and since then many health officers at airports around the world have politely handed back my medical documents after a close scrutiny. They are completely spurious, but that has been the secret of only myself and a doctor friend, who shall be nameless. Not even my editor knew. He still sent me the occasional cable: 'Don't take any risks.'

Chapter 1

THE INDIAN MYTH

The Indo-Pakistani war assignment had been doomed from the beginning, it had got off on the wrong foot. I had been a month 'on base' in Singapore after a spell in Vietnam. True, it had been a busy and exciting month with Malaysia's expulsion of Singapore from the still young federation, but the excitement was over and Singapore was no longer in the headlines. It had been good to be back in my own home for a change, and June's cooking was as superb as ever. But the war-clouds were gathering over India and Pakistan, the question of Kashmir was boiling to a calamitous head, and all Pakistan's scheming and plotting to force the issue with internal uprisings by the predominant Moslems was being ruthlessly and cruelly met by the troops of the Indian Prime Minister, Shashtri, and his Indian government, who greedily clung to the territory they had dishonestly and bloodily acquired when partition, supervised by Earl Mountbatten, had given the old India independence some eighteen years earlier.

For a well-trained student of world affairs – for that is what I was – whose job was to smell trouble before it happened, nothing appeared more obvious than that the long-awaited clash over Kashmir was imminent. Threats and counter-threats between the two sides had taken on a more dangerous significance than ever and it was rapidly becoming evident, knowing both sides as I did, that the clashes of a few months earlier were mere sparring compared with what was now being planned.

By the third week in August I was warning my London office of the coming danger. I should be there, I told my foreign editor several times by cable, but each time the reply came in words such as, 'Request you stay Singapore momently'.

Strange, perhaps, but not unusual for the powers that be in great national newspapers to consider that their knowledge of world affairs is far superior to that of correspondents they are paying to be in a particular area and making a study of it over years.

Stranger still when many executives, even editors, have seldom travelled farther than a few of the Mediterranean countries, and only for holidays. But then, all the master minds of the journalistic world do not last forever; as so often happens, others are constantly behind them, coveting their plush offices, their chairs – and their secretaries. Overnight the correspondent discovers that he has a new boss, someone else who became a world 'expert' just as suddenly as he got the job.

It happened, of course. India fired the first shots. She was at the throat of Pakistan with all her Hindu cunning, and Pakistan was ready for her. I was twiddling my thumbs in Singapore. My newspaper did not have a correspondent within two thousand miles of the conflict, but others had had their men there for days. Doubtless, they were already cabling their first despatches. It was now the first week in September.

The telephone rang. A call from London, I was told. Amazing! This was the first call from London office in three years. Telephones were regarded as expensive; a cable usually sufficed and often arrived when I was already winging my way to some far-off troublespot. The voice of the Foreign Editor was urgent. 'The war has started in India,' it said, and appeared surprised when I replied, 'I know'. But the situation had to be discussed, and quickly; which side did I think I should take, India or Pakistan. Obviously I would take the most difficult one; they would get a reporter out from the London office to cover the other side. There was no hesitation necessary; obviously, I would try to get into Pakistan. The Indian side would be simple to cover in comparison, I knew, and already Indian claims were coming over the radio of vast gains by their already victorious troops.

The decision made, the next thing was to work out how to get to Karachi. It was nearly midnight in Singapore although London had put through its call at around four in the afternoon, London time. My timetables showed there should be a plane to Karachi, leaving at seven in the morning, but even as I found it a thought struck me: the direct route to Karachi was by flying over India, and if India had closed her airspace, or civilian pilots decided it was too dangerous, they would make a southern diversion to Colombo and thence, perhaps to Teheran or Beirut. From either of those two places I would then have to get back, flying eastwards, to Karachi. It could all take two days. Another two days lost. I telephoned the airline and they confirmed my seat. Yes, planes were still flying direct to Karachi, I was told, but the situation could change at any time, even before the morning.

Why every plane in any direction I ever wished to go left Singapore at an ungodly early hour in the morning I never really worked out, but here I was, following the customary pattern: decisions made late at night, cajoling airline officials to find for me reputedly non-existent seats, and packing for the trip, an operation over the years I had perfected to ten minutes flat, or less if really in a hurry. Two tropical suits, the usual array of shirts and other necessities, typing paper, maps and every newspaper cutting on the war I had collected over the past few days. The normal traveller would have stopped there, but I was no normal traveller and Pakistan was by no means a normal country at that moment. Into the case went two bush jacket suits, one khaki and the other jungle green, and desert boots; they were only a part of the large wardrobe of military style equipment I had always at the ready, but I hoped they would suffice. I checked my passport, medical certificates, credit cabling and airline cards and piled them ready with travellers cheques and a roll of dollar bills.

Beside the case I put my lightweight portable typewriter. I telephoned the local taxi office to collect me at a quarter to six and arranged an alarm call with the telephone operator for five o'clock. Just in case anything should go wrong, I set my own clock for the same time and then sat down with June for a last drink and to brief her on a dozen-and-one things which always had to be attended to whenever I went away. She took it calmly, as always. So many times had she gone through the same process and so many times she had seen me leave, not knowing when she might see me again. Sometimes it would be days, sometimes weeks or quite often months. I have never ceased to be amazed that any woman would wish to be married to a foreign correspondent, especially one working in such troubled areas as I had done for so many years. Such wives are a very special breed.

It was still afternoon when we landed at Karachi. Flying west we had gained a couple of hours and the flight had been smooth and uneventful. Several times before, I had landed there but now it was different; the usual great throng of baggage boys, taxi drivers and others whose purposes one never really discovers, shouted and hurried hither and thither in their shapeless slacks and shirts, dhotis and roughly-wound turbans, with an animated sense of urgency which I certainly had never noticed before. Women in gaudy, sheet-style gowns, carried babies, somehow managed to hold another two or three young children, simultaneously handling their cheap cardboard suitcases and vast paper parcels. It was a mad crush. Hundreds appeared to be on the move, but to where? Could it be a panic to get out of Karachi before the bombs dropped? I could hardly imagine that development in this particular war. But those clamouring for tickets and plane seats evidently did not share my views. A few days later India was to prove them right.

On the tarmac I had seen the lines of troops with their full kit and British style, flattish tin hats waiting, I presumed, for air transports to carry them north to the war zone. Around the airfield perimeter anti-aircraft guns poked their thin barrels into the sky and crews had dug ditches for shelter. I had not heard radio news of the Indian claims for many hours, but my arrival at the airport was now making me wonder, if perhaps, they were not true. I found a taxi and began the sixteen-mile drive into the city I knew so well. It had always been nerve wracking, with countless motor trishaws buzzing in all directions, but today the road was choked to capacity. Cars and trucks loaded with people were piling out of Karachi, weaving among and around army convoys. And just as many appeared to be making their way in.

Karachi had never been one of my favourite ports of call. Most of the city had the appearance of years of neglect: streets were broken and dusty, goats, sheep, oxen and camels seemed to wander at will; the people looked unwashed and filthy; children played in their thousands on rubbish dumps and waste ground, their only toys the litter which lay around them. Of course, Pakistan was poor; she was still living mostly on foreign aid, but (as I had thought in so many other Moslem countries) surely the dumps could have been cleared, at least sometimes, potholes by the thousand could have been filled in, a coat of paint could have been put on public buildings and offices, and above all, the people could have kept themselves and their clothes a bit cleaner. This was the Karachi I had seen before, and in parts it did not appear that a war in the city could have made it much worse. It was depressing; it had always depressed me. I had always looked with distaste at the prospect of staying in a Karachi hotel, with its faded and decrepit rooms and furnishings, sheets which were never quite spotless and white, and the incredibly bad food. So it came as more than a pleasant surprise to find myself being driven up the approach to one of the most shining new and modern hotels I had come across in Asia. It had been working hard since my previous visit; the staff wore smart uniforms and service at the reception desk was slick, something unknown in Karachi hitherto. There were cocktail bars and well-carpeted dining rooms, a superb menu and a nightclub where an Italian band and a sultry singer were still performing. I relaxed for a short while in the luxury of a room with its own private bath, built-in radio, and push-buttons which brought a drink in record time, with ice, cocktail stick and a napkin. At any other time I could have enjoyed a few days here, I thought, as I looked down on the most inviting swimming pool I had seen in months. But it was not to be, I knew. The war was several hundred miles away, near the border, and that was what I had come here for.

No one in Karachi appeared to know the true war situation. The British Embassy had no information that I had not already gathered from the radio. On the hour the Indian radio pumped out its claims and the Pakistani radio did little to refute them. But could one believe all that the Indians said? Hard experience had taught me to treat with reserve anything that was issued 'officially' in New Delhi. Rawalpindi, the new capital in the north, was the only place to work from, of that I was sure. To its east lay the borders with India and Kashmir. And I heard that several correspondents had already taken off for Rawalpindi.

The airline office was not very helpful. Few planes were flying to Rawalpindi, they told me; most of Pakistan's internal fleet had been taken over by the military. Those still carrying civilians were hopelessly overbooked; government and embassy officials were hurrying back and forth between Karachi and their new embassies and offices, and only one plane would be going the following morning.

'Give me a ticket. I will take the chance,' I said and gathered that if I could get on the airline bus to the airport there might be just that slim chance of boarding the plane. It turned out to be a fight, almost, to get on the bus at six o'clock the next morning, and one man was fighting as hard as I was; in fact, he was blocking my entry and there were only three seats left. I gave an extra push and he turned, protesting. Then we recognized each other. It was Joe Alex Morris of the *Los Angeles Times*, we were old colleagues from the Middle East and we knew how to work together in a crisis. We joined our efforts, repeated them at the airport and finally sank into seats on the Rawalpindi plane from which we defied anyone to move us.

Three hours flight in the Viscount took us to Rawalpindi. We had not flown near the border, of course, but we strained our eyes for most of the way, trying to find any movements on the ground, any sign that might suggest that the Indian army had made a breakthrough and was, as Delhi radio was saying that morning, 'occupying large areas of enemy territory'. But no: not a trace of smoke from smouldering ruins, no convoys on the roads or any other signs of war could be seen below us, although one can never imagine the life going on below when one flies high over an unfamiliar land. Everything looked tranquil, one could almost say gloriously peaceful. Rawalpindi airport, too, did not have the appearance of being on any urgent war footing, unlike Karachi. I could see just two anti-aircraft guns on the far side of the perimeter and there was hardly a uniform to be seen. But then, over a hundred miles lay between us and the area where the war was rising in a rapid crescendo. It could have been a thousand and it was immediately evident that my newspaper could never project me from Rawalpindi as 'Our Man on the Spot'.

Why anyone should have chosen Rawalpindi as the new capital of Pakistan, unless it was the sheer conceit of president Ayub Khan, whose family came from that area, will always be beyond me. On the outskirts of the town, and a very small town at that, stood some modern but practically deserted government buildings. Gardens had been laid out around one or two, but they had that uncared-for look. Two miles outside the town the straggling and untidy diplomatic residential area was being built. The nations which had diplomatic relations with Pakistan had been forced to buy land and build or rent from an unscrupulous building developer when they had perfectly adequate embassies and residences down in Karachi.

It was simple to distinguish the rich nations from the poor; the new American embassy and the ambassador's residence shone out as a palace from among less ostentatious and often dreary attempts by Pakistani architects to create something 'modern'. The British Embassy was on the outskirts of the main town: two floors over some unoccupied shops, reached by plain concrete stairs, which had not seen a brush in weeks, fronted by a broken pavement which had hurriedly been laid over sand and became a muddy quagmire each time it rained.

Foreign embassies could not move completely from Karachi; it was still virtually the capital and any main government business and decisions still appeared to emanate from there. Apart from this it would be many more months, if ever, before new building at Rawalpindi could possibly accommodate the vast numbers of foreign embassy personnel. Consequently files, secretaries and ambassadors went back and forth between the two places, scrambling for seats on a hopelessly inadequate air service. And none of them could ever guarantee to be in the right place when they were needed. Ayub Khan obviously had followed that stupid mania of rulers which we see at Brasilia, the new capital of Brazil. King Idris of Libya went even further: he made capitals of both Tripoli and Benghazi and then decided on yet a third, a brand new capital at Beida, miles and miles from anywhere east of Benghazi. It might have been a convenient spot for King Idris to build yet another palace; he already had five, but for years the diplomats of the rest of the world have been praying that this self-glorifying habit of overnight presidents and dictators, even a potentate, would become the least fashionable thing to squander money on. After all, the money never had belonged to the all-powerful men who had thought up the great decisions. And none of them seem to keep their jobs long enough to see their dreams come true.

And then we came to Flashman's Hotel, the only inhabitable hotel in Rawalpindi. The taxi swept us into the narrow forecourt in front of the main building, single-storeyed and large enough to accommodate no more than a tiny reception office, a smallish bar and a restaurant which was probably no larger than the American Ambassador's main reception room two or three miles away. But there was a vacant suite – just one, the receptionist told us as he explained, 'We have not been so busy at Flashman's since the British left years ago'. We were led behind the main building to our new abode, through a door in one of several long and low blocks of dilapidated military quarters, built when the British army and its families had to make do with what was given them. The furnishings were unspeakably old, uncomfortable and dowdy: an unemptied ashtray lay on a rickety cane table, the beds were army style and the bumps of the springs showed clearly through the off-white sheets and army-style blankets. I looked into the stone-floored bathroom and saw the brown-stained bath. I pulled out some filthy and threadbare pieces of cloth, handed them to the boy and demanded, 'Clean towels, please. We will pay for them.' Joe had already opened a bottle he had in his bag and was cleaning two glasses with a handkerchief. 'Pity Intercontinental didn't get this far,' said Joe. To which I replied, 'They never will, not even at gunpoint'.

We did not wait to unpack but took a taxi to the office of the government information officer, Ibrahim Shalabi. We needed accreditation cards to join the troops, permits to travel and any cars we would hire. And we wanted them now; both Joe and I were expecting to be on the way to the front in a couple of hours at least. We expected, too, to find the government information office bustling with activity; instead we found it deserted and the time was not yet midday.

The government offices were the low, drab sprawl of buildings, similar to Flashman's Hotel, which had doubtless been left over by the British and had never been renovated. We went from one room to another, from one building to the next, calling and shouting, and eventually a sleepy-eyed clerk came from a back room, which was called the newsroom.

Where was Shalabi, we asked, and the clerk replied, 'Gone to lunch. Everyone is at lunch.' We must speak to Shalabi, we insisted, but the clerk said, 'Very difficult, he is at home.' Finally we got Shalabi's telephone number from the clerk, but this took another ten minutes. It took another ten, through the military exchange, to get Shalabi, but then all the satisfaction we derived from our efforts was, 'There is a press conference at three o'clock. Everything will be arranged then. Nothing can be done before, absolutely nothing.'

Three o'clock became four, but this did not appear to worry the group of Pakistani reporters gathered in the conference room. A young British journalist, although I did not remember meeting him before, recognized me and confided that he had been sitting in Rawalpindi for two days, and still had no permits to leave the town. Shalabi arrived with two 'spokesmen', one for the army and one for the air force. For fifteen minutes I was forced to sit and listen to 'communiques' and pleasantries between the spokesmen and the local press and, despite a dozen probing questions by me, all we had gathered was that 'operations are proceeding according to plan'. I tried again: were those advances or withdrawals? The spokesmen did not have, could not or would not give another useful scrap of information. No wonder the Indians are getting away with it, I thought, 'Do you realize that a hundred journalists are sitting at press conferences twice a day in New Delhi, being fed with information, true or false, which is being pumped out all over the world and the world is believing it?' I asked and the local reporters looked at me aghast for daring to speak to their spokesmen like that.

'I came here to project the Pakistani side of this conflict,' I added, 'but if this is all you are prepared to do for me I may just as well go home. Give me the permission to go to the front and find out the truth for myself. At the moment Pakistan is losing the war, probably only according to Indian propaganda.'

I had thought back to the days, three years before, when China attacked India. The Indian information officers were babes in the business then, but a bunch of the toughest world correspondents had knocked them into shape in record time. Two and three press conferences a day and any spokesman, general or minister, we demanded; information, the fullest it was humanly possible to get, searching questions, facilities to go where we decided, although not one of us actually saw the whites of the Chinese eyes. The Indians were retreating for practically the whole war, but we did leave a fairly efficient information setup, trained by us, when we left New Delhi; we had even decided which hall in which ministry would be used for the conferences and briefings. I could imagine it now, packed with journalists from far and wide, listening to Indian spokesmen giving them full and, presumably, authentic details of every Indian gain and Pakistani loss. Twenty Pakistani tanks destroyed, eight thousand Pakistanis taken prisoner; and I could imagine the journalists scribbling away delightedly – first-class copy, wonderful story.

Another thing we had taught the Indians in 1962 was to give journalists top priority in cabling their stories. This was done; the always efficient Indian cabling system worked overtime for us; never were there delays and, doubtless, there were no delays now. The Indians had learned a lot about the information business from their western journalist teachers. I was not to know it then, but during the whole of the three weeks war with Pakistan not one journalist writing from the Indian side was allowed within a hundred miles of any front or battle. Every gain, every claim, was issued in New Delhi by the Indians themselves; what at first were exaggerations gradually became blatant lies; if they could not win the war militarily they would win it by propaganda, the Indians had decided. And win it they did, at least that is what most of the world thinks even today and all the front-line battle reporting I and a few colleagues did from the Pakistani side could not alter it.

Mine was among several newspapers which completely misled the public at the time; the reporter they had sent to New Delhi was on his first big foreign assignment and can hardly be blamed. But his reports reached London hours ahead of mine, which were delayed by censors and the almost insuperable difficulties of getting back well over one hundred miles from the battlefronts to Rawalpindi to send our despatches. By the time they reached London the front pages were set; some newspapers had made up their minds that India was winning hands down and poor little Pakistan was taking a horrible beating. No Indian who knew the truth at the time could ever be proud of the 'victory'; there were too many lives to be counted afterwards and it would take years for India to build up her arms, tanks and planes before she could ever dream of going to war again. Equally, many editors cannot be proud of their journalistic expertise during those three crucial and dangerous weeks. But then, that was 'yesterday's story'. And Reuters, that great British worldwide news agency, was not really assisting from the Pakistani side in the first week of the war: it relied on a local Pakistani 'stringer', or local newspaperman agent, for all its war coverage until it flew in a good, solid, and most companionable staffman.

My straight talking to Shalabi and the official spokesmen had its effect. There were some quick telephone calls from Shalabi's office to military headquarters and by six o'clock those who wanted them had their permits, and forward headquarters had agreed to receive us the following morning. More correspondents were arriving and a British television cameraman and a London newspaper photographer made up a batch of ten. Strangely, none of the Pakistani reporters were clamouring for permits or facilities. I cannot really remember seeing one of them anywhere near the fighting during the following two weeks.

Back at the hotel we set about arranging cars. They had to be good, reliable ones and fast; forward headquarters was over one hundred miles east. Two drivers flatly refused to take us, but eventually, and after telephone calls to other hire car owners in the town, we came to agreements for the morning with three drivers who had, for Rawalpindi, fairly good and modern-looking cars. At five o'clock we were to start and I began to brief Ali, the driver I had chosen, on what he should bring: extra cans of petrol and some good spare tyres, and food, I warned Ali. We had no idea how long we may be away or exactly where we would be going. As proved to be the case, I had made a good choice in Ali; his driving was hair-raising and he had to be calmed down eventually, but he was fast and speed was essential in the long drives at night back from the front to cable our despatches from Rawalpindi. And Ali had no nerves at all; at times he drove me within half a mile of a battle, tucked his car out of sight from any attacking planes and sat contentedly, waiting for me to return, often hours later.

I was reasonably pleased with progress so far. There was no way of catching up on the lost days while I had sat in Singapore, but at least I was not wasting much time now that I had got as far as Rawalpindi. I repeated 'five o'clock' to Ali and was turning into the hotel when a shout came from a car pulling to a stop near the entrance. Out climbed two figures, but for the moment I recognized neither; they were covered from head to foot in brown dust and it was impossible to make out what original colours their clothes might have been. But I recognized the voice and the favourite greeting, 'Hello mate'; it was Don Seaman of the *Express*, a great colleague of many years, whom I had not seen for two years, since we parted somewhere in the Yemeni desert.

It was good to see Don again and we gripped hands, but there was a look of amazement on Don's dust-plastered face as he looked at my clean shirt and slacks. 'Where've you been?' he asked. 'I've been expecting you to be somewhere around for the past week. I've had the place to myself.' This was not like me and Don knew it. Over the years I had established some sort of a reputation for being 'first in', Don was in a hurry to get his despatch away and briefly I said, 'London office. They thought they knew it all.' To which came Don's reply as he and his photographer hurried off to their room: 'Christ, are they crazy? See you later in the bar.' Already he had done some fine reporting of the start of the war and now he was about to write his account of the huge Pakistani push into Kashmir. Throughout the war his newspaper remained balanced in its coverage from both sides, even if our despatches were held up by censors and arrived in London a day late. Don's were published, most times disclaiming completely the wild and untrue claims from New Delhi which had already appeared.

Five o'clock in the morning; it was still dark and we groped around the cars, piling in cameras, typewriters, bags and army packs with which some were equipped and sandwiches and flasks of tea which we had ordered from the hotel. The three cars swept out of Rawalpindi in convoy and Ali quickly took the lead. He had set himself two hours for the one-hundred-and-ten-mile drive, and he made it with three minutes to spare. But not without at least a dozen near heart attacks among the passengers; there was little on the road except for bullock carts and Ali appeared to think that even they had no right to be there. With klaxon screaming, Ali drove straight at them if they were taking up too much of the narrow road. Most times they moved with much fist-waving from the cart owners, but often there was not time. It was we who went off the road without slackening speed, but with a shout for the hundredth time, 'For God's sake, Ali, slow down.'

Forward headquarters had few troops to be seen as we arrived; masses of them were at battle stations somewhere along the border southwards and beyond Lahore, facing six Indian divisions massed in Free Kashmir. In several places the Indians had attacked but everywhere, until then, the Pakistani lines had held. General Mohammed Musa, their C-in-C, briefed us on where another large part of his army was deployed. Proudly, with a map, he showed how he had outflanked the Indians in the north and had driven a wide salient into Kashmir to Akhnur, twenty miles on the Indian side of the truce line. The General was feeling pleased with himself; he had just signalled his commanders: 'You've got your teeth into the enemy, bite deeper until he is destroyed.' A little premature, as it transpired two days later, the thousands of troops flooding into the salient had to drag themselves out fast when the major Indian attacks came elsewhere. But it was into the salient we were going this morning and Landrovers had been laid on to take us.

It was a trick I had learned years before, but if travelling in any sort of convoy in a parched and dusty country such as Pakistan in the fearsome September heat, the most comfortable vehicle is the leading one, especially over ground where tanks and other heavy weapons of war have travelled before. It was just a matter of getting out of the conference room a couple of steps ahead of the rest, and though for the first half hour over solid roads it would not have mattered, the sudden end of the comparative comfort and the lurching on to deeply furrowed tracks across country more than made me realize that a little experience can be more than useful. The dust from our wheels rose in vast clouds and any breeze blew the choking, brown powder in through the side windows, however securely we had closed them. I could feel it on my lips and it was covering the lens of my dark spectacles, my neck, already damp with sweat, was getting into a sticky and gritty mess and I tied a silk scarf around it to keep off as much dust as possible. I imagined what it must be like in the two Landrovers following, although I could see nothing behind except that towering, brown cloud. They could do absolutely nothing but drive into the dustcloud, bumping in and out of holes and sliding in and out of the furrows and over the ridges. It was completely blind driving. For twenty minutes we ploughed on until we came to another road and by then my face and bare arms had changed colour, but as we slowed to a halt the sight of the occupants of the following Landrovers had to be seen to be believed. They all looked alike; from head to foot they were the same shade of dust brown and there was no way of knowing what their clothes may have looked like before: their faces, their hair, their arms and their boots. As they piled out of the Landrovers I saw a group which could have been mistaken for men from another world; only the whites of their eyes contrasted with the all-over brown, and there were roars of laughter as they regarded each other. I could not tell who was who; for the next ten minutes it was a game of guessing on which colleague would emerge from the brown coating as we all set to, slapping away at each other, shaking out shirts and getting the worst of the dust off faces with handkerchiefs, scarves or any bit of rag which could be found. It was just one small discomfort of going to war as a correspondent; several of them, straight out from London, must have been wondering whatever made them agree to take on the assignment. But they all had learned something; there were good-natured, but most pointed remarks at me and the other two who shared my Landrover. I found it increasingly difficult to stay in the lead vehicle from then on.

Soon we were catching up with the signs of war. Villages of closely-packed mud-and-brick houses lay flattened in ruins, and not a sign of life could be seen. Rough wooden telegraph poles and lines lay in tangled heaps and a gaping hole in the dome of a small mosque showed the shattered mosaic interior.

And then I smelled it, the corpse. Whether it was animal or human, or half a mile off, this was the unmistakable stench of death and war that I knew so well. Even now I can bring its sickly sweet but foul odour to my nostrils' memory; on and off I had been with it for fifteen or more years, and once experienced it is a stench never to be forgotten. I spotted a cow on its back, upturned with three of its legs sticking straight upwards; then another, a bullock, goats and the headless carcass of what appeared to be a camel. The pungent smell increased until it became almost unbearable. Surely there must be humans around too, I was thinking.

We were crashing over the remains of a road between a dozen scattered and broken hovel-like dwellings when we came across them, lying in crazy postures among the rubble: three had been adults, although the filth prevented any attempt to decide the sex, while four small bundles of blood and flesh were obviously children. Just a few days before, perhaps, they had played gaily in this tiny hamlet. War had come suddenly and relentlessly, killed and passed by without time to give even a simple burial. They had not asked for it or taken any part in the decisions which had brought it their way. Toughened as I should have been, I had to steel myself against the lump in my throat. Each time I had come on such a scene the same thought shot through my brain: the sickening stupidity of war brought on by the greater stupidity of politicians, generals, power-crazy fanatics and religion which took no account of mere civilian, innocent lives.

From then on the sickly, disgusting smell stayed with us; the whole countryside was littered with rotting humans and beasts, but I saw only those I could not avoid. To allow one's thoughts to wander too far could only lead to a revulsion which would make it impossible to carry on. We had hit the tail end of the advance; the road was becoming crammed with huge transports filled with stores, petrol and the thousand and one other things which eventually roll in behind the forward fighting troops, the young officer driver wove his way in, out and around them, bumping along unmade side tracks and raising the acrid dust to the annoyance of the soldiers in the troop carriers.

The vast convoy crawled and snarled its way for at least five miles, nose to tail, before we finally shot past four tanks in the lead into open and almost deserted country. All was uncannily quiet and we could have shot off in any direction, friendly or enemy, with no gunfire to guide us until we waved down a jeep speeding from the opposite direction and a captain shouted, 'Six miles straight on. Second Infantry signpost off to the right behind the hill.' Another three miles and a straggling, unhappy crowd of Indian prisoners blocked the road, slouching in their dirty green uniforms and Chinese or Russian-style tin hats into captivity, despite the efforts of khaki-clad Pakistanis to make it a disciplined and brisk march. Thousands of Indians had given themselves up in the fighting in the Jaurian area and now the countryside was becoming littered with their equipment, hastily abandoned as they came out of foxholes with their arms high. Half a mile on we stopped to look at a small, French-built Indian tank which was completely burned out. A terrible stench made us look around and then we spotted it. One of the tank's crew had somehow jumped from the incinerator; the corpse lay on the ground, clothes and flesh burned into a blue-black mass, the helmet and head welded into one ghastly and charred shape of the same colour. We looked at each other and someone said, 'Let's get on'. We hurried away.

It was not long before we found the Second Infantry sign and it pointed off to the right and up a climbing track behind the hillside. From the tracks there was only one way to go and soon they took us through a gate and up to the top of the hill into a thick clump of trees. Under them we saw the light guns, and troops lay sprawled around, asleep. A corporal appeared and after we had introduced ourselves disappeared into a tent which was hidden among some nearby bushes.

Two minutes later we saw the astonishing sight of a major and a captain coming to greet us. They were freshly shaved and their hair was well brushed; their uniforms were perfectly pressed and their boots shone as though they were prepared for a ceremonial parade. In a perfect English the major said, 'Awfully nice to see you chaps, could I offer you some tea?' and then we squatted around his maps as he gave us the battle situation.

'You've missed the big show by two hours', the major told us. 'Rather noisy, old man.' He led us through the bushes and we looked down into the valley beyond. 'My chaps are well spread out over the hills two miles north and south,' he said. 'The Indians are down there in the valley, but I don't think they'll want another scrap for a few hours. They took an awful beating and we have several thousand in the bag since yesterday.' We went back and squatted near the tent, passing cigarettes, drinking tea and chatting. 'Casualties?', I asked, and the major stroked his neat military moustache as his face became set, losing the perpetual and friendly smile it had had till then. 'I've lost some damned good chaps,' he said. Some good officers among them.' The major and the captain exchanged looks; some of their best friends would never be walking into an army mess again, but the major went on: 'But light, old man, very light considering we've come this far.'

The more we talked as I watched these two Pakistani officers, the more I thought of a similar scene and a similar conversation years earlier in Normandy, shortly after the invasion of France. I tried to remember if the British officers had appeared quite as beautifully groomed as did these two Pakistanis so soon after a battle, and I rather doubted it. 'Sandhurst?' I asked the major and he beamed. 'Of course, old man. Sandhurst, where else?'

It was now a question of waiting, perhaps for many hours,

for more action, or trying to get some sort of despatch away to the Rawalpindi cable-head by Ali, the driver, and returning to the hillside later. Not much action for the British public today, I was thinking, but this seemed the logical thing to do in view of what the major had told us and the fact that he was anxious to give his men some sleep after thirty-six hours of continued advance and fighting. We got up to go and there were handshakes all round, 'If we're not here when you get back, old man,' said the major, 'see you tomorrow in the night club in Akhnur.' We enjoyed the parting joke. A night club was the last thing we would expect to find, although, at that monent, we had few doubts that the Pakistani advance could take in Akhnur and many places beyond within days, if it met no stronger resistance than that which it had encountered so far. But there had been surprisingly few Indian tanks in action in the salient and Pakistan had found it necessary to use only small numbers of hers. Where were the armoured divisions of India, equipped with the latest in tanks, the British Centurions? The major, I had gathered, had not seen one Centurion so far.

We were a mile along the advancing column when I saw the planes; six of them at about 3,000 feet had suddenly appeared and, strung out in a long line astern, they went into a huge circle above us. I knew that the Pakistanis had no fighters but fairly old American Sabre jets; and these were British-built Hunters. What they were doing, circling in that stupid fashion, was quite beyond me, but this was no time to argue, 'Run for it,' I shouted as everyone became aware of the planes in the same split second. We piled out of the Landrover and scrambled over the rough field and dived into the nearest slit trench some fifty yards away. The planes still circled and by now guns were manned all along the column. 'Bloody fools,' I was thinking. Here was a perfect target for air attack. The Indians could have played havoc if they had come in, unobserved, at nought feet and plastered the column from nose to tail. But here they were, announcing their presence and giving time for the troops, those not on the guns, to take cover under their vehicles or in slit trenches. In my days as a fighter pilot, this would have been asking for certain death. Who the hell had taught these Indians to fly?

It was almost a slow motion film. Up there sat the pilots looking at a superb target, working out how they should attack it and there was not a Sabre in the sky. Incredibly they chose to come in from the north, *across* the column, I could hardly believe my eyes as I saw the leader turn into a dive and point his plane directly at us. 'Down,' I shouted, and the other three ducked as low as they could in the slit trench. My own training had come into action. From 3,000 feet even a Hunter would take a few seconds to get down to around 400 feet before it opened fire. My eyes were glued to it – it had been years since my own fingers had been on the gun button, but I was shouting, 'Pictures, it can't hit us.'

The Hunter's flight line was no more than one or two degrees deflection from where we crouched, but I was certain we could not be in the centre of the gunsight. The TV cameraman was in action practically before I had finished shouting those five words and there began the most brilliant series of film shots to come out of the Indo-Pakistani war; the camera was turning from a fraction of a second before the pilot fired his rockets – until the rockets and cannon shells ploughed over the heads of the gunners, now blazing away from the transport column, into an abandoned tank a hundred yards to our left in the field. From then on, as the other five planes came in to attack, all following the leader from the north, I continued to act as film director. At times such as this, one had to have a lot of faith in one's colleagues, but sometimes the cameraman was standing to his full height at my shouts of 'OK camera'. He was dedicated to his job of filming that war or any other; never once did I see the camera shaking.

So the air war had started; this was the first time the Indians had thrown in planes and I was surprised that I had seen no patrolling Sabres, although they well and truly got the measure of the Indian planes later, as the war escalated. There was no doubt that the tiny Pakistani airforce eventually proved itself far superior in tactics, airfighting and courage, although it was heavily outnumbered. There was no improvement on World War Two tactics, but the Pakistanis proved they had trained well and remembered those tactics in a fashion far superior to that of the Indians. On the ground, the war developed into classic 1939–1945 military strategy, and at times more closely resembled World War One, as men were thrown against men and armour against armour. In fact, I refer to it as 'The Sandhurst War'; but then, so many officers on both sides had passed through the portals of that worthy establishment.

Six times that day the Indian planes were to come in to the attack before we reached forward headquarters. Half an hour after the first attack our Landrover was momentarily and inextricably stuck in the column when the Hunters came in, yet again from north to south. One reconnaisance plane, flying high, could have supplied the details for the pilots to set direct tracks onto the five-mile column for attacks along it, east to west. But no; each time they circled high and gave us ample warning. We tumbled from the Landrover and, determined to see the results, took cover under some nearby bushes instead of throwing ourselves flat under trucks as did most of the troops. Why we imagined the bushes would be any type of shield against cannon shells or rockets I will not attempt to explain, except to say that journalists and cameramen are an inquisitive species; they like to see things as they happen, which sometimes makes them overlook the fullest precautions in their quest for news and pictures. This time the gods were with us; two trucks loaded with jerrycans of petrol were hit and went up with a roar, but 150 yards along the convoy. We got as near as we could; there was a lot more good footage of film to be had although the casualties did not make a pretty sight. More than twenty men had been killed in that direct hit and as many others badly wounded.

It was slow going, with more stops in which to decide on taking cover or not, but the farther we drew away from the column the less we had to worry that Indian planes might be looking for us specifically. It was decided unanimously that we should make for Rawalpindi: films had to be got away and any writer had had a good day with which to plaster the front page of any newspaper. There was really only one more obstacle to cross: a hundred or more yards of river. We had forded it that morning; the water was no more than three to four feet deep and at the time I had thought I would not like to be caught halfway with planes around. Then, of course, there had been none; army vehicles had been crossing and recrossing without interference. This time I was regarding the river somewhat differently.

Two miles before reaching it we caught up with the second of the three press Landrovers; the London newspaper photographer was jubilant at the day's results, but it was not only I who had been thinking of the river. We agreed to cross it well spaced out, so as to make as small a target as possible; the other Landrover would go first and we would follow when it was well across. We stopped at the river bank and scanned the sky; there was no sight or sound of aircraft and the leading Landrover nosed slowly into the water. We still watched the skies until it was three-quarters of the way across before we drove in, our feet high to keep them dry.

Then, and no more than twenty yards out, I spotted it! A French-built Indian Mystere was tearing down the river at us at no more than twenty feet. I yelled 'Planes!' and threw myself over the side into the river and my three companions were not far behind me. Water would have been no better shield than had been those bushes, but it was the only thing to do and it was done automatically. I heard the crash of cannon as I hit the water and stayed down for the few seconds it would take the plane to pass; then we all surfaced, a sorry-looking bunch but unharmed. We stood by the Landrover with water up to our waists for a full ten minutes, but no more planes came. A lone fighter, it proved to be, perhaps one of a flight which had already made its main attack on the column and caught sight of the sitting ducks as it was streaking off towards the Indian lines. I certainly could not have resisted the chance in my piloting days and was hoping that this particular Indian had had the same instructions as had been indelibly printed on my mind: never turn back for a second pass at a target, its the fastest way into trouble from ground fire.

Eventually we made the opposite bank, but already we had seen that all was not well with the other Landrover. With little more than fifteen yards to comparative safety they too had baled out into the river. But the photographer had been hit; something had made a nasty gash in his ankle and there was a lesser wound higher up his leg. He was obviously in great pain and his wounds were bound with soggy cloth, but his main thoughts were for the pictures he had taken that day, both his cameras had gone under the water with him.

It was then I was to witness a stroke of sheer genius which brought the pictures into the photographer's newspaper the following Sunday. 'I must find something to hold water,' he said and we rushed around until we found a battered tin can. He filled it with water and dropped his cameras into it; at forward headquarters they were transferred into a bucket of water which was carefully nursed the hundred miles back to Rawalpindi to stop the films from drying. There they were unloaded in a darkroom and the developed results were near perfect. From his two practically ruined cameras the photographer built one with parts from each which functioned well for the rest of the assignment as far as he was concerned and until, reluctantly, he obeyed instructions from London to pull out.

The drive back to Rawalpindi was, I am sure, one that none of us will ever forget. It was dusk when we set out and Ali put his foot down hard; darkness came and then inky blackness. The car's headlights had been hooded but it made no difference to our speed. Ali still scheduled the journey for two hours and he was determined to make it. Indistinguishable shapes flashed by as Ali made last second and miraculous swerves. Screams from his passengers would not deter the intrepid Ali and mercifully I sank into a deep and exhausted sleep which saved me at least forty minutes of terror. I awoke as we drove through the outskirts of Rawalpindi, but there were no lights to greet us; the Government had ordered a complete blackout throughout the country. Flashman's Hotel was functioning only by the light of a few candles and windows were heavily covered. There was no doubt that the fear of air raids was being taken seriously; in fact, I quickly detected a sense of panic among all I spoke to, especially when two shadowy figures jumped on me as I got out of the car and all but pulled a cigarette from my mouth. Surely the Indians would not bomb open cities, I thought, and just stopped myself from making my views quite clear to the two Pakistanis who were saying some most unfriendly things. But there was something much more urgent to be attended to; somehow my despatch had to be written and we found candles and set up the dining room as a communal office. A hotel messenger boy rushed each sheet to the cable office as it came out of my typewriter, to be rewarded when he returned from the sixth and last trip, with a receipt upon which I had insisted, with twenty rupees. Now the next priority was a much needed shower.

Joe was already in the sitting room of our 'suite' when I arrived. By candlelight he had arranged the thick curtains and now we set about shading the one small table lamp we had. I went outside whilst Joe switched it on. 'Fine', I pronounced and Joe poured out two drinks. We had just had our first sip of the nectar when there was a furious banging on the door and angry voices were shouting, 'You have a light. Put it out!' We obliged, of course, and the muttered remarks about panicky Paks which passed between us could never be included in our despatches; so off to the bedroom beyond we took the candle and emptied our glasses. From there, with apologies to Joe, I took the only means of illumination into the bathroom and threw off my filthy and bedraggled clothes. Then I quickly returned the candle to a grinning Joe as more furious banging and shouting came from the other side of the bathroom window. But a shower I definitely was going to have, even if the operation was going to be performed in darkness. I fumbled with the antiquated taps and discovered that at least one item on Flashman's Hotel glossy brochure was correct. The tap which provided hot water was evidently more efficient than the cold tap. I jumped from the bath like a frightened cat as a cascade of scalding water hit me and it took me another ten minutes of juggling before I could adjust the taps to a safe but almost cold stream.

One soaping from head to foot was not enough. I was standing there, rubbing more soap into still matted hair; this was bliss and even if the next day I was going to be just as filthy again, no one was going to deny me a few hours of cleanliness. And then my thoughts, momentarily at peace with the world, were shattered. A crash came which I felt had burst an eardrum, it was so close. In a second it was followed by another and yet another. An anti-aircraft gun, unknown to me, had been positioned in the hotel grounds and had opened up.

With it came the staccato and echoing crashes from another twenty or more guns placed in and around the city.

Somewhere Joe's voice was shouting 'Get out of there', but I was still covered in soap and even in those few seconds my thoughts were telling me, 'Surely not; it must be panic. Surely the Indians cannot be dreaming of wantonly bombing open towns and cities.' Even as I thought this, I realized how wrong I could be; the terrifying whistle of a bomb came through the breaks in the shooting and my instincts told me that it was heading my way. The sickening explosion shook the building. The bomb must have landed no more than 500 yards away and it was followed by five more, luckily dropping at increasing distances from the hotel in a stick which straddled Rawalpindi.

The shower was no place to be. I was muttering to myself, 'Fools, mad, mad fools,' as I groped around for a towel and wiped some of the water from my body. I got through the door and stumbled over a bed. Joe was gone and the blast of the first bomb had blown out the candle. Somewhere I had clean clothes, but where? I fumbled over a chair where I had remembered some of them had been hung. Yes, here was a shirt and here were slacks. There was no time to think of socks, but I managed to get my hands on shoes. Outside there was shouting and from the distance I could hear the wailing of women.

By shouting through corridors of the rambling building I finally came across the tiny cable office, with its boarded windows and hastily arranged blackout, which now served as reception. By candlelight I wrote my despatch and marked it *Urgent*, but I need not have bothered. It took eighteen hours to reach London and was overtaken by the despatch of the following day which told the full horror of what had been deemed legitimate by India to prosecute a religious war.

Karachi, too, had been bombed that night; not one military target had been hit in either city, although by the next morning the Indian radio was claiming the destruction of many. It also claimed that Rawalpindi airport had been bombed and completely destroyed, although the nearest bomb fell three miles away. Wild and inaccurate propaganda was sinking in

STORY UNUSED

before the truth got out of Pakistan. Of the airstrikes in the salient the day before All India Radio was repeating with monotonous regularity, 'Indian aircraft attacked an enemy column, destroying over 700 vehicles, many of them tanks. The Pakistani advance has been completely cut off and thousands of enemy troops are surrounded.' Several of us who had been there listened grimly in my room to the broadcast and someone said, 'That includes us, but our stories this morning will stop the Indian lies.' Maybe they would have, if they had been published, but my newspaper's front page gave nothing except India's victorious claims. I received a cable saying—*Story Unused as Arrived too Late.*

Rawalpindi was counting her dead, not in large numbers, for it appeared that only one Indian Canberra bomber succeeded in its terror mission, whilst others had been frightened off by gunfire and had jettisoned their loads far and wide over the countryside. But the population was scared; there were enough homes reduced to rubble and enough grisly sights being dug out of them to start a frenzied digging of slit trenches. It was a day to concentrate on this new and senseless aspect of the war, forgetting, for the moment, the front line fighting, and the photographers and television men had plenty to film. What the real impact on the outside, civilized, world the bombing of innocents had made we had no means of knowing at the time, but to me, certainly, it was one of utter disgust and sadness. Did the outside world really care and did newspaper readers and television viewers really consider that such happenings mattered if they were not directly involved? I had time to think on these things again when a television colleague showed me his cable from London office. He had done no more than project the scene of wreckage and misery in parts of Rawalpindi that day and the cable read: 'You included fifteen seconds in news bulletin only as film considered biased.'

That was several days later. The days between had been taken up by mad rushes from one battlefront to another as the main Indian attacks came at three points south of the salient. The most dangerous was at Sialkot, which developed into an out-and-out slogging match between tanks; a second was directed against the city of Lahore from Amritsar, and another was south of the city. It was a pincer and encircling operation – at least it was planned that way – and the Pakistanis were forced to pull out every man and fighting vehicle from the salient as the Indian attacks quickly mounted in strength. If the Indian commanders had succeeded in their plan, three-quarters of the Pakistani army could have been surrounded and Lahore taken, and the rest of the country could have offered little resistance. In the event sheer determination of the numerically inferior Pakistani troops and weapons held the lines at all three places, although the front line on the Lahore thrust was no more than two miles from the city itself.

It was in Lahore that I made my new headquarters. The cable office there was still working with reasonable efficiency, but it was evident that somewhere down the line my despatches were still being seriously held up. The faithful Ali did not turn a hair at any request I made and was becoming expert at driving off the road at once at the mere sight or sound of planes or heavy gunfire. Into Lahore were coming the pitiful streams of refugees from the outlying villages and countryside, pushing their belongings on handcarts or carrying them in huge bundles on their backs or – the more fortunate ones – arriving in horse-drawn carts and farm trucks. The sounds of war boomed over the city and Indian shells landed on the outskirts. How near was Lahore to falling to the enemy?

I could have walked it. Batapur, where the Pakistanis were making their stand, was no more than three miles from the hotel, if I had reckoned without Ali. He was adamant: his job was to drive me, he insisted, and he threaded the car through the outskirts packed with refugee carts and foot-weary, laden families, heading they knew not where. The long, perfectly straight and treelined road into Batapur lay before us, deserted except for a military jeep rushing in our direction. An officer waved us off the road, so Ali took to the verge and slowly edged his way forward. But not far. An unearthly din of exploding shells broke out all around us and Ali rapidly swung into the shelter of a building which turned out to be a police station, still manned by one policeman. In fifteen minutes the shelling stopped, but in that short time hundreds of shells had been expended and most, I estimated, had landed on open ground.

Ali got back into the car, ready to drive on, but this time I made the decision: he would wait until I returned; I was proceeding on foot. It was the only time Ali and I had a stand-up argument until eventually, and most grudgingly, he gave in.

It is difficult to explain one's feelings as one realizes that one is apparently the only living thing moving on a wide deserted road in full view of guns only too willing to kill at sight. I cannot honestly remember feeling real fear since the day in 1943 when a German fighter was on the tail of my Spitfire and I realized that I was surrounded by Focke-Wulfe 190s. Apprehension perhaps, if that could explain the reaction when one has deliberately embarked on something, knowing full well the dangers. To me that morning the all-pervading reaction was one of acute alertness; I had no idea exactly what I was leading myself into, but a mile and a half down that road, obviously, were the Pakistani defenders, and if they had not been well and truly defending, Indian troops would have been flooding my way.

I kept under the trees, moving from one large trunk to the next. Here and there lay disabled tanks, and I used them as shelter as shells came over again. Then I realized that many of the deafening crashes were coming from the fields either side of me; Pakistani gunners were dotted all over them and well dug in, and most of the battle at this moment was between the artillery of both sides. Way down at what appeared to be the end of the road I could see clumps of buildings, one of which towered above the rest; this would be where the forward troops must be holding out, I decided. At times I took to the fields for short distances and crawled through the long, dried and prickly grass so as to avoid placing myself in full view of whatever might lie behind the buildings. Then I reached the shelter of the nearest, half-destroyed building, much to the amazement of four Pakistani soldiers I came across sitting behind a wall, two of them stripped to the waist and shaving. I needed a cigarette and stayed a while chatting; they could direct me the last two hundred yards or so and, most important, they could tell me the safest way to the command post.

It was on the other side of the large building, I was told, and the route needed some nimble negotiating, dodging a few yards at a time from one shattered house to the next. Indian snipers were in every building the other side of what I now saw was a barricade of tanks, trucks, concrete and every conceivable type of rubble, and the main idea was to stay below the line of fire from the tops of the buildings on the Indian side. I reached the large building and followed instructions to go through it and not round it; most of the roof had been blown in and gaping holes in the walls left much of the building exposed to the sun. Smashed machinery lay twisted in what had been a huge workshop and thousands of shoes lay among the dust and fallen brickwork. A ludicrous thought came into my mind; this shoe factory must have been built by the universally known Czech shoe manufacturer, Bata. Hence the name Batapur, the *pur* meaning town in English. What a fantastic advertising coup, I thought. This was, in fact, what had actually happened, and the houses around had been built by Bata for its workers. One day, later perhaps, it could add another line to its advertising copy: The Name which Defeated the Indian Army. Its workers were now far away; those who had survived the first onslaught were somewhere among the streams of refugees.

From the factory I got to the ruins which I felt sure was the command post. Again, troops were surprised to see this foreign civilian who suddenly appeared among them. I asked for the commanding officer and a lance-corporal disappeared into the ruins. Then it was my surprise; a major appeared, immaculate, and greeted me with the words, 'Hello old man, what are you doing up here?' It was the same major I had shared tea with at the most forward position in the salient only days before, with a smile which I was long to remember. Several weeks later I saw it again, when in Singapore I was visiting my tailor, the eighteen-stone, turbanned and white-skirted Akhtar in Coleman Street, who had dressed – in civilian clothes as well as uniforms – practically every senior British officer serving there. He waddled into his back room and appeared again holding a letter and a newspaper cutting. 'You were in Pakistan,' said Akhtar. 'Did you meet my nephew?' He handed me the newspaper cutting, and from it a face smiled at me, the face of the immaculate major. I read the announcement of his death on the Lahore front. He had been posthumously awarded Pakistan's highest military decoration.

How could one ever imagine this highly efficient, soft-spoken man as rotting flesh? He had the bearing, training and command which, if I had thought about it at that time, must surely have taken him into the uppermost ranks of the Pakistani army. 'I think you'd better get in here, old man,' he said as he led me into the ruins. 'It's safer here. We've not had a peek out of them for nearly two hours and on my reckoning something's due pretty soon.'

It came twenty minutes later, but shaving and cleaning up was over by then and every man was well in position. The major's infantry troops were stretched north and south from Batapur, holding a canal, he explained; a dozen times the Indian troops had attempted to cross it, in fact had done so at times and at points, but the line still held and not one Indian was alive or free on our side of the line.

The artillery began it, and as though a hundred fingers pulled triggers at exactly the same moment the air was filled with a mad cacophony of explosions, tearing air and petrifying whistling. At the same moment the Indian infantry opened up from the ruins, no more than sixty yards away, with machine guns, bazookas and rifles; mortars came lobbing over, but by now the Pakistani artillery was in answering action and the major's men were filling the air in the ruins and all around it with the acrid and choking smell from spent bullets. I did not see the major leave; one moment he was beside me and the next he was not. Through a crack in the thick wall I saw the greenish uniforms of Indians dodging from one piece of ruin to another towards the barrier, then the Pakistanis were out there, in the open and blazing away. Men on both sides were dropping, never to move again.

Thinking back on that half-hour of absolute hell, I have since asked myself if I was afraid. Afraid, no; but obviously there was some sense which was asking me if I expected to get out of it all alive. What I remember most is trying to make scribbled notes on bits of paper and the ludicrous moment when I looked at my watch to see that it was a few minutes after eleven o'clock. With five hours' difference between Batapur and London, the time there was now six o'clock and the editor would still be in his bed – from which he never sent cables in such words as, 'Don't take any risks.'

It was two o'clock when I finally got back to Ali and a great welcoming grin came to his face; from the police station stock he brought me cool drinks and fruit, and the policeman led me to a well where I was able to clean the worst of the dust away. The comfort of the hotel, the service for no more than half a dozen customers, the brandy and soda at the flick of the fingers as I sat writing, a meal and the bliss of a comfortable bed were heaven that evening. And to hell with the Indians! I had enough faith in the major and his men to sleep like a log after ordering Ali to do likewise with the words, 'Five o'clock start tomorrow'.

The Pakistani Air Force fighters were by now well into their stride. On several occasions I had seen dogfights overhead and although several fighters had crashed to the ground, pouring smoke, I had not recognized one of them, so far, as being Pakistani. A visit to the air headquarters had further convinced me that here was another Battle of Britain in progress and it is highly unlikely the huge board in the operations room, showing state of readiness and gains and losses, could have been altered for my benefit. Mine had been more or less a surprise visit and it was the Air C-in-C who greeted me and answered some very searching questions. So that I could see more of the true situation for myself he arranged for me to fly to one of the forward fighter airfields; even then I was loathe to base any writing on just figures I had been given, and the operations board showed that, out of their fighter force of just under a hundred dated Sabres, the Pakistanis had lost five against claims of over forty Indian planes destroyed in the air and many others on the ground.

For me the day was one of nostalgia; how strange it is that one can look back on a five-year war, remembering only the better times and forgetting the days when the squadron would land minus one, two or three of one's closest comrades. Here, among the young, fresh-faced, keen Pakistani fighter pilots exactly the same scenes were being re-enacted as were so many I remembered: Biggin Hill, Tangmere, Hornchurch or Kenley;

the Sailor Malans, Alan Deeres, Bob Tucks and Johnny Johnsons. There was the eternal discussion of tactics all the time the pilots were on the ground. They dressed as did our pilots and in the same colour; they talked and joked like them and grabbed mugs of tea, sandwiches and wads of cake between operations. Only the colour of their skins was different. I talked with them and these youngsters discussed their air strikes and battles completely free from inhibition, withholding nothing.

I stayed with them through take-off and landing from three operations and counted every Sabre safely back on the ground. I shared their whoops of joy or silence as a flight commander would say, 'Too much deflection, Mohammed', when the films from their camera guns confirmed or rejected their claims. A good day it had been for them; seven Indian fighters destroyed and two damaged for the loss of none. It was a story I was able to write with feeling, understanding and absolute authenticity. But what was one despatch against the flow of claims coming from New Delhi that the Pakistani airforce had been destroyed, several times over. My cable arrived the following day. *Story unused*, it said.

Early one morning at Flashman's Hotel I awoke to what my drowsy state could only persuade me was the invasion of Rawalpindi. The war was upon us. Quickly I threw on some clothes and hurried out to the front of the hotel, taking care to keep close to the walls of buildings on the way. Dawn was just breaking and the air was filled with ear-piercing shouts and yells and a thousand gunshots. I use the word intentionally, for by no stretch of the imagination could many of the fire-pieces that created the din be described as rifles. The Pathans, fierce and evil-looking tribesmen from the hills and mountains on the northern borders with Afghanistan, who had been the scourge of British troops around the Khyber Pass many years before, were in town and on their way to war, by any means at their disposal. For hours they poured into Rawalpindi in 8 horse-power cars of doubtful vintage, carrying as many as six and seven Pathans inside and another four or five miraculously balanced on the roof; in old trucks which, from their appearance, should have been abandoned years before, and now were crammed with fifty, sixty men and more, plus their bundles of belongings. That is the way they had travelled for hundreds of miles and for many days. Their turbans topped faces that were covered with fiery beards and great, drooping moustaches; their robes and embroidered waistcoats were all in the gayest colours imaginable; bandoliers, filled with bullets, hung from their shoulders, and they wore others, sometimes two, around their waists. Huge curved knives and swords in brilliant studded scabbards were somehow hitched on and pistols, most of them museum pieces, stuck out from robes and waistcoats or just hung among the rest of the armoury. And every one of the tribesmen was having the time of his life, loosing off shots into the air from inconceivably antiquated, long-barrelled guns. As I found later, less than a quarter of the Pathans could boast anything more modern than a rifle, no doubt stolen from British troops, which dated back to 1918 or thereabouts.

Here was patriotism of the highest order: the Pathans were convinced that the war could not be won without them and it was just a question of getting to grips with the Indian enemy. The imagination boggled at the thought of the carnage if they had been allowed anywhere near the flat open battlefronts, but who was to dissuade them? There were now thousands in the city and more on the way. To say that they were an embarrassment at this time is an understatement; army officials rushed all over Rawalpindi for hours trying to round them up and stop them from helping themselves to anything they fancied in the shops. Eventually they were led three miles out of the city to fields where they could have their own camp 'until going into battle'. The difficulties of keeping down their high spirits for the next week or so were tremendous and they had to be fed; daily promises that the general would allow them to fight 'tomorrow' were getting decidedly thin by the time the ceasefire came. I feel sure there would have been another war – Pathans versus the rest – if the war they had come to finish had not ceased anyway. Of course, the Pathans were an amusing sidelight and unexpected by journalists and cameramen; we trooped out to their camp, but only once. Too many curved knives were waved an inch from our throats and all of us were missing watches, pens and wallets before we left.

STORY UNUSED

With that one week to go before the efforts of America, Russia, Britain and United Nations Secretary General, U Thant – who personally flew to both capitals – brought about a ceasefire, it was evident that if any military conclusion was to be reached it would be on the Sialkot front. It was equally evident that both sides would be forced into some sort of compromise in the near future; India's tank, plane and personnel losses were mounting to levels of which she had never dreamed and it is doubtful if Pakistan had sufficient ammunition to carry on for more than another three or four weeks.

It was then that India made what was, perhaps, her major planned offensive. Into the Sialkot front she threw a tank division 200 strong, an infantry division and artillery: 50,000 men in all. And she failed. The Pakistani Air Force had command of the air and slammed at the Indian tanks as they came through in waves. Those which escaped were taken on by the Pakistani tanks and what became one of Pakistans best anti-tank weapons, bazookas mounted on jeeps. From foxholes I watched them; from their cover under trees they dashed into action against the Indian Centurions at speeds which took the Indian tank gunners completely by surprise. They were small targets and their weaving tactics presented difficult objects on which to train a heavy gun.

It is small wonder that the Indian generals were soon in disgrace for their dismal miscalculations, as they were, in fact, for their overall strategy of the war. As one wave of tanks came through to be mauled and defeated, another and then another followed. I saw many brave men die, but the grins on the faces of the bazooka men and tank crews, as the Pakistanis threw back attack after attack, convinced me that never before had I seen men with higher morale. Doubtless the Indians knew time was not on their side whilst so many high-powered nations were trying to force a compromise, and they desperately wanted a victory at Sialkot before that time came. But they failed and I could suggest many forms of retribution for the way in which the Indian commanders wantonly threw away thousands of lives. The thrashing they took at the hands of the Chinese should have taught them a lesson; unfortunately their conceit left no room for this.

The ceasefire came after three weeks of religious bloodletting, and it was agreed by both sides that all fighting should stop at noon the following day. Sialkot was the front from which to report it, but even at midnight the night before I could find no Pakistani commander who believed that it was over yet. The men, the tanks and the guns were still on constant alert, as well they might have been. At eight o'clock in the morning, just four hours before the official ceasefire, Indian tanks and infantry made yet another attempt to break through, another senseless attack in which many on both sides died. Noon came. Surely this must be the end, we thought; but still the Pakistanis did not trust the Indians. Two hours later the last battle was to be fought: the biggest attack for days was launched by India, and was repulsed by the Pakistanis. What trickery was this? Or was it fanatical hatred, exercised in the hope of slaughtering Pakistanis caught unawares? They were not, despite the fact that the Indians had blatantly broken an international cease-fire agreement. Pakistanis did die, of course, and so did Indians. My readers were never to learn of the mad deceit of that last day, for my despatch became just another 'Story unused'.

The morrow was to show the full and bloody results. As dawn came and not a shot had been fired since the previous afternoon, heads appeared both sides of the railway track which formed the ceasefire line. A quarter of a mile away we could see the Indians collecting and burying their dead and there was similar activity among the Pakistanis. Damaged tanks were being dragged in. Across the huge, open, shell-pitted plain I counted three disabled Pakistani Pattons. Then I counted the larger Indian Centurions: fourteen lay our side of the line and a Pakistani tank captain who had fought in the last battles drove me in a jeep to several of them. Upon one he climbed and opened the turret; inside was a headless body and thousands of maggots were already swarming in the neck. The captain closed the hatch and we climbed down; the stench was too much.

'That was Major Subramanian,' the captain quietly told me. 'I knocked him out yesterday afternoon.' But how did he know the name of the dead officer? 'We listened in to each other's radio,' he said. 'I knew he was leading that last attack. I recognized his voice.' The Captain pointed to the lettering on the side of the Centurion: 'Hobson's Horse', it read, the name of a regiment formed years before under the British Raj. The captain turned away. 'We were at Sandhurst together,' he said. 'We joined the regiment the same day, two years before Partition.'

For me, now, it was the inquest on the stalemate. Nothing had been gained by either side and much had been lost, much more than could be counted in tragic thousands of dead and disabled. Pakistan's hundred million people had for the first time been looking forward to some sort of prosperity; new vistas had been opened up for them by two five-year economic and industrial plans, with over £100m. coming as aid from western nations, and the World Bank had been about to give multi-million dollar loans. The current five-year plan was shattered and any confidence had been ruined among those in the west who had come to Pakistan's assistance earlier. India was in an equally sorry state financially and her Prime Minister, Shastri, was to die soon afterwards – taking a dreadful conscience with him, it may be hoped. Leaders whose first and only responsibility should have been to the poor and starving millions had squandered untold possible benefits in despicable and misguided dreams which had brought nothing but misery. I had seen enough of that in both India and Pakistan already, where people died of starvation without waiting for bombs and bullets.

For western-shaped military alliances the war had been a blow which was not to become apparent immediately; Pakistan was a member of the Central Treaty Organization, but throughout the war she had felt, and at times with good reason, that the West was siding with India. Zulfiquar Ali Bhutto, Foreign Minister at the time, had told me one evening in his Rawalpindi home that alliances were things of the past, especially any involving America. 'With America,' said Bhutto, 'it has to be black or white, there is no in between; it's time we looked to our nearest neighbours and became more friendly with them.' Communist China, notably, had been the only real hope Pakistan had had in the previous three weeks; she had threatened to move against India. It was strange to hear, over bacon and eggs in a field mess on the last day I spent with the troops, the same sentiments being expressed by officers whose speech, training, bearing and fighting could not have been anything but typically English. With 'Pass the salt, old man,' they enthused on the theme of friendship with China. Chinese weapons and Chinese military training. It was not long before they were being trained in the use of these weapons in Communist China.

Flashman's Hotel, the clinic and the bewhiskered face as I regained consciousness! Perhaps I had 'died' for no more than a minute, but there had been so many in three weeks for whom death was eternity. I thought of them in the luxury of the Karachi hotel where I had planned to stay for two days. I thought of them as I tried to sleep the night I arrived, only to telephone at four o'clock in the morning for a seat on the first available plane out, two hours later. I was on the plane. Beirut and friends were ahead of me. It was the only way: westwards, to connect with flights back east, to Singapore. A hostess brought me breakfast, but I was unnoticing; there were pictures in my mind of the charred body of an Indian soldier, crumpled heaps which had been living and speaking to me half an hour before, filthy remains of innocent children, mothers, fathers – bodies, dead bodies, hundreds of them.

Suddenly I was seeing more bodies, but now in Vietnam, fifty Vietcong here, twenty Americans there, lifeless women and babies on bloodstained streets, the moans of civilian victims of war as they breathed their last in makeshift hospitals, and over it all hung the stench of rot and decay. I was counting and I could do nothing about it. Was it three, four or five thousand dead bodies I had seen this year? I prayed. 'Please God, please – help me to stop.'

Chapter 2

THE CALM BEFORE

By my upbringing there was nothing more unpredictable than that my later life would be spent dashing across the vast distances of the world from one trouble spot to the next, delving into political plots and international chicanery which, for most of my days, have made certain that nations, creeds and isms are never allowed to live at peace one with the other.

My early life was music and religion, and for fifteen or more years, from my first recollections, music was to play the most important part in each day. Middle class, I suppose we would have been called then, although, on my father's salary as a civil servant and with four children, I would prefer to remember our status as 'lower' middle class. But father's accomplishment as a pianist kept us in the slightly higher bracket and ensured invitations to musical evenings if, in fact, we were not holding one ourselves and mother's beautifully clear singing voice completed the soirees that people then unconsciously recognized as the higher marks of respectability. Three times had father enlisted in the army, in 1914 and 1915, only to be sent home again as a suspected cardiac liability to His Majesty's Government; he lived for another fifty-three years with his beloved piano, and so my boyhood was spared the tales of Flanders mud, trenches, barbed wire, mass killing and the hated German.

My elder brother was developing well as a pianist under father's tuition, and I would doubtless have followed, if it had not been discovered that, obviously taking after mother, I had been gifted with a 'delightful' soprano voice. From then on it was the local church choir and very soon afterwards chorister at London's Southwark Cathedral. Naturally, the family's prestige rose considerably; it was then left to me to keep up with schoolwork at the same time as spending several compulsory hours a day, seven days a week at the cathedral. And, with so little time for anything but studying and singing, I missed much of the fun which so many others remember.

Every psalm and every hymn in the book I knew by heart; the prayers too, including those for peace and blessings on the work of the League of Nations. Politics, even local politics, were as foreign to me as were the words of young men extolling the virtues of a new and mysterious movement, communism. It was the Church for me; at least the Bishop – Dr Cyril Garbett, who was later to become Archbishop of York – had decided that I was good material for the priesthood. That might well have been my destiny if I had not won a public schools essay award. Someone close to the family suggested I should 'write for newspapers', although no one quite knew what that meant, and mother, who normally made the big decisions in the family, closed the whole subject of the priesthood with the words, 'We think the boy should be allowed time to make up his own mind; he is too young to make a decision now.'

I did, and it was newspapers. School rules were strict and decreed that no pupil should be seen without a school cap, wherever it might be. So I hid it in my pocket when I presented myself at the age of seventeen to the editor of a news agency. 'You have the job', he told me. 'Start on Monday and your wages will be twelve shillings and sixpence a week.' I confessed that I was still at school, but would like to begin at the end of term. Tommy McArthur, the editor and still a well-known figure in Fleet Street, hid a smile but promised to wait.

Music and singing, they were still so great a part of me, and the attempt to break from them became my greatest difficulty for the next few years. Twice I was almost pulled back and the second time I was actually in training, as a tenor, when the offer came for me to join a London newspaper with 'the biggest daily circulation in the world'. I accepted and for a year travelled the length and breadth of Britain. Twice I was sent to France and my yearning to see more of 'abroad' had begun. Then came the war and there was no need any more for me to struggle with the choice. Flying, hospital and flying again; the shock of mother's death from a German bomb; the comradeship of men from all corners of the earth; and although I often took part in concerts throughout the war years, my mind was made up when they were over. I would rather be a first-class journalist than a third-rate tenor.

I have never regretted the decision. The world became my hunting ground and with it the chance to know peoples, black, brown, yellow or white. Journalism gave me the chance to study individuals and to discover what makes a man pray to be left in peace, tilling his soil, or what magical power another has with megalomaniacal rantings which can sway illiterate masses, sometimes for good but often for evil. From Europe I went further to the Arab world, to Africa, Asia and the Far East, from Trinidad to Tokio, going eastwards. I found new horizons and my life became a study of humanity, always with something new to learn.

From my base in Beirut it was a life of continuous travel—Jordan, Syria, the Yemen, Egypt, Aden and practically every other country in the Middle East. Kenya, Tanzania, the French and Belgian Congos and Angola in Africa, Pakistan, Ceylon and India, Turkey, Cyprus, Greece and many more. It was the largest 'parish' any correspondent could wish for and stretched even to Madrid on one occasion when, bound for warmer climes, I made a last-minute diversion and spent a freezing December week clad only in thin, tropical clothes. Borneo during the uprising in 1961 I had seen, and Singapore; the startling change from desert to jungle, from eternal brown to luscious and brilliant green, intrigued me. It is said that one is either a desert lover or a jungle lover and one cannot be both. I have never quite made up my mind, for both have their beauty and both have their terror. But I welcomed the chance to return to the Far East in 1963, shortly before the Saudi Arabian desert had all but claimed me as a heatstroke victim.

Bustling Singapore, with its smells, its industrious Chinese, not so industrious Malays, Indians, Pakistanis, Tamils and Europeans; its religions – the many gods of the Chinese, the Buddhists, the Hindus, the Moslems and the Christians and the whole population of the tiny island's two million people sharing each other's religious festivals; Chinese food, eaten and cooked on the pavements of Kook Street, or Malay satay grilled on sticks over charcoal in the gutters of Beach Road; the vast lounge of Raffles Hotel and its dozens of rotating ceiling fans as it struggled to preserve its old colonial grandeur; the towering modern workers' flats, with multi-hued washing hanging from every window, sticking outwards on bamboo sticks; and the palm thatched huts of the Malays in their kampongs, soggy from the most recent tropical downpour. The steamy, torrid heat which could be guaranteed in April, June, September, any day of the year, and when shops decorated themselves with artificial snow and recorders blasted out that hardy annual tune, 'I'm Dreaming of a White Christmas' – this was the Singapore I had only glimpsed hitherto. Events were overtaking it, which were to cause me to make it my base and home for the next few years.

The Malaysian Federation was being steamrollered into being and on orders from the British Government nothing was to stop its formation. British diplomats sent out from the Commonwealth Office had their September deadline to put everything in order; and although many of them told me of their misgivings and doubts that the federation could ever succeed, it was more than their jobs were worth to pass these sentiments on to Whitehall. Malaya, Singapore, Sarawak and Sabah in North Borneo were to be joined as one, whether they liked it or not, and all Britain's responsibilities (except defence and foreign policy) were to be bundled together and passed over to a federal government, mostly Malay as it became apparent, to sort out for themselves. The Sultan of tiny Brunei in North Borneo had bitterly but steadfastly refused to take any part in the federation after realizing that he was only really needed for his oil riches, whilst being expected to take lower rank than Malayan sultans. And now, within hours of Federation Day, Malaya's Prime Minister, Tunku Abdul Rahman, was backing out as his fears mounted that this was some sort of trick which would eventually allow the Chinese, principally in the form of Singapore's premier, Lee Kuan Yew, to gain overall control. He was right, of course. If later events had not broken up the federation, inevitably over the years the Chinese, with their business acumen and drive, their superior political brilliance, their will to work where the Malays had little or none, must have become predominant.

Lee Kuan Yew was giving up a lot by changing from internal self-government in Singapore to all power invested in a central federate government, including his police force, as he was later to discover; but here was his dream of independence. And Lee Kuan Yew, regardless of the Tunku, the British Government or anyone, was going ahead with that. He would go it alone, he declared, and look after his own defence and foreign policy into the bargain.

It was my first meeting with Lee Kuan Yew, and I treated anything he said with caution. Many British officials had voiced their opinions on this lawyer who had obtained a double first degree in law at Cambridge. There were lots of question marks against him, the voices told me; he could be a dangerous man and his politics were too far to the left; it was even said that he was communist. How wrong were the British, but they have been wrong in so many of their deductions and the Malaysian Federation was to be no exception. Months later, when we had become good friends, I asked Lee Kuan Yew why he had apparently changed from the near-communist line he had taken during elections which made him Prime Minister. Openly, and this was one side of his character I always admired, he told me. 'I had to use them', he said; 'I needed their votes'. Lee Kuan Yew grinned. 'Then, when I was made Prime Minister, I put them all in jail.'

This day Lee Kuan Yew was just as straightforward in what he said and I had little doubt that he was prepared to declare independence for Singapore, although at the same time Britain would move heaven and earth to avoid it. I sensed that Lee Kuan Yew was as well aware of this as I was; he was playing a game of poker and, at the moment, he held the cards. Equally, he had a passionate belief that federation could work, that the conglomeration of Chinese, Malays, Indians, Pakistanis and the rest could prove to the world that race and religion did not matter. It was people who counted and they would gradually fuse into a new, although polyglot, nation. He had reckoned without the stubborn feudalism of the Malays and the determination of their leaders, whose personal coffers were already well lined, that nothing should interfere with their system.

Into the fray flew Duncan Sandys, then Britain's Commonwealth Minister. As he told me when I met him at Kuala Lumpur airport, 'I've come to bang a few heads together', and from that moment I felt more than certain that the federation would come into being. A year or so before, I had seen Duncan Sandys in action, 'banging together', the heads of Prime Minister Nehru of India and President Ayub of Pakistan. Indefatigably and without seeing a bed for days, he flew back and forth between Karachi and New Delhi until he had hammered out an agreement to which both leaders put their signature. He did it again this time, he was too much for Tunku Abdul Rahman, although the Tunku never forgave him for it, and a new date was set a few days ahead for Federation. Then Duncan Sandys telephoned me at my Singapore hotel, saying, 'I think I'd better get out of here until it's all over. I have an airforce plane. Would you like to join me?'

I joined the Hastings at Changi airport in Singapore and we flew to Kuala Lumpur to pick up Sandys. Then we set course across the South China Sea to Borneo and stayed there for three days, calling in at Brunei where, said Sandys, 'The Sultan has to have a slight rap over the knuckles. He's expecting it.' Sandys has been under fierce criticism and taken the blame for many things which happened during his term in the Commonwealth Office, some of them blunders. To me, as we flew high above the Borneo jungles, he offered an explanation, 'Governments make decisions', he said, 'and as the Minister it is my job to carry them out'. Few could deny that Sandys did just that, with considerable success. Then he let me into the secret of how it is possible to go for days and nights without proper sleep. He pulled a large silk handkerchief from his top pocket, neatly folded it and tied it around his head, covering his eyes. 'Catnaps', he said, and was sound asleep in one minute.

Hanging ominously over the whole drama of the formation of the Malaysian Federation hung the shadow of Indonesia. President Sukarno was rumbling his warnings, for he could

STORY UNUSED

see his dream of becoming emperor over a new Indonesian empire, stretching from Java to Thailand, fast disappearing. So far he had done fairly well in acquiring territory by threats, helped by American pressure on the Dutch, and Sukarno was still smarting under his failure to form his cunning concept of Mafilindo, a union between Malaya, the Philippines and Indonesia. The shadow was large enough to see and certainly the warnings to Whitehall from the fiery British Ambassador in Jakarta, Sir Andrew Gilchrist, that trouble was on the horizon, were strong enough to be considered. However, they were overridden, brushed under the carpet; it was success over Malaysia. Another federation had been formed despite the fact that others thought up by badly informed and misguided Foreign Office pundits were already failing. Success, success. How could the politicians see it as anything else, and who wished to hear of this fellow – what is his name? Sukarno? He had never been in their calculations, so why bother now?.

The ink was hardly dry on the accord signed by Lee Kuan Yew, Tunku Abdul Rahman and the chief ministers of Sabah and Sarawak, and Duncan Sandys was having one of his catnaps on the plane bearing him to London, when Sukarno declared war on the new federation. Not in those words, of course. Sukarno was far too wily for that and 'confrontation', he called it, a confrontation which was to keep thousands of British and hundreds of Australian and New Zealand troops, plus large parts of the British fleet and airforce, defending Malaysia for the next two years. If British politicians had not seen it coming it is to their great credit that the service chiefs had recognized it as a possibility and had already made contingency plans.

Sukarno's hatred was mostly against the British and he showed it in no time by burning down the British Embassy in Jakarta and wrecking, to a much lesser degree, the Malaysian Embassy. The last people he wanted around at the time were British journalists and he made certain that he kept us out – for the whole of that two years. It was not long before I was to meet this man, but I had to go all the way to Tokio for the introduction. Meanwhile there was little real action in his confrontation and another Far East situation was becoming most interesting. I took the plane to Saigon.

What a wonderful country Vietnam could have been; from the moment I left Tan Son Knut airport I fell in love with what still remained of sanity. Then, in 1963, it was still possible to see the countryside without the constant fear of a Vietcong ambush. Saigon itself, once its straggling suburbs were behind, reminded me of so many French provincial towns I knew: treelined avenues with gracious, French-style villas lying back in flower-grown gardens; the cathedral in the square and the familiar letters PTT above the nearby post and telegraph office. There were delightful restaurants and, even more delightful, French food and wines, served by French-speaking waiters supervised by the French patron who stood behind his counter beside the girl cashier. Outside on the pavements were the neatly-arranged chairs and tables where one could meet for aperitifs under gaily-coloured parasols and watch the world go by. There, naturally, the comparison with France ended, but I defy the Café de la Paix pavements in Paris itself to equal the scene of the slim and beautiful Vietnamese women in their national dress of wide and baggy, silk pantaloons, closely fitted, long-sleeved and high-necked, white dresses which reached beneath the knees with slits on either side, rising to a little above the waist. Raven black hair, well brushed and glistening, fell to that level and below, and a conical, round straw hat surmounted the exquisite picture. Motor traffic was light and every other girl appeared to travel by bicycle, sitting over drinks in the wide avenue of Le Loi, it was an intriguing sight never to pall as they daintily dismounted or flicked the rear part of the skirt onto a carrier above the rear wheel which, it seemed, had been specially designed for that purpose. Uniforms were little in evidence and the men, apart from those who dressed for business in western suits, wore the same type of baggy trousers and straight-cut, short-sleeved shirts, topped by the same conical hats. Pavements were lined with tiny stalls selling chocolate, cigarettes, wood carvings, lacquer work and a hundred and one other forms of Vietnamese bric-a-brac. Tu Do, Saigon's Bond Street, had its fashionable couturiers and tailors, with fashions which could have come from nowhere but Paris.

Saigon changed rapidly, but I shall be forever grateful that I was allowed, if for only a few days, to see the city as it might have been. The Vietcong had no intention of allowing Saigon to bathe in a sunny dream that was remote from a civil war. Grenades were tossed into pavement cafés which disappeared overnight, and the aperitifs of the future were to be sipped inside and behind stout metal grills which covered restaurant and café windows. As the American build-up grew, the main streets of Saigon were to become tangled masses of traffic and every third person, or so it seemed, owned a motor scooter. Bars, springing up like mushrooms, replaced many of the fashionable shops. Tu Do alone had over forty of them and each bar had that same number of bar-girls, whose sole knowledge of the English – or was it American? – language stretched as far as, 'You buy me a drink, Johnny?' The number of prostitutes increased a hundredfold and small children became thieves, homeless vagabonds who lived in parked cars. Sandbags were to surround small hotels which became American billets; thousands of American uniforms were to despoil what had been a city of charm, and as the Americans persuaded successive governments to get rid of the French – even doctors, nurses and teachers – the restaurant menus proclaimed the gourmet choices of double-decker hamburgers, Dagwood sandwiches, hot dogs, fries, coke and root beer. Although French wine stocks were dwindling, two particular names continued to appear in great profusion – Beaujolais and Chateauneuf du Pape. It took me some time and not a little indigestion before I was to discover that they were being manufactured, perfectly bottled and labelled, in the Chinese suburb of Cholon. And not a bottle had ever seen a grape. The shops and street stalls became stacked with goods which, strangely, should not have been seen outside the American PX store. Perhaps the saddest change came in the women; in their thousands they cast aside their traditional dress, cut off their tresses and donned blouses and short skirts, feeling that they looked western and agreeable to the floods of GIs pouring in. To my horror, I saw that nine out of ten

The Indo-Pakistan war of 1965. Photographs taken by the *Observer* cameraman show water damage after immersion in the river. See page 41

2. *Top:* Pakistani airmen at an airfield close to the front (Photo: *Observer*).
Bottom: Pakistani family in the ruins of a house in Peshawar, bombed by Indian planes in 1965. (Photo: U.P.I.)

females were painfully bow-legged; overnight they had become short and dumpy, unattractive. All that had decided me in my first few days that I was in the country of the world's most beautiful women had been thrown away.

Things were by no means as serene as they appeared on the surface during my first glimpses of Saigon, and very soon I was to become aware that behind the thin veneer lay terror and corruption, brutality and religious persecution among the 'free' Vietnamese themselves, which paled into insignificance the fear of being overrun by what was then, relatively, a small guerilla army equipped with home-made guns, bows and arrows, poisoned dart blowpipes and spears, its few and only more sophisticated weapons being those they had taken from South Vietnamese troops or police in carefully planned raids and ambushes. On my first night at dinner at one of the smarter restaurants I had seen them; well dressed and well groomed young Americans sat in pairs, threes or fours together at tables, and if I did particularly notice them I must have subconsciously bracketed them as some part of the American State Department, perhaps junior diplomats from the Embassy. But I was beginning to see too many of them. I do not know quite what peculiarities I had come to expect in recognizing diplomats, or journalists for that matter, but these young men did not fit into that bracket. There was a similarity about them, the way they looked at everyone who entered and their obvious secretive conversations, which stamped them as different, almost sinister. On occasions I tried to get them into conversation, but they were evasive and unforthcoming. It was probably two days before I learned the truth: they were CIA agents, America's third force and a law unto themselves, 'advisers' to the now hated Catholic convert President Ngo Dinh Diem, instructors to his vicious and cruel private army, and architects of the dreadful methods of suppression in which torture and violence were but a small part. As I was soon to discover, never were the CIA men actually taking part when Diem sent his troops against Buddhists, the chief object of his fanatical hatred, but these immaculate young men were always hovering somewhere in the background.

My main object was to get as complete a picture as possible

of the whole South Vietnamese situation and, being one of the few British correspondents who had so far taken such an interest, I was given a more than pleasant welcome when I dropped into the United States Information Services – USIS – offices in Le Loi. Pleasant, as I have said, the State Department had carefully chosen its men to disseminate its political line in Vietnam; more than one resigned in disgust when he found he was being forced to stay rigidly to it in the light of damning evidence which made it a mockery; but in those early days the real events were yet to unfold. After all, America's only role so far had been to supply 'advisers' to the Vietnamese forces, supply them with equipment and keep their puppet Diem solvent; and the whole financial outlay was less than a million dollars a day. If much of that was going into the pockets of Diem, his brother-in-law Ngo Dinh Nhu, his sister Madame Nhu and a few favourite provincial governors, why should the Americans complain? This was the attitude. And was Diem not their chosen bastion against the spread of Chinese communism?

A theory, of course, and as that was the considered, official political thinking of America it was natural that it should have been imbued in the minds of every American diplomat, embassy secretary, information officer, military adviser and CIA man who was sent to Vietnam or other eastern countries. But was not the theory more than a little naive, I found myself thinking as time and time again the domino theory – Vietnam falls and they all fall – was expounded? History had shown that the Vietnamese had fought the Chinese for fifty years and had fought the French for more than another score. They would do so again, I was convinced, as I began to understand them; they would fight any interference from wherever it came and for as long as necessary until they were left alone to arrange their own affairs. I had seen so many blunders in the wake of the John Foster Dulles doctrines of American foreign policy, a complete lack of perspective and childlike approaches to world affairs, a naïvety which had sent them into former British and French preserves with the sole object of unseating us in the all-powerful belief that these areas would automatically fall under their own determined spheres of influence. Many times in my Middle Eastern days I had argued vigorously against the American policy as they systematically eroded French, and British influence, in the area. At the time of the Suez invasion in 1956 I was almost physically attacked for advocating that the British and French should have gone right through, unseating President Nasser, in full opposition to American threats of intervention. If the American foreign 'experts' had understood the Middle East sufficiently, these sentiments might have been shared – and shared, too, by the ignorant British politicians who turned on Anthony Eden – and the chaos of the following years avoided. Vietnam was no concern of the British, but it had been of the French; the Americans, under the guise of friendship and assistance, had denied her supplies of arms when they were most needed, and the final defeat of France at Dien Bien Phu was not all that far away to be forgotten. America's next step in an illfounded plan came when she defied the Geneva agreement on the partition of Vietnam, backed Diem to the hilt and placed her foot firmly in the door. Now, in 1963, the signs of real escalation in the troubles which had fermented under Diem were becoming plainly visible. I could only hope that this was not to prove yet another major American blunder, but the more I observed the greater became my doubts.

Fourteen hundred American 'advisers', I was told, and it was impressed upon me that they acted in that capacity alone. With a couple of hundred attached to the South Vietnamese land forces, that left the great majority 'advising' in some other way, and as I discovered that they were all U.S. Army Air Force personnel I asked for facilities to join what was described as a 'transport' squadron. If nothing else, it could never be said that the Americans were not helpful and most obliging to visiting correspondents; perhaps much of it could be put down once again to naïvety, or perhaps the USIS officers knew little of what was happening outside Saigon. I had no reason to complain for the next few days; once away from Tan Son Nhut airport, I was able to wander at will.

The airfield to which I was being flown was some fifty miles south of Saigon and just away from the city outskirts I was to see why the delta area of South Vietnam was known as the ricebowl of the world. The sky was clear and visibility was certainly no less than fifty miles. On every side, and stretching as far as the eye could see, was one vast flat expanse of water, dotted with tiny islands which were villages or occasional small towns. From some of the towns thin ribbons of roads wound out across the water, their sides lined here with tall, spindly trees, or there with thick hedges. It did not occur to me then, as I looked down fascinated by the scene, that in these trees and hedges the greatest danger lay; now we were flying high and out of range of the bullets I was to learn about on the morrow. Under the water grew the rice, thousands of square miles of it. Here and there I made out minute figures, bent forward with their heads down, tending the rice beneath the surface. From this height was spread out the most peaceful scene imaginable; I did not know that beneath the water, too, lay the guns.

A steep and sudden descent dropped us into a main area base built on the only rising ground for miles around. A collection of huts lay to one corner, surrounded by high, sandbag walls; slit trenches were everywhere and gun positions were dug well into the ground manned by Americans in full battle kit. Rolls of barbed wire, forming deep perimeter defences, completely encircled the base and searchlights mounted on poles pointed to the soggy ground which, no more than one hundred yards away, disappeared into water, nothing but water. On one side of the field sat three 'Flying Bananas', obsolete helicopters, so-named because their long and bent, cylindrical bodies gave them the appearance of being just that. The main squadron was away somewhere over the delta, on a supply mission I supposed, and later, when I saw them come back in four formations of six, I could only wonder at what those supplies might have been.

No one appeared to notice me as I approached the buildings which housed the squadron offices, mess-halls and billets, and from then on I found my own way around. I located the adjutant, who gave me a curt 'Sure, we've heard about you' and no more, and walked into the nearest hut which offered any comfort and sat down. Three or four pilots, for this was their rest-room, wandered in and out, glanced at me and settled down to reading magazines or left again without a word.

It was the same when those who had been on the operation finally came in; a look from a few but not one nod. They sat around in groups and I could have counted no more than twenty or thirty words of conversation in the next half hour until someone said 'Chow' and they all trooped out. That was the most welcome sound I had heard all day; I had not eaten and I followed them into the mess-hall, to line up for my food and then sit and dine alone.

Back in the rest-room the atmosphere became that of a morgue once again; a few played cards, some just sat, whilst others leaned on the bamboo bar as a silence comparable only to that of a public library reading room reigned over all. Still I sat alone; my only efforts at conversation had been met with replies such as 'Sure' or 'Yep'. I was thinking that the best place for me would be a bed, if I could find one, when the crash came. Someone shouted, 'Christ, they're here again' and a second crash shook the wooden building, sending glasses to the floor. There was a rush for the door and I joined in, I had no idea who 'they' were and I had no particular wish to meet them alone. Into a sandbagged trench I went with half a dozen others and ducked with them as more mortars came our way. Guns on the airfield opened up and the floodlights stabbed out across the water all around; somewhere out there were the Vietcong and there was no way of knowing if the mortar attack would be followed up by an assault. I crouched, listening to curses, what the American pilots thought of Vietnam, the Vietnamese and, in particular, the Vietcong. Then came the mortar which hit a huge oxygen cylinder standing behind the mess-hall; sheets of flame shot into the air following the deafening explosion, and we were out of the trench, running to fire buckets and hoses. All hands were needed to save the camp from a major disaster.

The Vietcong may have used their last mortar or possibly considered that now they had achieved success; nothing more was lobbed into the camp and hard work for the next forty minutes saved the mess-hall and the nearby huts. It was a strange way to make friends and I had forgotten the earlier silence in all the excitement; in fact, it seemed quite natural, when it was all over, to hear a pilot with whom I had been working say, 'Reckon we need a drink', as he led me back towards the bar. We talked late into the night.

This had been the third Vietcong attack in a week. Raids on government army posts had become concentrated solely on acquiring arms. The mortar bombs which had hit the camp that night had been American; all over the delta the Vietcong were becoming stronger and more confident as they equipped themselves with real arms. Nearly every supply flight was now becoming a hazard; extra guns had been mounted on the Flying Bananas and the mission of that evening had been an air attack on a well-defended Vietcong position.

The pilot told me more. He was a captain who had flown in the Korean war; there he had met a nurse and had married her and he showed me photographs of their two small children. He had been in Vietnam for ten months and had to complete two more before his tour ended. He was weary, nervous and disillusioned. 'I'll be lucky if I make it,' he said. 'We're losing too many pilots, twelve a month. I was sent here to fly supplies; now they expect us to fight with these antiquated old kites. We didn't come here to fight their bloody war for them, but that's what we are doing. The South Vietnamese won't do it themselves. The whole setup stinks.' The captain had been in Vietnam long enough to know that all was not as it was carefully projected by the American information services, back home or around the world. He was bitter, and as he led me to a bed he said, 'Fly with me tomorrow and find out for yourself what it's like to be an adviser.'

At eight o'clock in the morning the Flying Banana was ready for take-off. Into it had been piled crates of stores, much of it ammunition, and a lot of canned food; half a dozen larger crates did not betray their contents. At the open side-door of the helicopter was a machine gun; thousands of rounds of ammunition were coiled in belts beside it, and the gunner was already checking that it was ready for action. In beside him went another gunner armed with three tommy-guns, and I climbed aboard to strap myself into one of the four metal bucket-shaped seats which faced the door. I had expected to be lifted vertically off the ground, but to my surprise we taxied out and took off just as would a conventional, fixed-wing aircraft, climbing gradually into the sky. How right the captain had been when he had complained that the Flying Bananas were 'antiquated'; they were totally unsuitable for the job or the conditions in which they were operating. To climb slowly anywhere across that countryside was an invitation to be shot at. The Flying Bananas' motors were not powerful enough to lift them off vertically under any load heavier than half a dozen men.

At 3,000 feet we levelled out; this height was considered safe from bullets, the gunner told me, but if he was suggesting that any stray bullets coming upwards would have expended their worth at that altitude he appeared to think that his could still be effective going downwards. He searched the water, the trees and bushes below continuously for any sign of movement and his finger was every ready on the trigger.

For me the vastness of the lake below was becoming more fascinating than it had been the day before; it still looked peaceful enough and the only sign of life were two or three figures bent over and working in the paddyfields. It was not long before I was watching them with somewhat more than passing interest and the gunner's words stayed firmly in my mind: 'Those are the bastards to keep your eyes on.' For half an hour we flew and still, incredibly, it was water as far as the eye could see. It was no small wonder that the Vietcong were concentrating mostly on this delta area in those early days: they had to eat and here enough rice was growing to feed the twenty-five millions of Vietnam, north and south together, as well as most neighbouring countries. To deny the area to the rest of Vietnam, to gain control of the main roads which took the rice into Saigon could mean disaster to the South Vietnamese government. Later, to a large degree, the Vietcong were to succeed as huge areas of the delta fell under their control, and to avert starvation America was forced to supply South Vietnam with tens of thousands of tons of rice.

As we approached, it seemed impossible that we could land on the minute island of mud. From the side of the helicopter I had seen it as the captain descended in a large circle, picking out his approach so as to avoid flying over the narrow, hedge-lined road with which it was connected and to avoid any figures working in the paddyfields. The patch – it could not be described as anything else, for where it was quite clear of the surrounding water it measured no more than fifty yards square – was nothing new to the captain. However, he had landed on it dozens of times before and today dropped the Flying Banana on to it in a last-second vertical descent, the mud softening the impact. Four Americans squelched their way towards us, and ammunition and food was lowered to them from the side door; their job was to defend the patch and they stayed there in the mud for days on end. One of them handed up a bundle of letters for posting, letters to America – I remember wondering at the time how it could ever be possible for a mother, wife or sweetheart to imagine in what conditions her boy was serving in Vietnam, however he might have attempted to describe it. Then we were away, climbing as before to 3,000 feet and in the air for twenty minutes before landing on another patch, but this time larger and close to a village, dropping supplies and picking up empty crates and mail.

We made two more such landings before letting down onto the largest patch of all; huts had been built on it and it was manned by twenty or more men. We climbed down and I followed the crew towards one of the huts. Our arrival had been perfectly timed to eat and I heard the welcome shout of 'Chow'. Long before I sat down I had decided that my desert boots and clothes were hopelessly inadequate for this sort of assignment; they were sodden and caked with mud. But I did discover what was in those larger crates, as from the cookhouse a little later came the shout, 'Hey, those lousy bums have sent me only one icebox. I ordered two.' The captain promised to pass on the complaint to the supply depot, which should have known better than expect men to be at war with only one icebox.

There were four more supply drops to be made that day and the sun was sinking low from a reddening sky when the call came over the radio. From our northern course towards base the Flying Banana suddenly swung off westwards and the gunner shouted me the message, 'One of our kites in trouble'. Taking off from one isolated supply drop, it had run into withering fire from a road whilst it was still at no more than two hundred feet. As I learned later, not one sign of the Vietcong had been seen in the area before, but here they were in a new 'nest'. Somehow, and perhaps under water, they had crept up on the landing patch and one gunner in the helicopter had been wounded in the first and surprising burst of fire.

Two more Flying Bananas were already in action when we got to the reported position. We had flown, losing height as we got near; the only way to attack was to fly low along the road, raking it with bullets and I could see the tracers tearing into a thin line of hedges. We circled wide, just above the water, getting into line astern of the other two; then we swept alongside that road, the machine gun and tommy-gun blazing. I was out of my seat and standing behind the machine gunner when I realized that many more 'farmers' were working in the paddyfields than I had seen at any other time that day. Plainly I could see their faces, under their conical hats, as they looked up, and there was no way of knowing if they were friend or foe. In any case it was the road on which we were concentrating and we raked it with fire three more times before the action was called off.

We were well on the way to base when one of the gunners noticed it: there was a bullet hole in the middle of the metal seat on which, earlier, I had been sitting. It could not have come from the road; any shots from there would have hit the Flying Banana from a side and slightly upwards angle and we had seen none. This particular bullet had come from directly beneath us, so at least one of those innocent-looking men had not been in the paddyfield to attend his rice.

The gunner from the helicopter which had been attacked was dead when they lifted him out at the base and, apart from my long talks with the captain, it was a silent rest-room and mess-hall again that night. It was fly, eat and sleep, nothing else; these pilots and crews knew they were trapped for a full twelve months unless they were carried out dead or wounded before. I flew with them for another two days in which we were engaged in minor battles; at times the gunners blazed away apparently at nothing, but on the third day one Flying Banana failed to return, later to be found in a paddyfield with all its crew dead.

The crews were living on their nerves. They were edgy and on several occasions I saw the edginess explode into bad temper. Normal conversation was rare and stilted. I saw one pilot leave at the end of his tour and the few farewells he got were given grudgingly; his departure was nothing more to the others than that they had six weeks or six months to go themselves, flying and shooting for these 'goddammed Viets'. They felt they had been tricked and thrown into a war which was no affair of theirs and in their bitterness counted the days, weeks and months until they could 'get the hell out it'.

Later, of course, we were to see a different type of morale among the helicopter pilots and crews; the veterans were replaced by young, keen and freshly-trained boys whose indoctrination had prepared them for the 'holy' war against the hated communism. Helicopters became the main weapon in closely-fought battles, and machines were designed solely as gun platforms; they were flown by 'death or glory' boys and no one can deny their amazing bravery. Eventually it was impossible for correspondents to obtain permission to fly with assault helicopters, so great were the losses. And by the end of 1969 over 1,400 helicopters alone had been lost in this war, which was to account for hundreds of thousands dead.

A second branch of the flying 'advisers' was attached to the South Vietnamese airforce, at that time a small force with no more than forty or so slow but effective, propeller-driven Skyraiders. Already obsolete, the Skyraiders were ideal for dealing with a guerilla type of warfare. They carried heavy bombloads and a useful array of guns or cannon. If only the American generals had insisted on putting them back into production instead of using supersonic jet-planes for ground assault, much more success might have come their way in the earlier stages of the escalation. But who could tell the Pentagon how to run a war? It was a long time before the generals on the spot were to learn that modern jets are not the weapons with which to fight a jungle war.

It was never easy to pin down the advisers flying in Skyraiders to exactly what their role might be. Officially they were instructors, 'training' the young Vietnamese pilots, but this training extended to operational missions. On several occasions I saw the Skyraiders in action and invariably two or three planes in the flight would press the main attack, flown superbly, whilst the rest circled and made weak and inexperienced passes at the target. It never came as a surprise to learn that American pilots were in some of those planes, 'sitting beside the Vietnamese pilot, as advisers'. More than that we were not allowed to know and certainly not see; correspondents were not welcome at South Vietnamese air force dispersal points. Soon afterwards the airforce became the deciding factor in the *coup d'état* which overthrew Diem; it might have been embarrassing if correspondents had been able to report that day that the cruel puppet dictator whom America had created, but over whom she had lost control, had in fact been attacked from the air by South Vietnamese air force planes flown by Americans.

Comparatively, life was pleasant in Vietnam on that first visit, or at least for the earlier and greater part of it. Visits to forward areas were easily arranged and there were no difficulties in discussing the situation with American 'advisers'. The war was not really regarded as such at the time; the Vietcong were not operating in great numbers, although they were better armed than before. Diem's brother-in-law Nhu was making claims of creating thousands of 'protected' hamlets on the advice of British experts of the Malayan emergency, and the overriding attitude of the Americans, as well as Diem's government, was that the 'communist' uprising would be under control reasonably soon, within months. The Buddhists were a nuisance but Diem, once a Buddhist and than a Catholic, knew how to deal with them, with the assistance of the CIA. Perhaps never before had any like situation been so completely overclouded with complacency. President John F. Kennedy was murmuring that it would not be long before he withdrew most of his advisers.

For me, between helicopter operations and visits to the troops, there were the comfort of the Caravelle hotel, pleasant cocktail and dinner parties, and drives into the fascinating and beautiful countryside around Saigon, where it was considered safe from the Vietcong. Behind the protection of diplomatic plates, I was able to spend a weekend at the once fashionable coast resort of Cap St Jacques, which still had its cafes, beach stalls and parasols of the days when Vietnam had been part of French Indo-China. But there was also time to dig beneath the surface of this fool's paradise, to discover that Nhu's so called 'protection' for the hamlets was nothing more than hastily placed barbed wire around villages which his British experts were never allowed to see. All this while Nhu and a few chosen provincial governors became dollar millionaires.

There was time also to discover that the Buddhists, well organized and directed, were preparing, as did the Vietcong, to rise against the tyranny of Diem; and to discover, through secret meetings with Vietcong agents, the strength of this ever-growing revolutionary army. The corruption, the persecution, the plotting, hatred and intrigue – it was all there, but conveniently swept under the carpet. We were a small band of correspondents, no more than fifteen, and most of them American; we wrote of the underlying dangers and warned of the holocaust which loomed on the horizon. We were viciously attacked as 'trouble makers' by the American State Department, the Pentagon and the White House itself. Chosen columnists were flown out for a few days, shown set pieces of 'protection' around hamlets on the outskirts of Saigon, 'briefed', dined and wined by US commanders, USIS spokesmen, American Aid officials and given an 'off the record' chat by the American Ambassador. We read their glowing reports of the success of the American programme for South Vietnam, and the complete containment of the communist guerillas, which was rapidly leading to their annihilation. And we read the castigations, the condemnation of their colleagues in Vietnam who, wrote one columnist, 'had been there too long to discern rumour from truth or right from wrong'.

This was a campaign, once started by the Washington politicians and generals, which gathered fast in momentum; this was the line they wished America to believe and, I had no doubt from the attitude of the visiting columnists towards us, the line which America wished to believe. The reputations of several journalists were in jeopardy; a few were recalled to America and two resigned their posts. It was several months before we saw most of them back on the scene, but by then the Buddhists had sparked off a chain of events which was to shock America into the realization that all was not as it should be in Vietnam or what it had been led to believe.

It usually began with an innocent conversation with a Vietnamese journalist, anxious to help a visiting foreign correspondent; then came the regular visits to my hotel; then, naturally, the talks quickly turned to politics. I needed every shade and every facet of opinion and, if I gently refused to give any opinions of my own, the Vietnamese had only one object: to decide if I were open-minded enough to listen to divergent views and could be trusted. From those visits and talks came introductions, invariably after dark and on car journeys designed to dim any sense of location or direction, to Buddhist leaders, Catholics and various political propagandists, and to actual agents of the Vietcong. Intrigue, admittedly, but legitimate intrigue, accepting the risks involved when one needs the answers to so many questions from so many sides, viewpoints and, one always hoped, a hint of possible moves before they happened. I had no illusion that each group did not know of my contacts with the others, but that was accepted provided they were sure of my journalistic integrity of never discolosing sources of information. For them, especially under the eagle eyes of Diem's secret police, it was an admirable although dangerous arrangement, a means of making their voices heard when, for some, it was a crime to speak at all. For me it was the building of a host of valuable contacts whose word could be weighed one against the other and against the Americans or Diem – and a means of getting as close as possible to unbiased writing.

I could never be sure whose voice it was that came over the telephone from time to time, but if there was a suggestion that I should be in a particular place, perhaps a bar or café, at a particular time I was always there. So it was when the high-pitched, musical voice told me, 'Go to the flower market at once'. I left the hotel immediately, crossed Tu Do and hurried along Le Loi.

Suddenly the screaming rose from the distance; I was running when I turned off Le Loi into the broad street, lined with flower-stalls, to see them streaming from every side-street, forming a wailing, weeping and hysterical mass of people a hundred or so yards away. At the same moment came the screeching of sirens, and the trucks and cars swept past me from Le Loi; from them jumped the troops, a hundred at least, and charged into the crowd, unmercifully swinging rifles held by the barrels, clubs and iron bars. I was seeing Diem's private army in action for the first time and it was horrifying to see the people being felled to the ground, streaming with blood. Women and children went down with the men; who it was appeared of no concern to the maniacal troops as they beat their way through the scattering hordes. They chased them into doorways and beat them senseless; I watched from the safety of a restaurant which had hastily closed and bolted its doors. Then, as the crowd cleared, leaving dozens lying where they had fallen, I saw the smouldering heap in the centre of the road. The Buddhists had begun their open protest against Diem: one of their monks had burned himself to death in public.

It shocked not only Vietnam and America; the burning shocked the world and our dispatches from Saigon that day spared nothing and nobody. Evidently it shocked my London office, and at the same time, no doubt, Saigon was seen as a first class source of eye-catching, circulation-building headlines. The following day the cable arrived, *See Vietnam etmalaysia future troublespots etfeel you obvious man projob stop wouldst agree leave Beirut setting up Fareast Bureau query.*

A Buddhist monk had to burn before they could 'see' the approaching dangers, although for weeks I had been predicting them from the painfully apparent undercurrents in both areas. This is the function of a 'correspondent' as apart from that of a 'reporter' – to study, understand and to be able to write of situations. But it had been a reporter's story which was now to decide my life for the next few years.

I agreed; I think I would have protested strongly against any other decision from London. The prospects had the possibilities of a correspondent's dream; although for Vietnam the following years were to be a nightmare.

The most difficult decision to make then, and for many months to come, was: when could it be considered 'safe' to leave Vietnam? As at this particular time nothing could be safely predicted in a jungle as thick as this, infested with intrigues and plots among the religions, erstwhile politicians and, as we were to see, among military officers who all considered that it was their rightful turn to have the pickings of the American dollars which flooded the country. *Coups d'état* became bigger news than the Vietcong, although the Vietcong never failed to take advantage of them and a suicide by burning of a Buddhist monk never failed to hit the headlines. But how to know exactly when they would occur was an impossibility, however many and wide were my contacts. It became a saying among visiting correspondents: 'Stay and nothing happens for weeks, leave and all hell breaks loose as your plane leaves Tan Son Nhut airport.'

I stayed another ten days after the burning of the Buddhist monk but Saigon stayed quiet, for it appeared that the Buddhists were loth to chance another such brutal beating from the Diem troops. My immediate priority was to transfer from the Middle East to the Far East and much had to be cleared up in Beirut and passed over to my replacement. At the same time, I would not be spending all my time in Vietnam and I would need a good, reliable stringer to cover events in my absence. So until I arrived in an emergency, I appointed John Sharkey, a softly-spoken, young and highly efficient American radio and television journalist, booked a seat on a plane and prepared to leave.

The airline bus was due to leave in half an hour when John's level and unhurried voice spoke to me on the telephone. 'Thought you should know,' he said. 'I've had a tipoff to be in the flower market at one o'clock.' One of John's contacts had passed on the information, but none of mine had been in touch. My bags were packed and the hotel bill paid. 'Reliable?' I asked, and John's next words decided me. 'Never let me down before, but I'll cover for you if you want to get off to Singapore,' he told me. 'Thanks, John, but that can wait another day,' I said. 'I'll see you there.'

I looked at my watch: there was almost an hour before the rendezvous, but this time I wanted to see more of what might happen than I had been able to see before. The flower market suggested only one thing: Buddhists and another possible self-burning. I walk leisurely down it and through the sidestreets leading off it, but all was normal. It was lunchtime for the

Vietnamese and in their hundreds they squatted on the pavements eating their rice and dried fish from bowls as the womenfolk cooked it over tiny charcoal fires. Fifteen minutes to go and I made back to where the flower stalls ended and the road opened into a broad square; if anything was planned it must, as before, happen there.

I walked into a nearby café and ordered a beer. From the window I could see no sign of John and there was little movement in the square. Continuously, I studied my watch as the hands came up to the hour.

I was deciding that I had wasted my time when I spotted the saffron-robed figure emerge from a street opposite and walk towards me across the square: a Buddhist monk, carrying a travelling case. I watched him fascinated as he reached the middle of the square and placed the case on the ground. He opened it, took out a small box and placed it beside the case; then from the case he took a large can, unscrewed the cap, lifted the can high and poured the liquid it contained over himself from head to foot.

At that moment I realized I was not the only witness. From the nearby streets had come the people, running, but no sounds came from their lips; they formed a crowd twenty yards back from the awful sight of the Buddhist monk making his preparations for what was the greatest deed he could commit on earth—burn himself to death and join his ancestors and gods in protest against those who defiled and persecuted them. In the few second in which I had to take in the scene I saw John and two Vietnamese photographers, all with cameras in their hands, standing in a shop doorway opposite, where they had been waiting for this moment. Now the monk was kneeling and reaching for the tiny box. As he struck a match a sheet of flame enveloped him. He placed his hands together and bent his head forward, saying his prayers as he roasted alive.

From the crowds the shrieking and wailing came as the flames spread, setting light to the road surrounding the monk. Hundreds more were rushing from all directions and the café doors were being slammed shut. Awestruck, I sat as through the flames I could see the kneeling figure turning black, agonized, but happy and unafraid. Then the piercing sirens filled the air:

Diem's men again. But however tight had been their grip on the city, once again they had been just those seconds too late to foil the Buddhist plan. At first I could not see them; they were hidden by the thickness of the crowd, but from the rising screams I knew they were doing their cruel work rapidly and efficiently as the people scattered.

The monk still burned as they broke into the scene they should have prevented and in their frenzy they turned on the people again. Up the sidestreets and along the pavements the butchery spread; young or old figures were dragged out of the doorways and shops and were beaten unconscious, or worse. Then I saw the troops wielding their clubs and rifle butts over where I had last seen John; I caught sight of him ducking and running away, only to be surrounded by more troops, one of them swinging an iron chair until he fell to the ground.

Nothing could have been more obvious, with his western dress, camera and appearance, than that John Sharkey was a press man. For some time Diem had hit at the press in every way in his power, short of violence. Visas had been suddenly cancelled and residence permits withdrawn and the American Embassy could do nothing. In some cases they had not wished to act. Now we found that direct instructions had been issued to Diem's men: 'Attack the press.'

For John it meant several days in the American military hospital before being flown to America. There the beautiful but infamous Madame Nhu, Diem's sister and wife of minister Nhu, had been invited to appear on a television programme 'Meet the Press'. With her flashing smiles and glib tongue she felt sure she could persuade America, with confidence, to increase the dollar aid to the Diem regime – the only possible saviour of South Vietnam. John Sharkey appeared on the programme, his head and arm swathed in bandages and Madame Nhu laughed as she asked, 'Whatever happened to you?' Perhaps the shock to America was as great as at the burning of the monks when John calmly replied: 'Your secret army did it. They beat me up in Saigon last week.'

For me it was a search for another stringer, but only temporary, for John was to return. The burning of two Buddhist monks had aroused a storm which surely must burst over Diem's head before long. Even the American diplomats in Saigon realized that and were busily fishing to discover from where the winds might blow. The CIA were in disgrace and their well-dressed young men were hastily dissociating themselves from the many facets of the regime into which they had infiltrated. But when would the blow fall – days, weeks or months? I decided on weeks and gave myself two to get to Beirut, clear up my affairs and return. My reckoning was wrong – by four days.

After Saigon, the so-far trouble-free air of Singapore was a welcome tonic, despite its heat and steamy humidity, which meant a change of clothes at least three or four times a day. Undercurrents of friction between the Chinese and Malays were forgotten in what were the first flushes of enthusiasm at being an important part of the new Malaysian Federation. The National Anthem of Singapore had been dropped for the rousing Malaysian one, hopefully composed to arouse the hearts of a multi-racial society. I liked Singapore, its hum of commerce and its feeling of busy efficiency, and I like the Straits Chinese, who were certainly the mainstays of both. How different from the Arabs among whom I had spent some years; I would not be sorry to leave them. I decided that Singapore was to be my new base, as against that other haven of journalists, Hong Kong. President Sukarno was not showing signs of great activity just yet, but I felt sure that would come. I could be sitting in one 'troublespot' whilst being within easy distance – two hours by plane – from the other great potential, Vietnam. With a lease signed on a small house surrounded by bougainvillæa, hibiscus and orchids, I flew off to Beirut, the home I had by now all but forgotten. One week I had given myself to move my household, close accounts, give a farewell party and attend all those I expected to be thrown by the host of friends June and I had made in over three years, then it was to be three days of complete relaxation before the move to Singapore.

Six days later the last packing cases were being moved out when the telephone – it was now on the floor – rang. The foreign editor from London was announced, but I got the words in first. 'Yes, I know. Diem has been overthrown in a military *coup d'état* in Saigon. I'm booked on the first plane and should be there by tomorrow.'

Chapter 3

ROUND TRIP

If there had been any slight sadness in leaving Beirut during those few hectic days of packing and farewells, they were quickly forgotten as the plane climbed above the mountains and headed eastwards over Syria. They had been happy years, perhaps the more so for June, who had been able to discover more of the beauty of the Lebanon than I had found time for; but ahead lay new surroundings, new peoples and customs. If we were leaving friends, a host of new ones were to compensate fully for our temporary loss. We were not to know it then, but many old friendships were to be renewed, like a magnet the east was drawing towards it senior diplomats of many nations, and among them were familiar faces we had seen in capitals thousands of miles from where they next appeared.

Much-needed sleep was the first priority as we flew through the short night and into a rising sun which clipped hours off the approaching day. Teheran, Karachi and Calcutta were left behind and I wondered when, if ever, I would see them again. The Orient was beckoning and from my brief views of its fascinations I was already feeling that I could stay there forever. For June it was a world unknown, armed only with an address in Singapore and the strange name of Punch Coomeraswamy, a Tamil lawyer I had met earlier in Singapore, who lived in the next house to ours and who, I was sure, would give June all the help she needed. For I was leaving the plane at Bangkok, bound for Saigon. June was moving into Singapore alone, and if she had some slight trepidation, many such upheavals in the past had trained her not to make it apparent.

Tan Son Nhut airport was darkened and quiet when I landed. Armed troops surrounded it and patrolled the streets as I was driven into the city under curfew. President Diem and his brother-in-law, Nhu, were already dead, discovered and shot by an over-zealous young officer who conveniently dispensed with the necessity of lengthy trials and all the ramifications of the colossal corruption they might have revealed. 'Big Minh' – Major General Duong Van Minh – had headed the *coup d'état* which overthrew Diem, and he was now being acclaimed as saviour. The Americans were murmuring that he was a fine man, an honest general whose recognized capabilities would quickly defeat the Vietcong and bring peace to South Vietnam. It was the signal for America to increase her aid and, if only she had realized it, the signal which added to the impetus of the jealous and squabbling generals to get their avaricious hands on it. More serious, the Vietcong immediately stepped up their attacks, well armed as they were now becoming, and to their horror the Americans realized that Big Minh's only answer to it was to fall into line with the latest solution being put forward by President de Gaulle: for the south to make friends with the north and neutralize the whole country.

Big Minh had to go. Nothing was farther from the minds of the American generals in the Pentagon, who were hell-bent on having a war against the communists somehow. With the assassination of President John F. Kennedy they found even easier clay to mould into their way of thinking in the form of Lyndon B. Johnson. It really did not matter who would replace him; the Americans were willing to back anyone who could unseat Minh and they succeeded, within three months of the fall of Diem. What they got in Minh's place was an even more bitter blow; a young upstart by the name of General Nguyen Khan cocked a snook at them for over a year until he had amassed a personal fortune and finally agreed to go quietly into exile. His first move when he took over from Minh was to appoint his brother-in-law as consul in Hong Kong, a conveniently close clearing house for financial manipulations, and gradually move his family there. Safely out of South Vietnam, Khan demonstrated how much he despised the Americans for their stupidity of the preceding years by spending some of his ill-gotten gains in the country from which they had come. He bought a large house on Long Island, New York, but this was hardly noticed in the new fever which was sweeping

America. Johnson had bowed to the dictates of the Pentagon and had ordered the fighting troops into Vietnam. The real killing had begun.

Through one crisis after another I was to shuttle in and out of Vietnam until it became my second home. But now, with the move from Beirut to Singapore, I was anxious to know more about my number one home, and with Sukarno's rumbling turning into something more positive I was hoping that I would be spending more time there than had ever been possible in Beirut. June had settled in beautifully; our new neighbours, the Coomeraswamy's, had been wonderful in those first days and already she knew the local shops, the local foods and prices. I arrived to find a household running perfectly; in the kampong among the palms and the beetle nut trees a hundred yards away from the house June had found Ah Li, a most capable Chinese woman who had become our amah; a Tamil gardener was tending the orchids and the garden was already neat and trim. And then, as though it had been specially arranged as a welcome, a Chinese travelling theatre moved into the nearby field and for the first time we were able to share, with everyone from the kampong, the delights of a traditional Chinese play with its gaudily, but magnificently, dressed characters sing-songing in their high-pitched voices for over two hours to the accompaniment of clanging cymbals and a thousand flashing lights.

With the coming of the independent Malaysian Federation, Singapore was having a boom; foreign businessmen were exploring the new possibilities which, despite Indonesian confrontation, were rapidly opening up; new hotels were already rising from their foundations and the price of property and land had rocketed, seemingly overnight, four, five and sometimes tenfold. Trade unions – Lee Kuan Yew was eventually to regret this particular innovation which he had copied from the British Socialism – were becoming strong and wildcat strikes were breaking out like a rash. But they were exciting days. The shops were full and we spent hours in Orchard Road, Raffles Place, Change Alley and the Thieves Market. To my great joy I found that one could bargain for anything and I was as adept at it as were any of the dealers – my training had been among the Arabs. Our main furniture had not yet arrived and there was so much we had disposed of before leaving Beirut, which could now be replaced at prices far lower than we had ever seen in the west. We found Tan See Chong, the carpenter whose carving was still as good as it had been in Shanghai, where he was taught many years before; we found Ah Chum the tailor, and a dressmaker for June. Many new clothes were to be needed for these seldom varying temperatures and this clinging humidity. And we found the clubs, an essential part of my requirements for keeping in touch with everything which could or did go on.

The Singapore Town Club I had been introduced to on my earlier visits and this became my first meeting place. High above Collier Quay and in the hub of the island's business community, I soon found it invaluable; here gathered the senior members of firms which operated all over Malaysia and some still had connections in Indonesia. For feeling the political pulse in the new federation the club was ideal; so wide were the ramifications of many of the firms and so long had been their presence in this part of the world that most of the directors knew more of a situation than did the diplomats who came and went. It was the natural meeting place for all those in commerce throughout the Far East during their visits to Singapore and many were the times when I was able to gather the best possible information on what was going on in such faraway places as Laos, Thailand, the Philippines, China, Formosa, Japan and even Vietnam. Originally the club had been founded when Singapore had been part of the British Empire and none but western faces were seen on the premises; now the membership had been thrown open to all, provided, of course, that the recommendations were approved by the committee. A typical lunchtime gathering would include Chinese lawyers and stockbrokers, Tamil and Malay businessmen, as well as the British, Australians, Dutch and the occasional American who was in town.

The clubrooms were large and comfortable and the service and food excellent, but it was not long before I decided that the club had its dangers, enough to ruin a working day. How they survived I shall never cease to wonder; a hard core of members were at the bar before midday and it was nothing unusual for them to be on the same stools at five o'clock in the afternoon, before returning to their offices 'to sign the letters'. Then it was back to the club for a few more drinks in preparation for the evening social round. I developed a routine of dropping into the club when the lunchtime drinking sessions were well under way; seldom did I stay more than an hour, except for a particularly important lunch, and I chose my drinks carefully. For my day was just beginning. I would be working on many nights long after the businessmen, stockbrokers and lawyers had gone to their beds.

As exclusive to the business community as was the Town Club, the Tanglin Club was open to all, that is, if one was lucky enough to be 'spoken for' and could secure the signatures of twelve 'sponsors' who were committee members and to whom one was, supposedly 'well known'. Victorian and colonial down to the smallest amendment in its rulebook, the Tanglin was suffering the pains of realizing that no longer were things as they had been under the British and that the club, if it wished to continue as such, must abide by the rules and laws which had crept up on it under the new constitution. One was that every club must open its membership to any and every race, and the committee went as far as it dared to keep the club 'white' with its rule of twelve sponsors. How ludicrous was the rule I had no difficulty in proving: in half an hour one lunchtime at the Town Club I completed my list of signatures from members of both clubs. The Tanglin Club need not have feared an Asian invasion; few bothered to join when Lee Kuan Yew discreetly let it be known that he had his own plans for the club premises if it continued its 'colonial' ways.

Honour had been satisfied and there is no doubt that the Tanglin Club had its rightful and useful place, serving the needs of a large expatriate community. For the family there were the swimming pool, tennis and squash courts, and within the rambling jumble of buildings were the ample facilities of cardrooms, library, bars and an excellent restaurant. It was a meeting place for the young and old such as existed nowhere else in Singapore; here every section of the foreign community foregathered, the service officers, the diplomats, the grocers, the salesmen and the rest – with their children. Not to have been a member is almost like admitting that one has never seen Singapore, although on our first visit to meet the committee we did wonder what we might discover next when we came face-to-face with a woman arriving for dinner in a long and sequined gown, complete with pearls, long white gloves and a tiara.

I will always think of it as the most exclusive club in Singapore; but then, one would not have joined it if one were not interested in horses and that great game – polo. Perhaps my one sadness at leaving Beirut had been that Mabsoud, my magnificent grey Arab stallion had, perforce, to be left behind. I had schooled him and taught him the first lessons in jumping until my daughter arrived to bring him up to standard for shows and competitions; he followed me like a dog and nuzzled me affectionately. In Arabic his full name was 'the gentle one', but on a long ride across desert or dunes he showed all the fire known to his breed. On arriving back in Beirut after a long absence, Mabsoud's excited greeting was an eagerly awaited part of the homecoming; he was every bit a member of the family as a dog becomes – and he was being missed.

Mabsoud was never replaced, but the Polo Club in Singapore had some fine animals. More than that, lying peacefully in the luscious green, away from the city, it had an atmosphere of close friendship which other clubs lacked, shared on the field or under the whirling fans of the clubroom terrace after the evening ride with its members and riders – generals, colonels and captains, a naval commander, a Chinese rubber broker, an Indian shipper, a baby-food salesman, a couple of diplomats and a hard-riding American priest. There were the tournaments when our guests came from Johore, Perak and Pahang in Malaya, or from the Philippines. Stable boys and sultans, a Filipino millionaire and a young Marine Commando lieutenant. With our womenfolk we all gathered together for dinner and dancing after the games; nowhere could it all have been more democratic. And, although I had not planned it, I found I was learning more on quiet rides, exercising the horses, about Sukarno's confrontation and the defence of Malaysia than I would ever have expected from, or been offered by, the British Forces Public Relations Department which existed for that very purpose.

Among the men who staffed the Public Relations Department at this time were some who were only too anxious to make clear that they were not really used to handling news and information, but had been seconded from other military duties. And in the anxiety not to make mistakes or to do anything that might invite adverse criticism from their superiors, they were determined to take no chances whatever of giving out information of a possibly unpleasant nature. In fact, to say nothing or to deny a story already circulating was the safest policy. Of course, there were, as public relations officers for the three services, some first class men who writhed under instructions to withhold as much information as possible. Consequently, as confrontation took on more dangerous proportions and British forces who were taking the main brunt of defending Malaysia found themselves in actual jungle battles, the Department met every enquiry with the words, 'About any action involving Malaysian Security Forces we can give no information; you will have to ask Kuala Lumpur.' Neat, evasive and totally dishonest. British commanders were directing every facet of what had now become war with British troops; the one time that Malaysian troops were put on the Borneo border, they were caught unawares by Indonesian guerillas whilst they bowed in sunset prayers and were wiped out. True, there were periodical defence meetings in Kuala Lumpur, but they were more or less routine; there was not one Malaysian officer with sufficient experience or who could be trusted to make a major decision.

On occasions it was suggested that the Tunku did not wish Indonesia to know that British troops were involved; it may have been some vague Asian Moslem reasoning, but it was difficult to imagine how the simple facts which were known throughout the world had somehow not percolated through to Jakarta. And even more difficult to disguise the British ships, British planes, British Gurkha regiment, Marine comandos, paratroops and other British units which built up the defences rapidly as the situation worsened. It was also suggested that 'we' – and that included me – 'should be nice to the Tunku'; it had not taken him long to grumble that the British had brought all this trouble down on his head by pushing him into federation. But here were the British boys, fighting under wretched conditions with no recognition or thanks from the people they were fighting to defend. The war operation rooms were in the British bases in Singapore and in the British forward headquarters in Kuching, but nobody, least of all the people of Britain, were to be allowed to know of their existence or what they were doing. I did not have to be told of the immediate security precautions; these were natural considerations. And I definitely refused to accept the evasions of the Public Relations Department, knowing that no information would ever come out of Kuala Lumpur when British boys were being killed.

It was a fight, a stupid one so far as the Department was concerned, for if it was not prepared to give me information, it was reckoning, too, with many troops and officers, some most senior, who could not agree with what became official policy, whether decreed by the Department or the British Government itself. It began with the death of a Royal Air Force chaplain, shot down by Indonesians as he visited front line troops in Borneo by helicopter, hopefully arranging Christmas services in jungle clearings. A 'member of the security forces' had been killed in Sarawak was all that Malaysian radio announced and, apart from being referred to Kuala Lumpur, there was silence from the Department. 'We would like to tell you, but those are our orders and it's more than our jobs are worth to go against them,' the individual public relations officers told me then and many times later. Finally I would ask such questions as, 'Are they British, Gurkha or Malaysian?' and, painfully trying to help whilst at the same time obeying instructions, some such answer would come as, 'The second could be right, but please do not say you have spoken to me.'

The horses were saddled at the Polo Club that evening of the broadcast and four of us trotted out together. We had not gone far when one of my companions asked, 'You've heard about the padre? Shot down over the border. Wonderful chap. He was on his last tour. Begged to come out here.' The club was not my only source of information but many were the service members who were sympathetic to the cause I had taken up. Later that evening I had the pleasure of disturbing one officer's dinner and a statement had to be issued that the padre had been killed three days before. A Marine commando was next to be killed and then two Gurkhas. Sukarno was hotting up the jungle war and British Defence Minister, Peter Thorneycroft, flew out to study the new crisis. In Kuching I told him my views on his public relations and Thorneycroft promised to go into them in Singapore; whether he did or not, nothing appeared to deter those in charge of information, for the following day they issued a complete denial of a despatch I had sent, telling of a British counteraction in which I became involved just two hours after the minister left Borneo. It had never happened, that was the official line.

It may be that somewhere in the back of the official mind there was the idea that this was the correct interpretation of a directive from somewhere above. That is all I could say in favour of such behaviour. Too much publicity regarding the British forces in the local Malaysian press could possibly have dampened the will of the Malaysians themselves to rise and defend their federation and, God knows, that will was damp enough anyway. But to deny news of the British to their own kith and kin was unforgiveable and dangerous; letters from worried relatives in Britain did not help the troops involved and families of many of them back in Singapore had become nervous and upset with every new mention of 'Malaysian' casualties. They were resentful, too, and had every cause to be when they saw the Tunku fly to Borneo to visit the survivors of that one and only action – if action it can be called so far as the Malay troops were concerned – in which real Malaysians were involved, handing out decorations to all, alive or dead, and large sums of money to their dependants.

It took me another five months to end the ridiculous situation. I wrote an article headlined, 'Why are they lying about the British dead in Borneo?' showing the British casualties, dead and wounded, at that time as thirty-six. Not one of them would have been reported if it had been left to official channels, I said, which brought forth a scathing attack in print, not in the British press, where the article had been published, but in the local English press in Malaysia. I was able to reply and my letter laid the blame fairly and squarely where it belonged. There were quick changes of personnel, but I do not remember receiving invitations to any farewells, if, in fact, there were any. The Ministry of Defence issued instructions that details of all British casualties would, henceforth, be released subject to security precautions existing at the moment. Deep were the sighs of relief everywhere at the change of attitude, and not least were they heard in the forces Public Relations Department, which settled down to providing a first-rate and friendly service to the press, radio and television for the rest of Sukarno's abortive war.

After more than two years without respite from the heat of deserts and tropics, Tokyo in winter appealed to me more than anything else I could imagine in January, 1964. From the heated wardrobes which guarded them from the ruinous mould and mildew of Singapore's humidity came clothes I had all but forgotten. The fact that I was now a hot climate person and that within a week I would have gone anywhere to escape the biting cold, rain and sleet, was never in my mind. I suppose, like most men, I still liked to feel that I was something special in an expensive Savile Row suit, and the few I had trailed around the world I had had little opportunity of showing off. Here was the opportunity to get away from the eternal shirt and slacks, a tie only out of respect for the person one was visiting, or a jacket for formal occasions, but only if there were air conditioning. Tokyo, the big city of the east, which I had so far had no chance to see – the grandeur of Hong Kong, its tensions and delights, could wait until later, I thought as we briefly put down there *en route*. I was perfectly happy at the prospect of Tokyo and the exquisite food and drink on the Japanese Airlines plane – seldom surpassed in all my travels before or since – and the traditional Japanese courtesy with which it was served, all made for one of the happier journeys I care to remember.

It also gave me ample time to consider the reason for my visit and I was finding it incredible that President Johnson, so recently in the saddle after Kennedy's death, should find this an opportune time to interfere in the Indonesian-Malaysian-British dispute. From what I understood, Johnson wanted Britain out of the fray; leave it to the Asians to sort out their own affairs was his advice. But was this the counsel of his Jakarta embassy where once his ambassador had had the ear of Sukarno but was being noticeably cold shouldered by the Indonesian president now that America had ploughed in untold millions in arms and aid? Only fools could fail to see that Sukarno's plan had been to grab the North Borneo states of Sabah and Sarawak the moment the British pulled out. Already he was being supplied with Russian arms, whether he intended to pay for them or not, and he had engaged in a close courtship of Peking. This could be but the beginning. Where was the sense at this moment in placating him and putting pressure on Britain to withdraw her troops? And wasn't America in enough trouble with Vietnam – or did she still not notice it – to dream of allowing communists in any form to creep up from the south in Java, where they all but held the reins, and gradually eastwards, engulfing large parts of the area from yet another direction? How much credit could be given to the American conviction – or was it conceit? – that she understood these peoples of the east? She had burned her fingers with the Arabs, misjudged Sukarno already once and showed little signs of any real comprehension of the Vietnamese mind. Did she know herself?

With Sukarno's known intransigence, it was difficult to see how Johnson could expect much success for this 'peace mission' – talks with Sukarno, who had agreed to meet in Tokyo, President Macapagal of the Philippines, Tunku Abdul Rahman in Kuala Lumpur and finally with the British Prime Minister, Sir Alec Douglas-Home and his foreign secretary 'Rab' Butler in London. But then came the next imponderable – why had Johnson chosen United States Attorney-General Robert Kennedy to lead the mission? Was this little more than political in-fighting by Johnson? I could not remember that Robert Kennedy had played any major part in international politics before and he was hardly the man for this task. At the same time, and whilst America still mourned its late President, here was the perfect opportunity to damage the reputation of Robert – the man Johnson might have most cause to fear as a future presidential candidate – by presenting him with an almost certain failure. This had all the makings of a most interesting assignment, I was thinking as I sipped a final champagne and the plane began to descend on Tokyo.

I had given myself two days before the scheduled arrival of Robert Kennedy and the first person I wished to meet was Sukarno. It was purely incidental that Kennedy should be meeting him there. Tokyo was one of Sukarno's favourite playgrounds and he had agreed to meet the young Attorney-General during this particular – but one of many – holiday in the Japanese capital. One of the world's biggest spenders, Sukarno kept millions of American aid dollars in the banks there and a select embassy staff to organize his every whim. A whole bevy of women were retained on call for his visits, at whatever price they demanded and, far from any thoughts of state confrontation or of Kennedy, Sukarno was engaged in his favourite pastime when I called at his hotel early that evening.

At the reception desk Japanese hands were raised in horror when I presented my card and asked that the President be told I wished to see him. A finger pointed at a large clock. 'Nobody must disturb the President before seven o'clock,' I was informed and now it was but five-thirty. 'Then get me someone on the President's staff,' I demanded, 'and tell him my visit is important.' It was one of those occasions which needed the strong approach; hotel staffs can be so obstructive. I stood over the receptionist as he made the short telephone call and his eyes showed that at least he was impressed with my importance. Then he put down the phone and gave me a slight bow. 'Mr Ganis Harsono will see you, but he is not quite ready. We will take you up in fifteen minutes,' I was told.

Ganis Harsono, it was a name I knew well but, being barred from Indonesia, it had never been my pleasure to meet him. He was credited with being closer to Sukarno and his views even than Subandrio, the Foreign Minister who was due to arrive from Jakarta for the Kennedy talks. No one appeared to know just what was Harsono's official position in the strange hierarchy Sukarno had gathered around him, but on many occasions he had acted as Sukarno's spokesman, and to my knowledge had always been a pretty sound prophet of any move the President was to make. Sukarno I had come to see and that was still my object, but if I had to wait Harsono would make an interesting interlude. I was wondering what sort of person I could expect as I was shown up the stairs to his room, with Japanese precision, exactly fifteen minutes later. Whatever it was, I was not expecting it. As the page knocked on the door it opened and a gorgeous Japanese girl hurried past us; Ganis Harsono stood there dressed only in shirt and slacks. 'Come in,' he said and grinned. 'Help yourself to a whisky.'

The fact that Harsono had mistimed my arrival at his room did not disturb him in the slightest. I refused a whisky. He suggested champagne and from the bottles around the room, untidy as he had made it with clothes lying on practically every chair, I could see that any drink I might like was there. He opened a bottle of the best French champagne, rang for fresh ice and poured himself a long whisky. The bed was in a great state of disarray, but he appeared not to notice as he lounged on it, glass in hand. Oh yes, it was a great pleasure meeting me. He remembered my name well. I had written some very bad things about Sukarno, wasn't that right? It could have been the beginning of a short and not too friendly conversation, culminating in a request that I leave. I was quite prepared for it from that first remark. But no, this fellow Harsono was astute in his own particular Asian way and he seized the opportunity to tell me what a great man was Sukarno. 'He laughs at what the British press says about him,' said Harsono. 'He enjoys it, and if you met him he would greet you as a friend.'

This was just what I wanted to discover for myself, but I did not broach the subject at once; better to get to know Harsono more. It was far more useful to be regarded by him as reasonable and friendly and allow him to imagine that he was persuading me into his point of view. I might need him later. For nearly an hour we drank and talked; with every whisky Harsono became more confidential, and when I remarked on the beauty of his recent visitor it was received as though the firm bonds of friendship were already tied. 'Good, yes,' said Harsono. 'Good, but we have better, you will see. I will give you the best women in Tokyo.' My thanks were profuse and my enthusiasm must have seemed genuine, for Harsono went on into more detail of the delights of his visit so far. But I was looking at my watch; it was now six forty-five and I was thinking it was time to get back to my main purpose. 'You've told me a lot about your President and I have never met him,' I said. 'It could help both our countries if I talk to him. Would you arrange that for me – now?'

Harsono put down his glass and looked at me for a full ten seconds, weighing in his mind any opinion he may have formed of me and whether or not he might have been successful in his own attempts at propaganda. Then he said, 'Yes, it is a good idea. I will talk with the President.' He picked up the telephone and spoke; my name was the only word I understood but Harsono was nodding his head. 'Ten minutes,' he told me. 'I must dress.' He disappeared into the bathroom, but not before saying, 'Drink more champagne.'

In a strange way, although I could never admire him or the regime of which he was part, I have always had a certain regard for Ganis Harsono since that first meeting. On several occasions more I was to meet him in eastern capitals and he never failed to greet me as a friend and welcome discussions on the situation in which his country was involved. I was to find that, however ready he was to defend Sukarno and his policies, Harsono could and would listen to sound reasoning. We had formed a link which enabled me to send notes to him in Jakarta and, as far as he was able, he sent replies. Finally he personally arranged the visa which got me into Indonesia, but by the time I collected it from the Indonesian Embassy in Bangkok, Ganis Harsono was rotting in a Jakarta jail with so many others of the Sukarno entourage. He was corrupt, of that there was no doubt, but his profits from the millions salted away by Sukarno and his ministers were almost nothing by comparison. He enjoyed the prestige of knowing Sukarno's thoughts and the high life that went with it but, misguided as he might have been, he showed a degree of sincerity of which the majority of Indonesians are totally devoid. I used him in Tokyo and perhaps he had not realized fully that I had been an adversary in a battle of wits. One thing I am sure he believed, that he was doing the right thing in arranging a talk

3. A Buddhist monk commits ritual suicide by burning in the centre of Saigon, October 1963 (Photo: U.P.I.)

4. *Top:* Ngo Dinh Diem, President of South Vietnam prior to his deposition (Photo: U.P.I.). *Bottom:* Robert Kennedy with President Sukarno at the Tokyo talks in 1964 (Photo: Assoc. Press)

with Sukarno. I had said that it could help both our countries and, as far as getting any sort of truth out of Sukarno, it did that. At least Britain was to know what to expect for another couple of years. Malaysia knew where she stood in Sukarno's plans and America should have realized that her meddling, however designed, was to have no effect.

Harsono led me to the lift and up to the top floor of the hotel, which was almost wholly occupied by the 'royal' suite. Outside the door sat one of Sukarno's staff at a desk and two others stood guard nearby. A word with the man at the desk and he rang the bell; another member of the staff opened the door and I was shown into a large hall, thickly carpeted in wine-coloured red and lit by Japanese hand-painted lamps. We waited there for a full two minutes before another door opened and we were beckoned in. Here was the moment of meeting the man whose power and personality had held sway over one hundred million people for years, the man who was seldom photographed out of a magnificent uniform bedecked with fifty medals. Such moments before meeting kings, dictators, leaders of revolutions or statesmen who had become names to the whole world never failed to conjure up mental images of what to expect, however momentary. Any that may have been playing around my mind were shattered the moment I passed through that door.

The room was vast and sumptuously furnished. Great oil paintings adorned the walls in their heavy gilt frames and a giant chandelier glistened. I took it all in – the thick pile of the carpet, the palace-like atmosphere – but my eyes were fixed on the three figures reclining among the silk cushions of the massive couch. On the left sprawled a beautiful blonde and on the right, her feet tucked up beneath her, was an equally beautiful brunette. She could have been Eurasian but I had no time to decide just then. Both girls were draped in long and fabulously embroidered negligées – partly transparent, as I soon became aware – and between them half-sat, half-lay a paunchy figure of an ageing man, clad in an open-necked shirt, baggy slacks and slippers. In front of the couch was a carved and gilt table and on it was a magnum-sized bottle of champagne in its ice bucket. The man waved his hand and said, 'Come and have a drink.' This was Sukarno and he was not wearing the black, velvet Pitji, the pillbox-shaped hat which covered his head in every known picture. The great man was showing what only intimates ever beheld – a large bald dome.

For some time no one had doubted that Sukarno did not care a damn what others thought, whoever they might be; here he was demonstrating that he did not care a bigger damn what they might see. He was perfectly relaxed and made no attempt to rise as Harsono, in their own tongue, explained who I was. Then he laughed. 'A British journalist – one of my enemies. Sit down – Ganis, pour the champagne.' It was a scene which would have been a joy to write about in a gossip magazine, but for the monent one which had to be put in store. The fact that I was holding a drink should give me time for a few salient questions and the fact that Sukarno was fondling the hand of first one girl and then the other I conveniently appeared not to notice.

With small talk about where I had come from and did I know Indonesia, the first glass emptied and Ganis was ready with the bottle for a second. Then Sukarno looked at his watch and shooed the girls away. 'Go and dress, we are going out,' he said. They unwound themselves and departed through one of the several doors. Sukarno pulled himself to his feet and began pacing the room. 'What do you want to know?' he asked.

All the answers to that question could have taken me hours and I was considering I would be lucky if I had minutes. What views did Sukarno have on the Kennedy peace mission, I wanted to know first; surprisingly, the answer came straight and to the point. Sukarno was now on an imaginary platform and his arm was thrown high, his fingers outstretched.

'I don't know why he is coming. I don't want to meet him,' he said, and his voice rose with the pacing of the carpet. 'If the Americans think Malaysia is a better substitute for combatting communism than Indonesia, let them take it and leave us alone.' American aid? Sukarno stopped and looked at me; he was bent forward and raised a clenched fist. 'Drop confrontation or America will drop you, is that what they are saying?' Sukarno laughed. 'I take no orders from anyone; if they are threatening that, they can get out. We get practically nothing from them now anyway.' I was not prepared to waste time on the possibility of Indonesia already being in the grip of communism to a large degree; I wanted rather to know whether or not Sukarno could compromise over the formation of Malaysia. 'Of course not,' he said. 'Not until the British get out. This is our own affair and it's too late to talk with Britain now. If we accept any terms, Britain will expand into Indonesia itself. No, I will fight – for years if necessary.'

The well-known megalomania was showing itself. Sukarno's temper was rising, but I was getting my answers and, watching him, I knew that he meant every word he said, even if he had no clear idea how he would put them into effect. He went on for a while, but his phrases added up to one thing – to hell with America, to hell with Kennedy, to hell with Britain; in fact, to hell with everyone and everything. Suddenly he stopped his pacing, arm-waving and ranting, turned to me and smiled. 'Tell them that, tell them all that,' he said. 'You're a good man. Come and see me in Jakarta.' I mentioned something about needing a visa and Sukarno laughed. He slapped me mightily on the shoulder and made for one of the rooms. 'You'll have one soon,' he said. 'When we get the British out of Malaysia you are all welcome.'

It had been a most interesting twenty minutes and Harsono was feeling that he had done a good job as he suggested a drink in the bar. We went down to the ground floor and took a table near one of the huge windows. I was in no hurry; darkness was falling here in Tokyo and I had a particularly important despatch to write. In London it was still morning and my editor would just about be arriving at his desk.

I was glad I stayed. Harsono still wanted to talk and I was willing to listen, especially about Sukarno's companions. 'He prefers the blonde,' Harsono told me and grinned broadly as he added, 'She's American, she's agreed to go to Jakarta for three months if we put fifty thousand dollars into her bank here.' Harsono found it highly amusing and to a point it was. At least one American was getting something back from the millions American Aid had allocated for agricultural development in Indonesia. And she got the money; Garuda, the

Indonesian airline, sent a special plane to collect her and I had several reports from Jakarta over the following weeks of her appearances there.

Arrogance was a facet of Sukarno's character which he had no intention of hiding. In a few minutes we were to see a squad of police clearing the large, crescent-shaped drive leading into the hotel. Small but controlled crowds gathered at the gates, sure that all the fuss must be for visiting foreign royalty. They could have been right. Uniformed porters opened the main hotel doors and bowed low as Sukarno appeared to the flashes from half a dozen press cameras. The blonde was on one arm and the brunette on the other and both girls wore the most expensive mutation mink coats over shimmering gowns and open enough to reveal the glistening pearls at their throats. Sukarno was taking them to an official government banquet and Harsono smiled approvingly as the enthusiastic clapping came from the crowds. 'The people here love him,' said Ganis and I had no reason to argue. After all, Sukarno had made one Japanese bar girl into a very rich woman when he took her as his fourth wife. And the Japanese Prime Minister, I was told, did not raise an oriental eyebrow when next morning he paid a state call on Sukarno to find the blonde and brunette sitting there throughout the entire visit. On the best possible authority (Harsono) I was assured that they were dressed.

As enlightening as my meetings with Harsono and his President had been, I felt I had seen and heard enough for the moment when I politely excused myself from the earlier offer of a lady companion and left Ganis for the silence of my hotel room. Kennedy, so far as I knew, was still in Washington, being briefed for his mission by Johnson, and I was hoping that my despatch would be published in good time to assist them both. But this was my first night in Tokyo and it was still young; to eat American style in the hotel, as the menu suggested, held no attraction and, my cables away, I set off in search of a Japanese restaurant, leaving the unholy din of roadmaking equipment behind me. The 'West End', with its gaily lit stores, arcades, modern buildings, flashing neon, theatres, cinemas and restaurants was fully and vitally awake and proved more fascinating than I had ever remembered London's

Piccadilly or New York's Broadway. It was more alive and even if the majority among the milling throngs were bent on nothing more serious than pleasure, they were doing it with a sense of purpose. The dress was mostly western, but occasionally it was possible to see the attractive and traditionally dressed women in their kimonos and bustles and their hair piled high. They were always with their escorts, out to see a film, a show or to dine.

I chose a restaurant on the assumption that, having seen several kimonos pass through the lantern-surrounded entrance, there was less chance of being presented with a western menu there than at several others I had noticed, which were more modern. I was not disappointed; the waiter was an excellent interpreter and his suggestions provided me with a meal in which any international gourmet would have been proud to share. It was after leaving my solitary feast that I discovered Tokyo's triple-theatre – Japanese plays on the groundfloor, vaudeville above it and striptease at the top. The shows would be continuing for several hours yet and many were the exotic photographs which bade me to choose which floor I preferred. I decided that I had seen enough feminine beauty for one day; it was time to sleep.

The shock of the drastic change in climate between Singapore and Tokyo came next morning and it reduced me to a shivering mass from the moment I left the hotel until I hurried into the warm sanctuary of the Tokyo Press Club. The rain poured down, changed to sleet and then back to rain again. With it came blasts of icy wind. They cut through my Chinese-made, padded short coat and through some of the best and warmest material which had ever come out of Bradford. It is said that one's blood becomes thin after years in hot climates and whether or not I had chosen to believe it in the past I realized now that mine was as thin as water. There had been so much I had planned to see, but it was all forgotten as I plodded, drenched and miserable, though the streets, vainly waving at what seemed to be a thousand taxis, but every one of them occupied. I suppose I took a few wrong directions in my ignorance and I walked for all of forty minutes; then a taxi stopped and completed my journey – all two hundred yards of it – to the club which lay at the far end of the street in which I had found myself.

The London Press Club had its attractions, if one considered the bonhommie in its crowded bar, its reasonable restaurant and the big armchairs in the library, which were mostly used for afternoon naps – if one remembered the stuffy heat of an exceptional English summer and the icy blasts which swept up the stairs in the winter. The Washington Press Club was disappointing from most aspects. The New Delhi Press Club was like a barn at any time of the year, and the back room on the upper floor of the Cricket Club in Singapore, where the few journalists met once a week to have their brains picked by the information officers of the various Commonwealth High Commissions, was hardly worth remembering. But the Tokyo Press Club – it had to be seen to be believed: it was the Ritz, the Waldorf and Mayfair's Mirabelle all rolled into one, and its sumptuousness obliterated the outside elements in the time it took me to get halfway down my first drink. The reception rooms, the lounges, the carpets and furnishings made White's, Boodles, the Athenaeum or the Bath Club pale by comparison; the library, with its packed shelves and courteous, quiet attendants, the shower rooms, the cardrooms and the charm, efficiency and the food of the restaurant made me wonder how for so long the press of the rest of the world had been content to exist as second or third class citizens.

Correspondents descending on any place where news is being made have an unfailing sense of finding the central meeting place, whether it be a hotel, club or the best eating house. Normally, somewhere attached, is a bar and the time is shortly before lunch. In Tokyo we had the natural and palatial Press Club; it was the obvious place and, as usual, the right time. Within an hour I had met a colleague from Hong Kong, others from Saigon and Manila and the chief of an American news agency bureau in Tokyo I had not seen since he left the Middle East, three years before. Apart from the friendliness and pleasure of seeing each other, and apart from discussions on the particular assignment in hand, these get-togethers were invaluable. So often we had flown in from widely varying directions and places and, over a drink and lunch, we were able to keep each other informed on the most up-to-date situations and political moves and gossip throughout much of the vast areas the few of us covered. From the American news agency man there was little he could pass on of the optimism or otherwise of the Kennedy mission, but Kennedy was due to arrive next morning, he was able to tell us, and with him was coming a planeload of political correspondents from Washington.

The presses were still rolling in London and I had no idea if, or how much of, my Sukarno despatch was being published. Better not to mention it for the moment, I decided and, in any case, everyone would know soon enough when the agencies in London saw it and flashed it around the world.

None of us hurried over lunch; I had no appointment until six o'clock at the British Embassy and I am sure, like me, the others preferred the warmth and comfort of the club to the abominable Tokyo weather. It was one of those occasions to relax and enjoy. For a roving correspondent they were all too rare; in twenty four hours he might find himself in a slit-trench.

The large and rambling buildings of the Embassy compound looked cold and forbidding, but at least a car had been sent to pick me up from the club, and I was pleasantly and thankfully surprised to find that the great and high-ceilinged halls and rooms were well heated. The political counsellor was an old acquaintance from Istanbul and the ambassador I had not met before; but he was in the Embassy and as it was still too early in the London Foreign Office for anyone to be stirring I was hurried in to be introduced as soon as I mentioned my talk with Sukarno. For the Ambassador my visit was heaven-sent; not always did embassies abroad know what was happening under their very noses, but here was the opportunity for the Ambassador to send off the signals which would arrive, nicely timed, on the desk of the head of the Far East department as he arrived from that hated commuting train journey from Surbiton. It was all a question of the Ambassador, for once, being able to begin his signal, 'I am reliably informed that...', instead of receiving an irate signal from the man, already in a bad mood from the trial of negotiating Waterloo Station and the underground railway to Westminster, who had not deigned to read a particular and so-called 'popular' newspaper that morning and was only too willing to excuse his oversight when it was drawn to his attention, beginning, 'Did you know .. ?' I could have told the Counsellor or the Ambassador the night before, of course, but from experience I had no intention of allowing a diplomatic 'leak' in London to the opposition press. They understood and were grateful; Sukarno's words only confirmed the pessimism they had felt since Kennedy's visit was announced, but, being British and directly involved in the Malaysian dispute, they had to stand well clear during any talks which were coming in Tokyo, and from any of the personalities involved.

The evening passed pleasantly enough at the home of the Embassy Counsellor. It hardly matters where in the world one accepts such an invitation, but one can almost forecast the menu long before it is time to sit down for dinner. There was one other guest, and knowing that, diplomatically at least, he was not any more important than was I, it would be 'Number Three Menu,' three courses only: soup, English style main course, which could be steak and kidney pudding or a roast meat with two vegetables, one bottle of wine between the four, plenty of fresh water and the inevitable crème caramel – all prepared by the Japanese cook whose only instructions need be one, two or three menu. He had been doing it for years for a succession of Embassy officers and he knew that this night he did not place the port, brandy or cigars on the table for the men to pass round when the womenfolk, in this instance just the Counsellor's wife, left to 'powder their noses upstairs'. Old-fashioned and correct as that custom still is, it often seals a dinner party as a success or otherwise for the women; if the conversation upstairs is mainly on babies and servants it is a failure, if it develops into a round of malicious, gorgeous gossip it can be a big success. And bigger still, if the hostess has her own bottle tucked away somewhere up there.

That night the Japanese servant brought the tray of liqueurs to us as we sat comfortably in armchairs and they were served in minute glasses. Long practised in the art, I carefully sipped mine, knowing that it had to last through two cups of coffee. Sometimes a second brandy would be offered, but one could never be sure that the end of the second coffee automatically meant the signal to rise and make excuses that it was getting late. We were approaching that moment when the telephone rang and the counsellor disappeared from the room to take the call; in three minutes he was back, grinning broadly at me and saying, 'Have another brandy – that was my opposite number in the American embassy asking if I knew where to contact you. You've caused a stir with that Sukarno story. The Americans are in a shocking flap. Says he would like to meet you if you go to the American Embassy in the morning.' The second brandy was much more satisfying than the first. 'Did you say that I might be interested in meeting Kennedy too?' I asked, and the counsellor smiled. 'Of course,' he said; 'what did you expect?'

The meeting with Kennedy came the following afternoon, at the American Ambassador's residence, and it was a painful experience. No worse envoy could have been chosen by Johnson and I realized at once that this man who spoke mostly in monosyllables knew nothing of foreign affairs. Perhaps he was well aware of this himself; his embarrassment he covered with weak smiles and at least four times he attempted to answer questions with the words, 'My late brother, the President . . .'.

Why had Johnson done this to him? It was nothing more nor less than political slaughter. Sukarno would play with this immature youngster, spank him gently and send him away. I recalled that the American Secretary of State, Dean Rusk, had often said that there would be no South Vietnam crisis if only the Vietcong would stop attacking. Did not Mr Kennedy consider that the same might apply to Sukarno's guerillas in North Borneo? A pathetically weak and slow reply came, no more than a short sentence and unfinished: 'Well, when I talk to President Sukarno . . .'. Would Mr Kennedy put any pressure on Sukarno in an attempt to end the confrontation? Kennedy looked away, visibly blushing, and murmured, 'Well, I'm not here with any threats and, eh . . .'. Did Mr Kennedy agree that Britain should stand by her commitments and defend Malaysia? The Attorney-General was becoming more and more flustered, searching for words which his lack of experience would not produce. 'Well, I'm sure my late brother, the

President, would agree, this is an Asian affair and, eh . . .'. So did Mr Kennedy advocate that the British troops get out and leave it to the Asians?

I would have felt sorry for Kennedy if it had been possible, but his limp and unsure intervention could be playing right into Sukarno's hands. It was the last question he made any attempt to answer: 'Well, the Asians should be allowed to, eh . . .'. Was America following that policy in Vietnam? I was too disgusted to raise the point. It was all too obvious that, even if Kennedy had ever been briefed on a possible suggested solution, which I doubt, it had gone overboard the moment Sukarno's words to me became known. Sukarno had already won the first round, before the two men came face to face, and that's how it turned out. He and his Foreign Minister, Subandrio, in no mean terms, told Kennedy that if he wished his peace mission to succeed there was only one way to do it – get the British troops out of Borneo. Yes, said Sukarno, he might agree to summit talks with the Tunku, but he made it clear his terms would not alter; the infant abroad went on his dreary and uncomfortable way to see Tunku Abdul Rahman and then on to talks with Sir Alec Douglas-Home with nothing more to offer than that. To talks, but only at foreign minister level, the Tunku did reluctantly agree; on the question of the British troops, Kennedy got the same reaction in both places. The words were couched in somewhat more polite terms than Sukarno would have used, but they meant the same – 'Go to hell'.

Lamely wandering along in the wake of Sukarno's troublemaking was a frightened President Macapagal of the Philippines and, as at the same time there was strong feeling there at the continued presence of American bases, Kennedy had been instructed to pay a courtesy visit whilst he was in the area. For me it was the opportunity to see yet another country in my parish and, with the outcome of Kennedy's Tokyo visit plain for all to see, I saw no reason why I should stay on there until his scheduled departure. Manila, fifteen degrees above the Equator, with its sunshine and warmth, was beckoning me vigorously, and I could not leave Tokyo fast enough. I endured the freezing and wet drive for two hours through the slums –

arranged by the airline – and went through the airport so fast that I forgot the customary memento of any new country I usually bought for June. We had left the North Pacific and were over the Philippine Sea when I remembered it, but my teeth had stopped chattering.

The hot breeze coming in from the sea caressed me as I stepped from the plane. Now I was hopelessly overdressed in my European clothes, but it was a joy and would be remedied as soon as I reached the hotel. Immigration formalities were simple, practically non-existent, and customs were left behind with a mere wave of the hand from the official who appeared bored with the whole operation. Anyone and everyone, I thought, could pass through here without a check on security aspects or baggage and no one seemed to care. But I did not realize at that moment that now I was in one of the most lawless countries on earth. What did it matter if a few more undesirables found their way in? They would be a drop in the ocean of crime, murder and corruption which was accepted almost as the normal way of life. Petty crime appeared to be everyone's right. I noticed it as three baggage porters hemmed me in but seemed more interested in getting their hands on my watch than on the baggage handles. This was my first lesson and the next was that taxi windows should always be kept closed. Twice on the way to the hotel motorcycles drew alongside us in the traffic and the first time I pulled my arm from the window in the nick of time as a hand came through to grab that little circle of gold on my wrist.

It was a new, popular and comfortable hotel overlooking the sea and, as I was to find, regarded as being in a reasonably 'safe' area. As used as I was to seeing armed troops in so many countries, it did not strike me as being particularly untoward when two uniformed figures, armed to the teeth, stood aside from the main doors as I arrived – until later it was explained that these were private security guards. Everyone with any property to protect had them, sometimes two or three with tommy-guns, pistols and knives and their own sentry boxes at the firmly locked gates of villas surrounded by high walls and topped with barbed-wire. Residents of modern blocks of flats paid into a fund for their own protective private armies, but complained that they got little protection from frequent marauders; so they employed more guards to safeguard their homes from the men they were already employing for that very purpose. It was a situation which, had it not been so serious, would have been laughable, but a situation in which one was obliged to learn quickly which streets one should use even in daylight, for to walk in the wrong area at any time was an open invitation to thugs who always stood waiting to attack any unwary person, to beat him, or her, to the ground and steal everything of value.

In Manila you were a crook or you were not, and if you were not you carried a gun against the crook. I saw them being handed it at a nightclub cloakroom as casually as a hat might be exchanged for a ticket of receipt, and next morning, when the information officer from the American Embassy visited me at the hotel, he took a pistol from his pocket and laid it beside his drink with nothing more than, 'Sorry about that, but it gets so goddammed heavy in my slacks'. When I was with a friend from the British Embassy I asked where he kept his gun, to be told, quite seriously, 'Everyone tells me I'm crazy, but I don't carry one. However, I've been lucky so far.'

My roomboy at the hotel was a mine of information, and from the first moment we met he gravely impressed on me that I should go nowhere without first consulting him. I must not take a taxi unless it was one parked inside the hotel forecourt, he insisted, and told of the easy pitfall of hailing a taxi in the street and being driven to a quiet spot where thugs awaited. An honest person, I thought, and so he was in a particular way; he did not agree with violence and could not have been more helpful with his advice, especially when I ordered a drink in my room. He looked at me in amazement. 'You musn't order a drink in the hotel,' he explained. 'One glass of rum will cost you five pesos here. Give me ten pesetas and I will go out and buy you a bottle.' I handed him the money and he was back in five minutes with a most palatable brand of the Filipinos' national drink. 'You only order the lime and soda in the hotel,' he confided, 'they are cheap.' Then he picked up the telephone and spoke to the bar, adding, 'with ice'. He was welcome to the profit; I saw the same brand in several shops – marked '8 Pesos'.

After dinner the boy was beside me as I made for the hotel entrance; he chose the nightclub I should visit and the taxi which would take me, and collect me at an agreed hour, with the words, 'Remember, sir, no other taxi'. I gave him a small tip, but he politely returned it and the taxi driver nodded as it was explained that they had their own arrangements in such matters. If he had similar connections with the night club which, incidentally, I could have reached on foot in two minutes, and had telephoned it of my arrival, I was not complaining. It was a gay evening as the Filipinos know how to be gay, among themselves and without the need for expensive hostesses. I placed the Filipino women among the most beautiful in the world as I studied them dancing with their husbands and escorts, and the long, white and embroidered, frilly shirts worn by the men as the accepted evening wear, I made a mental note, would be at the top of my shopping list. I had sat alone for no more than ten minutes when an invitation came to join the table of two Filipinos and their glamorous wives; I was to curse Kennedy, Sukarno and the rest once again, later, when I was asked if I would care to join them the following day at their beach villa. Alas, Sunday was a working day for me like every other and the American Attorney-General was due in Manila.

Coffee, lots of it, newspapers and solitude is my perfect beginning for any day; never am I seen in a hotel dining room for breakfast and gossip with friends or colleagues. Those first hours after waking I cherish as my own, whenever circumstances permit; they give me time to plan the day and take complete stock of the job in hand and I have no wish to be diverted by the opinions or suggestions of another. The morning was perfect as I drew back the curtains in my Manila hotel room; a few people wandered on the beach less than a hundred yards away and small children played under the palm trees. Below, in the courtyard, a group of Americans in brilliant-hued shirts and ghastly Bermuda shorts were piling ciné cameras into a taxi, preparing to 'do' Manila and everything around it in the short twenty-four hours allowed them in their world package tour. It all looked tranquil enough and this part of the coast, slightly away from the city, was not lacking in tropical beauty; my hosts of the night before had been charming and I had had a thorougly enjoyable time. Could this be the lawless place that I had been led to believe it was, or was it that, for his own reasons, my faithful roomboy had painted an overcoloured and terrifying picture?

I rang for coffee and the local newspapers and they were placed on the table by the time I came out of the shower. The *Manila Times* lay at the top, folded and I could see that its front page was carrying a huge picture. I poured myself coffee and settled down to gather what local opinion, if any, there might be on the Indonesian confrontation issue, but the moment I unfolded the newspaper politics of any kind immediately left my mind. The picture covered three quarters of the page and it was a closeup of a dead man; entering the neck at the side and reappearing at the front was a viscious metal dart and underneath, in big letters, was the name of the victim; 'The latest sling-dart killing in the new gang warfare which is sweeping Manila', I was informed. I read on to find that the young man, 'a known gangster, suspected of three murders himself', was number eighteen on the list of fatal casualties in the past two weeks since the new and lethal playthings were introduced by the gangs. Charming, I thought, but now the word was in a different context.

I read on: page after page of violence, stabbings, political killings with President Macapagal accused as instigator, corruption among the police, customs officers, merchants and doctors, a photograph of a girl, raped and put to death, and a murderous and pillaging attack by 'brigands' on a village somewhere up country of which I had never heard. The *News of the World* and the *New York Daily Mirror* would have come nowhere in a competition to report brutality if they had been put together; this was Manila, this was the Philippines, and the editors of the *Manila Times* and the two other local newspapers had no intention of hiding it. Just as a contrast, and an invitation to the crooks and burglars to decide on their next hapless victims, each paper published 'society' pages, filled with pictures and accounts of receptions and parties and what the fashionable women wore – including their sparkling jewellery. There were political columns, but I had to search for them. I found that all three lambasted the President for being scared of Sukarno and, most vociferously, told him exactly what they thought of him for backing Indonesia in its fight with Malaysia.

It took me a while to drag myself away from the columns of vice, calculated trickery and blood, but this unanimous view of the Asian conflict was interesting and I wanted to know more about it. My telephone calls and meetings that morning only confirmed that the columnists had been right; the Filipinos who thought about the situation declared Macapagal to be misguided and the rest had no wish to get involved anyway.

But what were Macapagal's views? They interested me too and I put through a call to the presidential palace. He was not in Manila and would not be back until the evening. I decided on the next best, the Foreign Minister, Salvador Lopez, and asked the operator to get him at his home. The voice of Lopez answered me, 'I have a lunch party, but would you care to join us?' I was asked and I readily accepted, saying that I would take a taxi at once. 'No, no,' said Lopez, 'you musn't take a taxi. I will send a car for you.'

When a Filipino is rich he is very, very rich and there was everything to indicate that Lopez had hit the top bracket in his few short years of politics. His white villa, surrounded by at least a dozen guards, was huge and the rooms, from what I saw of them, were filled with classic Spanish antiques. The lunch guests numbered between thirty and forty and they were gathered beneath the hanging wisteria on the great terrace which led down to a beautifully landscaped garden. The champagne flowed and the silver-littered buffet tables displayed the gastronomical delights which were to follow – from caviare to paté, turkey and wild boar. Everyone there, it seemed, was in the millionaire class too and beauty abounded among its own trimmings of diamonds, rubies and pearls. In the centre stood the short, tubby figure with, despite his thirty-five years or so, a shiny bald head; like the other men he wore the white and frilly shirt and I felt pleased that I had packed a rather sophisticated creation, French style, I had had made in Saigon.

Salvador Lopez came to greet me as a servant hovered with a silver tray bearing a glass of champagne. As I had seen the night before, Filipino hospitality could be more than genuine and Lopez exuded it now as he welcomed me. With apparent pride he introduced me with the words, '. . . a famous journalist from London', and it was some time before I was to gather why I was being regarded as the honoured guest. In Manila a journalist carried more than a little importance and influence and one from London – why, it was natural to expect that he wielded a power certainly as great, if not greater, than a prime minister. Salvador Lopez had been a political journalist before becoming one of Macapagal's entourage and realized that his ex-colleagues could still make or break him. For all that, I decided, he never would have lived and entertained quite on this scale as a journalist. Lopez had made it and was determined to enjoy it to the full – until the next election when, inevitably, he was to lose office but retire gracefully on the pickings of five years in a cabinet post.

It was one of the nicer lunches to remember, the ambience was perfect and equalled by the food; I was among the most exclusive set in Manila and only the fact that I was a prisoner of time and events kept me from accepting the many invitations I was offered. Then, with the last of the guests sweeping away through the gates in their Cadillacs and Chryslers, Lopez led me to chairs placed in the shade of a low palm. He called for more coffee and brandy – it was time to talk.

Perhaps I should say it was time for me to offer advice, for that, it quickly became clear, was what Lopez needed and was looking for. It was not unusual; on many occasions before and since I have found myself with leaders of foreign countries who are completely unsure of themselves and have not known exactly how or why they had become involved in a particular situation. They rely on a correspondent who has studied it from every angle to fill in the gaps they have overlooked or failed to grasp, and, strangely, they are often prepared to accept his views. Salvador Lopez was such a man, terrifying as it may seem that, as Foreign Minister, his personal actions or words could lead a country into a war which nobody would have wanted and precious few understood. He was gullible too, amazingly so, and seldom have I found it so simple to lead a man in such a position into discussing things which would have deserved dismissal if they had come from any Filipino ambassador who worked under him. He knew, Lopez admitted, that Filipino sympathy lay with Malaysia, but to recognize the federation would antagonize Sukarno. With no thought of how Sukarno might, or could, express his displeasure, and no idea what might be the reaction of nations friendly towards the Philippines, Lopez said, 'I am afraid of Indonesia; she has one hundred million people against our thirty million.'

On another issue he was worried. 'We've made it so difficult for ourselves now that we have claimed parts of North Borneo,' Lopez told me. 'How can we drop that? I wish I had never listened to Subandrio. It was his suggestion.' The slight pomp he had shown before his guests had left him; he enjoyed the fruits of office but was betraying that the job took him completely out of his depth. Pathetic, maybe, but dangerous. Lopez was not and never will be alone in a world which tolerates avaricious politicians and their criminal incompetence. 'I wish I could turn the clock back,' said Lopez, 'begin all over again.'

We talked for nearly two hours and at the end Lopez was more relaxed. Kennedy was suggesting summit talks and it would be more in the interests of the Philippines than against them to add their weight to a possible peaceful solution. The claims to parts of North Borneo could be discreetly left on one side and settled legally later; Tunku Abdul Rahman had already hinted that he would agree to this. He should refuse, on any pretext, to make any declaration against Malaysia and resist any persuasion to become militarily involved. If Lopez was asking for advice, these were the main points even if, with others, they left him sitting on the fence during what could develop into a serious clash. He had gone far enough and had made a mistake; he agreed that he had been caught up in a net which contained far bigger fish than the Philippines and that the best way to stay alive was not to make a noise on either side. That is more or less what happened during the next two years of Sukarno's confrontation. I am not claiming credit, for others had power as well as reasoning to add to their advice; but that afternoon, as we left to go to the airport to meet Kennedy – Lopez insisted on driving me there – another babe in the big world of political machinations and skulduggery was relieved, grateful and profuse in his thanks. 'Tonight I will tell the President what you have said,' he told me. 'I know he will be pleased. He is so worried.'

I stood beside Salvador Lopez on the tarmac as the Attorney-General's private Boeing came to a halt. I had not asked or tried to join the official government reception committee, but Lopez would hear of nothing less. I do believe he would have presented me to Kennedy – I was now friend as well as adviser to Lopez and another lunch was arranged for the following day – if 5,000 teenagers had not broken throught the police cordon and surged forward, mobbing Kennedy as though he were a film star. It could be, from their age, that they imagined he was. Ethel Kennedy was swept aside and separated from her husband for a full ten minutes before order was restored, time enough for me to slip away from the possible embarrassment of Kennedy, who astounded the screaming youngsters by declaring, 'The reason for my visit is peace in South-East Asia'.

Despite the hospitality of Salvador Lopez and the excellence of his champagne and food, the chance of a night at one's own home was not to be missed. Kennedy was not due in Kuala Lumpur until the following day; there was an early evening plane to Singapore and it would be a simple matter to be there well in time for the next round of the 'peace talks'. My arrival was no surprise to June; she had long become used to my sudden appearances, just as she took for granted the sudden disappearances which could be short, or could be long. There was, however, the slight hope that soon I would be able to spend a little time in Singapore.

June informed me that some time must be spent on house-hunting, for, taking advantage of the soaring prices, our landlord had sold the house, and unless we were prepared for a legal battle a new home had to be found within a month. That would not be a simple matter; rents were bounding upwards everywhere and houses were being snapped up at any price in a commercial invasion of the island, confrontation or no confrontation. It was a problem which would be dealt with somehow; we had had many and similar ones before. If I thought of it again that evening it was nothing compared with the problem which faced Robert Kennedy at that moment – his whole reuputation might depend on the success or otherwise of his mission, and the cards were stacked against him.

If one can accept the slow pace, the incompetence of the Malay civil servants and the general couldn't-care-less attitude of 'Allah will provide', which is peculiar, I have found, to all Moslem countries, Kuala Lumpur has an attraction all its own. It lies flanked by the highlands and surrounded by rubber plantations, palm forests and tin mines. The bulk of the city is old, paint-starved and uncared for and dotted with the colonial mansions which in so many cases have fallen into a sad state of disrepair. Then suddenly, among it all, rises a large and modern office block with shining and chromed shops beneath and invariably bearing the names of Indian or Chinese proprietors.

On an industrial estate on the outskirts large factories have arisen, their impressive façades and structures hiding attempts by foreign managers to raise production to half of what it should or could be if they were not hidebound by government laws that insist on Malays being given preference for the jobs available. A large and sparsely populated university complex lies behind, some of its approach roads surfaced and others forgotten, which accepts non-Malay students to make up for the scarcity of Malays who decide to rise to academic heights. There are two or three new hotels to contrast in their gaudy interior decoration with the dinginess and complete lack of comfort of others into which one may be forced if a booking has not been made well in advance. New and costly villas straggle out in another direction, let at exorbitant rents to the large influx of foreign diplomats and businessmen since independence; and then come the kampongs, either Chinese or Malay, among the beautiful and gently rolling hills, the palms and the flowers.

In the slums of the city centre Malay cafés serve their food on roughly made tables which stretch out onto the broken pavements and from kitchens which would hardly bear an inspection for cleanliness, whilst the Chinese eating houses nearby invite one in with clean linen and cutlery and waiters who at least have bothered to change their shirts from the ones they had worn the day before or the day before that.

There is the new parliament building, of course, and then there is the vast monstrosity which is proudly pointed out as the mosque the Tunku had built. The architect who designed it surely deserved a prize, as well as his fee, for the most hideous and garish monument ever erected in the name of religion. But the Malays love it; the mosque was a special present to them by a benevolent government. The same thing was happening all over Malaya; instead of giving better housing, schooling and modern amenities, the Tunku squandered state funds on providing mosques, hundreds of them, hoping to keep the lower classes happy. Up to a point they did, under a feudal system which has existed for centuries the Malay does not ask much of life, especially if little or no work is entailed. He prefers to leave that to the Chinese and Indians, perpetually grumbles that they control most of the country's business, whilst at the same time accepting the fact that the very rich Malays, even the Sultans, made their vast wealth by getting the Chinese and Indians to work their land for them. Second-class citizens though they be and less privileged, the Chinese, by their own efforts and saving, were educated to a degree far superior to the Malays; they were prepared to make something of Malaya, despite the fact that they would never be able to claim it as their own. They had their poor classes as well as the rich, but the country would have rotted but for the industry and intelligence of the Chinese, plus the need to live, and therefore the labour, of the Indians. Despite this these two races were obliged to accept control by Malays in government, police and everything else and the Malays never ceased to resent them. Here was a potential volcano always on the point of eruption; small eruptions were soon to come and one hesitates to ponder on the consequences if ever one of these should reach the proportions where this inbred and jealous hatred on the part of the Malays gets completely beyond control. Unlike the Dutch in Indonesia, who beat the Malays to make them work, the British colonizers took the easy way out and imported the Chinese and the Indians to make up for the local shortcomings.

The British left a heritage in which it can only be hoped that common sense will prevail.

For the avid sightseer in Kuala Lumpur, and I must confess I do not belong to that particular breed, the Royal Palace, ornate and gilded, must be included, for the city cannot boast of being over rich in history and there are few other 'places of interest' which could not be taken in during a two-hour tour. Soon after moving into the new Malaysia, I was surprised one day to find that the 'Queen' had opened a women's bazaar in Ipoh; so the local newspaper told me and I could not imagine how a visit by Elizabeth – for Malaysia was in the Commonwealth – had escaped my notice. The following day the front page showed me a photograph of the 'King' and even if a mistake had been made in Prince Philip's title this was by no means his likeness. But Malaysia does have its own king and queen and they reign for five years; they are chosen from among the nine state sultans and by the sultans themselves. All very democratic, of course, among the sultans, but they are all Malays, and when Singapore, Sabah and Sarawak were included to make twelve states of the federation they were excluded from any say in the election of the next king and queen because their leaders were not of 'royal' blood. There was little possibility of any sultan having two terms as king, for when succeeding to a previous sultan they went to the bottom of the list and many died off before they were again anywhere near the top. The ballot was secret and no sultan ever knew who was for or against him; each one of them had a tiny rubber stamp bearing nothing more than one thick line and on election day all they had to do was use it on nine papers, striking out one word on each in a sentence worded, 'In my opinion, His Highness the Sultan of . . . is suitable/unsuitable to exercise his functions'.

For the lucky one there was a Privy Purse worth £30,000 a year plus another £4,000 for his consort. There was the 'royal' proclamation, and several months later the coronation, with all its pageantry, pomp and glitter as the 'royal' turban, decorated with a crescent and star of platinum, studded with diamonds, was placed on the head of the 'king', standing in his 'royal', silken and embroidered gowns around which had been placed the 'royal' belt embroidered in gold and with a ruby-studded buckle. For five years he and his wife could live it up royally, dotted along the way with tiresome state functions, the opening of mosques and conferring of honours. Even as a sultan he had never enjoyed the bowing and scraping which was to be his for five years; he was supreme authority in the land, religious leader – all Malays are Moslems – Commander-in-Chief of the armed forces and with the power to appoint the Prime Minister. Then he gracefully retired, to return to the more mundane job of governing his own state and spending his own money – safely estimated at a value of a hundred times that of the Privy Purse.

Tunku Abdul Rahman – the title *tunku* meaning prince – was from such a family. Much of his younger life had been spent in Europe 'studying', but he holds one of the time records as a student before he graduated in law. He loved the bright lights and the gaiety of nightspots and was reluctant to return to his own native land; once there, however, he found he was accepted as a political leader in a country where politics were in their infancy and, during the Japanese occupation of Malaya, acquired the reputation of being reasonably efficient and, more important, co-operative. He disliked the Chinese, envied them and at the same time feared them; with independence for Malaya and with few others in the field, he was the natural choice as Prime Minister and, as the constitution of the new federation of Malaysia had to be heavily loaded in favour of the Malays – the Tunku would have had no part of it if it had not been that way – there was little or no other choice for the premiership of a new parliament when he led by far the largest political party.

Speaking and acting without thinking was one of the Tunku's greatest failings and many have been the times when an unconsidered remark or decision has had to be speedily reversed, usually with protests that he really did not mean this or that in the way it had been interpreted. It was one such lapse which led to the formation of Malaysia, something which the federation maniacs in Whitehall at that time were dreaming of as another package of British interests to be got rid of. The Tunku was speaking as guest of honour at a lunch given by the foreign press and, preening himself on the success of Malaya under his leadership, his tongue ran away with him and he continued, 'I would like to see the federation expand, to take in Singapore and North Borneo in one great brotherhood . . .'.

There was no chance of going back now; before he knew it, the statement had been flashed over news agency wires and was picked up in Whitehall as a heaven-sent opportunity by the federation fanatics who had failed to sell the idea so far. The same evening, in parliament, the Tunku's 'statement' was hailed as from a far-seeing and brilliant statesman; the British Government could only agree with his wisdom and would put every assistance at his disposal to ensure that the federation was formed in the shortest possible time. Down came the dust-covered files from the Whitehall shelves. Federation had already been worked out, down the the last detail; the Tunku had bought it, did not know what had struck him, and was totally unprepared for the mad rush into Malaysian Federation which was in being within months. Unfortunately for him he had really been dreaming of something far larger, the idea of an economic, cultural and friendly union between Malaya, Indonesia and the Philippines which was the brain child of Sukarno, who was successfully selling the idea of Maphilindo to his ethnical brother, the Tunku. It would have been Sukarno's first heavy foot in the Malayan door, the first part of an imperial plan was to take over the North Borneo states. No wonder Sukarno was beside himself with fury when Sabah and Sarawak came under the Malaysian crown; he had been thwarted and if he wanted them now he would have to fight the British for them. Maphilindo was in tatters before it had got beyond summit talks, and Sukarno was blaming the scheming British. So was Tunku Abdul Rahman, for spoiling a quiet Malayan life and bringing trouble down on his head; but I'm sure he never quite realized what he was blaming them for – the wrecking of Maphilindo or for Indonesian confrontation.

For all this the Tunku had become a father figure to the Malays and some credit must be given him for holding down the more fanatical and racial elements he had allowed into his party and government. When Kennedy arrived it was a question of one man, totally unsure of himself or the situation, talking to another, the Tunku, who had not grasped why it had all

STORY UNUSED

happened or why his old friend Sukarno was now against him. The British kept out of the discussions, although their Deputy High Commissioner, Jim Bottomley, kept his brilliant ear well to the ground during Kennedy's short stay. There would have been no need to interfere, even if that had been possible. Sukarno fired a torpedo just when Kennedy was persuading the Tunku that the Indonesian leader was a reasonable man and only wished to talk the whole thing over. From Jakarta Sukarno declared, 'Onward, never retreat – we must crush Malaysia.'

A bright official spokesman at the Foreign Office in London said that there was 'a serious suspicion that Mr Kennedy had been a victim of a double-cross by Sukarno'; this profundity was seriously offered for the edification of the British public through its newspapers. In Kuala Lumpur the Tunku was shocked and it gave Kennedy food for thought. He immediately changed his plan from flying north to Bangkok to a hasty and panicky visit south to Jakarta.

I was at the airport that day, but not to see him off; his visit had coincided with a state one by that unpredictable monarch of Cambodia, Prince Sihanouk, and there was an important matter I wished to clarify; why was the Prince barring me from entry into his country? We stood talking in the VIP lounge and the friendly but smooth Prince was explaining that it was all a mistake. Of course I could have a visa; he would instruct his consul in Singapore. He did, and cancelled the visa almost immediately; but that is away from the point.

The cavalcade of American Embassy cars drew up in front of the airport building as we talked; Kennedy saw the red carpet which had been laid out for the Prince across the tarmac, took it as a charming farewell from the Tunku to himself and began to walk along it, waving to the small crowd which had gathered. In time a protocol official noticed it, stopped Kennedy and led him back and out of sight of Sihanouk who, a split second later, walked out of the lounge and onto the carpet to his waiting plane. An international incident was just averted, America was Sihanouk's particular whipping block at the time and the sight of Kennedy could easily have brought forth some unkind words from this outspoken ruler of Cambodia. Five minutes later, when the Prince was safely away, Kennedy was invited from his hiding place, the red carpet had been rolled up and was out of sight.

So he proceeded on his mission of peace, to Jakarta where Sukarno assured him he was ready to talk, but that the British must go. Sukarno offered a ceasefire in North Borneo during discussions which, when it came a month later, meant little or no respite for the British troops defending the borders. Then to London, to be told by 'Rab' Butler, 'We want to be sure we maintain the integrity and independence of Malaysia'. Kennedy then stated his conviction that his mission had been successful. Why had he been let out of America? Was this all that a great power could offer? Why did Kennedy, before leaving London for his office in the States, have the temerity to tell the British government, 'I still trust Sukarno'?

Chapter 4

LAOTIAN MEETING

I have never been able to subscribe to the 'domino theory' – if one falls they all fall. Simple as it may have been for America to attach every happening in the Far East to that theory, and imagine it as further proof of the need for military interference, it showed a complete lack of knowledge of the complex racial make-up of the area. America's great fear, after Russia, was China and any uprising was seen to have the Chinese hand somewhere in the background. Never was it taken into account that individual countries, especially those of Indo-China, had their own internal aspirations and, with the final withdrawal of France and the Japanese, that new and powerful factions would come to the fore, determined to rule those countries in their own way. In American thinking there was no grey, only black or white: you are for the way we have decided or you are against it, and if you are against it you are communist.

Nationalism never fitted into the American pattern and no account was taken of it; that was the teaching of the American diplomatic and military schools, and every diplomat or general made sure his thinking went that way if he wished to stay in his job. Because practically all peoples of Indo-China are slant-eyed it does not make them Chinese and the slightest and discerning study of them brings out the stark differences in character, thinking, ways of life and aspirations. Unfortunately the Americans saw them all, using that disgusting American word, as 'gooks' – and thought they were all controlled from Peking. This was another fatal Washington miscalculation, and many are the young and academic young men of the State Department I have seen arriving for the first time in the orient as 'experts' – graduates of oriental studies, the study of the orient as seen from America.

One of the prime considerations they had when assessing any given situation was: 'Will this deprive the people of the chance of leading an American way of life?' Surely, they thought, the American way of life was something to which the whole world was entitled. If it did then it was 'those goddammed communists' who were causing the trouble and that particular country had to be given the means to defeat them. Communism was the number one dirty word; its true meaning had been entirely lost sight of, despite the fact that a true communist pattern was the one and most suitable for the mainly peasant Indo-Chinese. With this, after years of foreign domination, was allied an intense nationalism which demanded, 'Leave us to run our own countries, our own affairs.' It was never considered by America that the Indo-Chinese could be capable of doing just this. Splitting the countries into blacks and whites was no solution. Left alone they would undoubtedly have resolved their internal differences eventually but then, of course, this might not have had the American stamp of approval. Many sections would have gone under, but perhaps they would not have been missed and the end result would have been all to the good – for the Indo-Chinese. They were proud of their own countries, and western ways of life were not theirs. They had not schemed to take over each other's territories, but western intervention forced them into assisting each other against a common enemy. This was misery forced upon countless thousands of innocents.

Laos, tucked between Vietnam and Thailand, with Cambodia for its southern border and China to the north, was one of the countries of Indo-China evolving through the throes of self-determination into its own style of communism. An internal affair, one would have thought, as had been Vietnam's at the beginning, but western nations saw it as a dangerous finger jutting out from Peking and, with the greater pressure coming from Washington, fourteen nations met in Geneva in 1962 at a conference to assure the neutrality of Laos. China, of course, insisted on taking part, and so did Russia; in those days the split among the two had not come to the surface and, having seen the flagrant way in which America had defied the previous treaty on Vietnam, they could see the same thing happening in Laos – an American presence there, aimed solely at China. America, with the aid of her oriental study experts, saw the revolutionary Laotian Pathet Lao as Chinese in disguise, but they too, and again like the Vietnamese, would have fought China if she had dared to attempt to take over their country, something which Peking was not inviting.

A 'neutralist' government was set up in Vientiane under the premiership of Prince Souvanna Phouma, although none but fools could have imagined that the answer had been found when the Prince's own half-brother, Prince Souphannouvong, was expected to sit at a lower chair in government with him when Souphannouvong already controlled vast parts of the country as the Pathet Lao leader. Behind Souvanna Phouma was the small and ill-equipped Neutralist army led by General Kong Le, and if America was determined to act against the Geneva agreement on Laos it might have been expected that she would have looked on the general with some favour. But no; the Washington trained oriental specialists were deciding on another and devious plan. A General Phoumi Nosavan had been appointed as Neutralist Deputy Prime Minister and America backed him and his troops, which became known as the Rightist army. Money and equipment was rushed in to set up this third and 'powerful' force; lavish anything necessary on it were the orders from Washington.

If America ever thought that this Rightist army would go to war against the Pathet Lao they were sadly mistaken. But the army grew to a reasonable size, it offered the best and most comfortable way of living Laos had ever seen – grossly inflated rates of pay, good clothing and food, and family living quarters; certainly the possibility, or intention, of fighting did not enter the calculations of this toy soldier force, from General Nosavan down to the lowliest, but perfectly happy private.

Nosavan, with his new-found power and importance, saw the heaven-sent opportunities and became the director of the National Bank, as viewed from Vientiane; all he had to do was persuade America of the seriousness of the Pathet Lao threats and into it poured untold dollar wealth. Nosavan and his chosen lieutenants had discovered the greatest bonanza imaginable and enjoyed it to the full. They bought large houses by the dozen and filled them with women of their choice, they imported Cadillacs and the best in food and drink from anywhere they wished. America was supplying them with the means to embark on a debauchery such as had never been known before, especially to those against whom they were defending 'freedom'. Nothing could have been designed more to bring about the domino theory which had, in fact, not existed.

It is a recognized saying in Indo-China that every general has his day but Nosavan's lasted longer than many. He was not sharing the spoils equitably and when, in April 1964, two of his junior generals mounted a *coup d'état* in order to run the exchequer according to their own rules, the time came for me to turn my attention more fully to this small but important part of the eastern jigsaw puzzle. Using no more than five dollars worth of American bullets in their dawn descent on Vientiane, Generals Kouprasith Abhay and Siho Lanphouthacoul forced Prince Souvanna Phouma to take them to the royal capital of Luang Prabang to get the blessing of King Savang Vatthana.

It is difficult to imagine a greater farce, here was a king in name only, being presented with two pantomime generals declaring they were supreme overlords in a country which did not exist as such. Prince Souphanouvong walked out of the so-called Neutralist government to join his troops to the north and never returned; there was a flurry among the politicians in London, Paris, Moscow, Peking and a handful of other capitals. In Washington great heart-searching led to a quick reappraisal of the whole policy in Laos and, as the Rightist generals strutted and screamed but kept their troops in barracks whilst the Pathet Lao advanced southwards, an excruciating conclusion was reached – America had backed the wrong army.

Over many years of visiting new places I had learned never to anticipate what I might be going into – it was never what one conjured up as a picture and on the journey to Vientiane from Bangkok my thoughts were more concerned by the erratic flying of the antiquated DC4. Some twelve years before,

STORY UNUSED

I had looked forward to all the modern comforts of the Grand Hotel at Ismailia in the Canal Zone of Egypt, only to find on arrival that the Grand Hotel was a wooden hut and my 'bedroom' was a tent among the sand behind it. In retrospect I look back more kindly on the Grand Hotel; if nothing else, it was clean and the word cleanliness appeared to be forgotten or non-existent in Vientiane. The airport building, from the outside, looked neat enough, it was the one American edifice of which they had controlled the cost. Inside was the chaos of immigration and customs, but there was the pleasure of being met by friends – by name only so far. Simon Dring had arrived in Vientiane after three years of wandering eastwards from his first trip abroad from England – to France – as a student. He had picked up a little journalistic experience in Bangkok and had done a good job in holding the Laotian fort for me. Estelle Holt, a capable woman of around forty-five, was a name I had been given to contact from London office. She rushed me through the airport formalities as though she owned it and led me to a waiting car; immediately the three of us were talking as though we had known each other for years.

The road into town – I hesitate to call it a city – was long, flat and uninteresting, with scattered and roughly-built wooden houses at either side. It was the road taken by the Rightist army in their only warlike foray outside their barracks, I was informed, but now few troops or armoured cars could be seen. They preferred life in barracks with their families. Nearer town the road broke into a dismal state of repair and mud splattered the car from uncountable potholes; the farther we got into the maze of narrow streets the worse became the roads and each turn revealed more starkly a Vientiane which was a decaying ruin. Houses and shops were hovels which for years had never been touched by paint, plaster or repairing cement; pavements fell away into the roads among soggy mud patches and puddles; rubbish lay everywhere, stinking and rotten, and from the car I saw the giant rats which rummaged among it in hundreds, freely and undisturbed. Practically every person looked like a beggar, so tattered were their excuses for clothes.

Estelle must have noticed that if my first impression was not one of surprise it certainly was anything but favourable, for she hastened to tell me about the hotel. 'It isn't exactly a palace,' she said, 'but its the best one here and we have been able to get you a room.' Perhaps she felt that her words were not too reassuring, for she went on to say 'But it is centre of everything, everyone meets there.' I needed no further description, we were there and I stepped out of the car into mud up to my ankles.

The front of the hotel was no wider than the tumbledown shops and deserted ruins which faced it across the narrow street and flanked it on both sides; strings of bamboo beads hung down to the floor from the door and open window to keep out insects, but inside the air was thick with myriads of flies which settled on everything by the dozen. Among them wove the mosquitoes through the hot and humid air to feast off bare arms, legs and feet carelessly protected. I picked one out of my first drink and brushed a persistent squad of flies off the table and its remains of an earlier meal, as the three of us sat down to talk – a briefing I needed to bring me up to date.

The hotel keeper, one of the few smiling people in Vientiane and usefully French speaking, promised he would soon lead me to my room, but at the moment it was being cleaned. He suggested dinner in the meantime and we moved to the back of what was the bar, café and restaurant to continue talking over a meal in which I found only the soup palatable. But I was thanking Estelle and Simon, for a group of correspondents had crossed the Mekong river into Vientiane from Thailand that evening and descended on the hotel; they were packed in somehow, two and three to single rooms and some sleeping on the floor. I was considered lucky. I had a double room and invited one American colleague to take the second bed; his thanks were profuse, but neither of us had yet seen the room. That slight shock was to come when a rat jumped out of the first drawer I opened and we failed to catch it. The rat stayed on as our uninvited guest among the squalor of the two broken beds, a rickety wooden table and ancient dressing table, mosquito nets which did not stop the mosquitoes from eating us throughout each night and a roughly bricked 'shower room' in which the dribbling and erratic shower apparatus was mostly superfluous – a gaping roof which had long lost its tiles assured us of a more than adequate supply of water whenever it rained.

The war was escalating rapidly and it was mostly one-sided; only General Kong Le's small force was prepared to do much about the advancing Pathet Lao, somewhere north over the mountains on the Plain of Jars, and any information on the general's real position which filtered into Vientiane was scrappy and unreliable. But to get to him was a problem; four days trying to cut through the red tape were lost before I was to disappear quietly from the rest of the press corps and into that great unknown of craggy peaks which looked forbiddingly down on us from afar. Meanwhile, however, affairs were anything but uninteresting; in fact, America and China got closer to war with each other in those few days than at any time since the Korean war. America had trained pilots and given the Rightist army a squadron of T-28, propeller-driven fighter bombers; how effective they were I was to find later, but two or three times a day they rose into the sky in perfect formation and flew off north, ostensibly to attack the advancing Pathet Lao. On their return the pilots gave graphic accounts of their successes, but reports of further Pathet Lao gains hardly bore out the claims. America, facing the dilemma of the Rightist troops totally ignoring pleas to get out of their barracks, decided to act unilaterally. From the Philippines she brought eight F-100 Super Sabre jets and set them against the guns of the Pathet Lao. 'Escorted reconnaissance flights', the Pentagon chose to call them, but communist China gave an ultimatum that if America did not stop its acts in defiance of the Geneva agreement on the neutrality of Laos she would send in her planes.

It may have been a slow way to cover the diplomatic scramble which started in Vientiane, but taxis were almost impossible to find and, all the embassies being on the outskirts, I decided that the only reliable way of getting around was to hire my own personal bicycle rickshaw. Not that it worked out any cheaper than something mechanically propelled; the rickshaw man reckoned that the wear on his legs over twelve

Top: Soldiers of the Pathet Lao forces in the Plain of Jars, with Chinese-style caps and a Russian built truck. *Bottom:* Evacuees from the Plain of Jars in Vientianne (Photos: Assoc. Press)

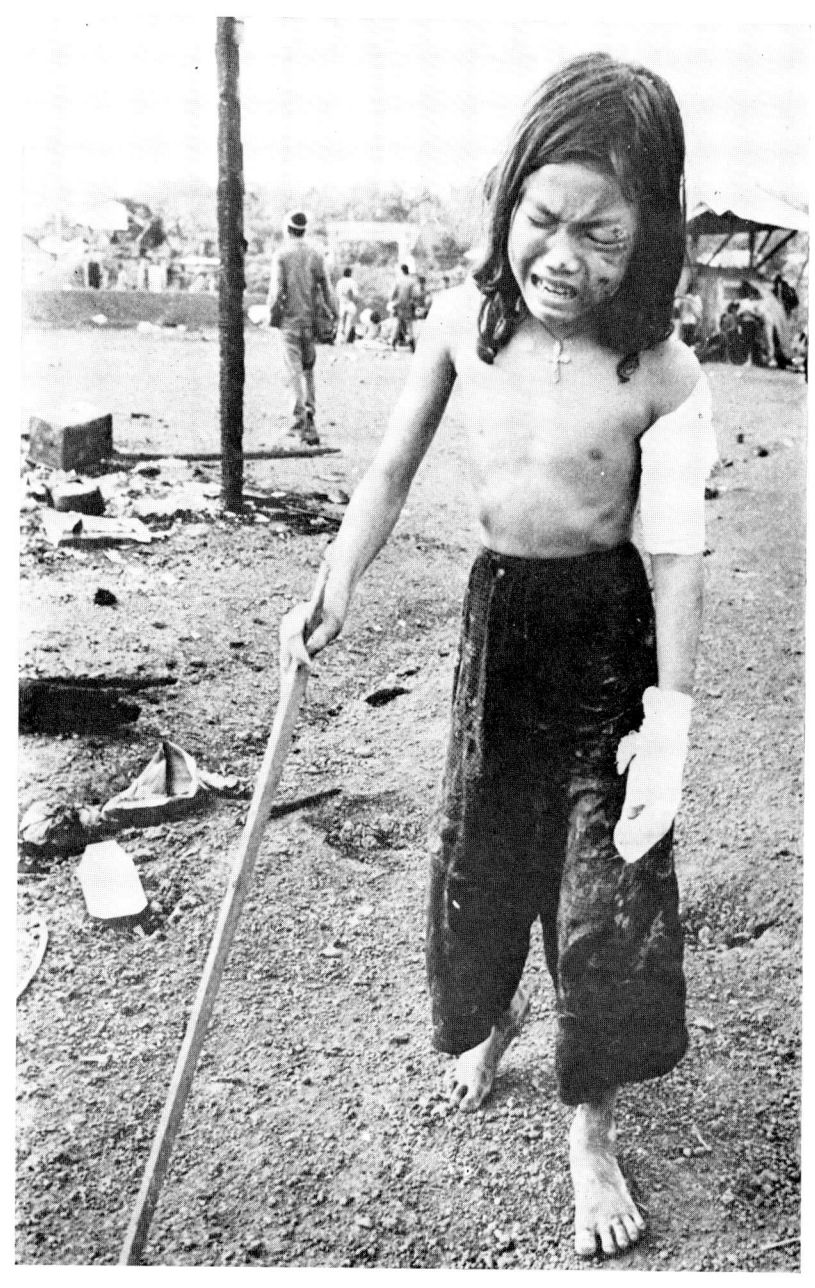
6. Twelve-year-old Vietnamese girl during the battle for Dong Xoai. Photo by Horst Faas (Photo: Assoc. Press)

to fourteen hours a day was worth every piastre of the hard bargain he forced. But he knew the embassies and was kind enough to steer around puddles whenever possible; he also knew the most backbreaking routes away from the main roads, but I had a smiling companion; and for perhaps the first time in his life the rickshaw man had a 'regular' job.

The British Embassy was the scene of most of the action. China had demanded that Britain and Russia, as co-chairmen of the Geneva agreement, should call emergency talks among all the signatory nations. Britain was willing and anxious enough, but Russia had other views – maybe she would have liked to have seen America embroiled with China – and she certainly was not going to get involved in any on-the-spot discussions in Vientiane. It was to his great credit that John Denson, the British Chargé d'Affaires there, never gave up, but it is hard to say that he made any headway; tenacious as he was – he was later chosen as head of the Peking mission – he could find no way of contacting the Russian Ambassador. If he sent a note over to the Russian Embassy it was returned, and if he took one himself the Ambassador was always out, or so he was told. Later the Russians closed their embassy door and refused to open it to Denson; if he pushed one of his strong notes under the door it was promptly pushed back until the Russian Ambassador left Vientiane 'on leave'. At the French Embassy there was a lot of shouting that if America had played the game in helping France to stay in Indo-China all this trouble never would have happened, but they refused to be any part of it here and now. Across at their small compound the North Vietnamese diplomatic mission were having a hard and rough time; accused of helping the Pathet Lao, they were under siege by Rightist troops, indignant that the North Vietnamese had threatened their chances of a continued, lucrative and peaceful existence. First the water was cut off and then the electricity; as the days passed the guards got more and more hostile and stopped anyone of the mission from leaving the compound to get food. The first time I tried to get in to see the Vietnamese, my faithful rickshaw man drove through the still open gate and past the guards; but I did not get into the house. Guns were waved and we were ordered back in what did not appear to me to be very polite Laotian language, and the rickshaw man received a hefty whack across the shoulder from the butt of a tommygun. It did not please him, but he took it with true oriental philosophy; several times he took me back so that I could hear the Vietnamese at the windows scream their accusations and oaths across the oleander bushes in unprintable French, against the guards, Prince Sihanouk, the Americans and everyone in general.

The Americans were, as they would say, playing it cool. No talks for them, no admissions and definitely no information on any involvement in Laos. The Ambassador and his staff carried an air of injured innocence and passed me on to the military attaché to be shown, with his maps, the great danger which was upon us as China took over country after country. I had heard it all before, but the colonel took it that he was preaching to an ignorant convertable. He invited me to his home that evening for drinks and there, on his lawn, as the only foreigner in a gathering of Americans, I realized to the full the thinking and teaching of the Pentagon at that time. 'We've got to bomb the lot of them,' I was told 'Atom bombs – that's the only way to deal with these gooks. We reckon that if we drop one atom bomb on Peking we'd kill enough of them to get the rest of China under control.'

One piece of paper with a rubber stamp on it was all I needed to start me off in search of the war. From the first day in Vientiane I had seen small, single-engined aircraft heading towards the mountains, and by discreet enquiries found that they belonged to a firm calling itself 'Air America'. The planes were not to be seen parked on the main airport, but next to it was a large compound, entirely surrounded with barbed wire, which housed the air company offices and control. All personnel, including the pilots, wore civilian clothes; they worked and lived inside the compound and were seldom seen in the town. Innocuous enough, on the surface, but Air America was owned by the American government; it was a branch of C.I.A. and the planes were used for a variety of undercover jobs. At the moment, I found, they were mostly engaged in an airlift of food, clothing and blankets for refugees who were crossing the mountains in thousands. Well away from the town I had seen the first thousand or two to arrive; they were crammed into old and ruined buildings and near starvation, forgotten by authority as it existed apart from a meagre ration of flour over which mothers and children fought and cried. I had also heard that ammunition was now going into the planes for General Kong Le, realized now as the only hope to stop the Pathet Lao forces from taking Vientiane itself. If the ammunition could reach Kong Le, I reasoned, so could I and, with a government press card I had obtained as my first requirement, I got past the guards at the Air America compound gates and presented myself to the air controller.

He was friendly enough and assured me he would like to help. Air America was a private company, he said, but orders were that no one must be carried on its planes without government permission. Just give him that permission, the air controller told me, and he would get me on a plane flying north, but he would not guarantee where it would take me or when they could get me back. Simple enough, if the government would agree, but who or where was the government? From one deserted office to another I went and then to the Defence Ministry, without success; if I did find an officer he would tell me to return tomorrow as his seniors would not be at the Ministry that day. I tried the headquarters of the Rightist army, but anyone high enough or with authority to deal with my request was always away or sleeping, not to be disturbed. After two days of time-wasting I went in my rickshaw to the villa of Prince Souvanna Phouma, on the outskirts and next to the residence of American Ambassador, Leonard Unger. The Prime Minister was not at home, I gathered, but a servant pointed to Unger's house. An affable Ambassador invited me in; for the first time I met the Prince and we sat talking for half an hour over drinks as Souvanna Phouma puffed incessantly at his pipe. If I learned anything it was no more than that the Prince realized that his country was in a complete mess and the fourteen countries which had guaranteed neutrality would be doing precious little to get them out of it. But permission to fly with Air America – the Prince raised a hand and shook his head. He was in no position to grant it and he said so frankly; he did not know if he were still officially the Prime Minister; I had better ask General Abhay or General Lanphouthacoul.

That was easier said than done. It was a question of finding the generals and I recruited all the aid I could think of to report to me whenever it was known that they had been seen. If they were purposely trying to be elusive they could not have been more successful, and I made half a dozen abortive trips to find they were not where they should have been, or had never intended going there, until, on the fourth morning I heard that Abhay had just arrived at the Defence Ministry. Simon Dring was at the hotel with me when a British Embassy friend telephoned with the news and Simon had his motorcycle outside; not even to Simon had I disclosed my plan, but there was no time to lose and, if I succeeded in getting the permission I needed, I would probably have to rely on Simon eventually for communications. Never was he known to drive slowly, but this time Simon's riding skill excelled itself. With me clinging on behind, we shot through the narrow streets and potholes to the Ministry to find a Cadillac standing there decorated with flags and four large metal stars. Simon found a captain he knew, who took us to a major, who took us to a colonel; in turn they scratched their heads and to my repeated requests that it was General Abhay I really wanted to see, the same heads shook, with mumbled words that it was difficult, the general was such a busy man.

If we had not known that Abhay was in the Ministry we might have given up in frustration and disgust, but we stayed talking and arguing until at last our patience was rewarded. Out of an office which Simon knew to be his walked, or rather strutted, a bloated figure, resplendent in a gaudy uniform bedecked with medals. 'That's him,' said Simon; I pounced, and a bewildered general found himself hemmed in and unable to move another step. For a minute or two he heard me talk of refugees and a permit as we were quickly surrounded by startled officers. I doubt if he really grasped what it was all about, but the words 'British journalist' appeared to have a suitable effect. Abhay looked at his watch and was probably thinking more of his champagne, lunch and a girl friend; he turned to the colonel, waved a hand and said, 'Arrange a permit'. It could have been that he saw this as the easiest way to stop me blocking his path.

It took us another half hour to get the piece of paper signed and stamped, for the colonel's original wording, in all probability, would have got me no further than the refugee 'camp' a few miles away and I had to insist on something more explicit. Eyebrows were raised and the colonel put down his pen when I dictated, 'To fly as a passenger with Air America,' but he quickly picked it up again when I said, 'The general understood this and it is his orders that you issue the permit – are you disobeying the general?' As on so many similar occasions the tactics worked, although the general might have been in jail within a week; now his command was supreme it was all a matter of persuading the colonel that a complaint to the general might have disastrous consequences for himself.

There was no wish on my part to arouse suspicions among the rest of the press corps as to where I might be heading or what my plans might be, and I instructed Simon to make a detour of the town and head towards the airport. He was beginning in journalism then and had thoroughly enjoyed the scene so far and what he had learned from it. Simon was a young man who learned fast; it was not to be long before he was distinguishing himself in Vietnam for a news agency before joining one of London's better newspapers. If he had been surprised at the way I had extracted the permit from the military headquarters it was nothing to the look of incredulity that we got from the Air America controller when I presented it. His crewcut hair got a sound massage as his interpreter read out a translation in English. 'Well,' he said, 'I've never known anyone else with one of these before, but there it is, you've got it and you're welcome.' He looked at his operations board and said there would be a flight out in about an hour. 'There's a canteen across the yard,' he added. 'Better get some chow; I wouldn't reckon on getting much more for a while.'

The hour was more than useful, and if obtaining the permit had been a reasonably easy operation the next one had to be thought out. To get oneself into the mountains, perhaps into the war, was one thing, but to get my despatches from there back to London was another. Air America was my only link and I instructed Simon to keep in touch with them throughout each day and collect everything I sent back. The Laotian telegraph system was so unreliable that it was unusable for anything urgent; Simon would take my despatches across to the main airport and find a passenger flying to Bangkok. There the passenger would telephone another of my stringers at a number written on the envelope, the stringer would collect it from the passenger and cable it to London under my name. That is how it worked, and worked well, for the next three days. Not one passenger courier failed us and the stringer in Bangkok knew his job; each one of my despatches, written in the mountains or on the Plain of Jars with General Kong Le, reached London and, with the help of the eight or so hours time difference, appeared in the newspaper the following morning.

I'm sure Simon thought he would never see me again as I walked out to the plane, and the pilot, an uncommunicative forty-year-old, had not exactly added to his confidence with a greeting to me of no more than, 'Hi, I'll get you as far as I can and then you're on your own.' He said no more than that until we were well away from the airport and the plane heading towards the mountains. I doubt if the next short conversation would have occurred if he had not been trying to fly the plane and at the same time wrestling with a pile of papers on his lap, filling in logs and forms which obviously had got well in arrears. Automatically my hand went to the control column where I sat on his right as the plane veered slightly to the left; the pilot had trimmed the controls and for a minute or so the plane had been flying unaided. Without touching his control column, the pilot looked up from his papers and across at me. 'Done any of this before?' he asked and I replied, 'A little.' That was good enough, or so it appeared. 'Great,' said the pilot, 'she's all yours.' He pointed to two peaks in the distance where the mountains broke into what could have been a valley. 'Head between those,' he said and no more. He settled down to his papers again.

For half an hour we flew across the plain north of Vientiane and I kept the plane in a gradual climb to around four thousand feet, the height needed to fly between the peaks; beyond them I could see more mountains, beautiful and unending, with tree covered slopes. I was through the gap between the peaks before the pilot looked up again and then it was only for a moment; he pointed to a valley between two mountains rising even higher and I climbed again. For another half-hour it was just instructions in monosyllables as we twisted up and around the breathtaking mountain scenery, then, suddenly, the pilot put down his papers as he said, 'OK, I've got her.' He looked down at a small gathering of huts on the mountain side and I saw the tiny landing strip, partly levelled off and no more than a hundred yards long. Down we went into a spiral, throttles back and following the emergency landing procedure for such a light plane – a controlled dive at the end of the strip and the control column pulled back at the last moment, losing speed and practically pancaking onto the rough ground. This was mountain flying and I was to see a lot of it. We rolled to a halt in less than sixty yards.

This was just the first call and the pilot did not stop the slowly turning propeller as two men ran from a hut and pulled two large crates from the plane. What they might have contained I had no idea. There was no time-wasting and the moment the door closed we swung around to the end of the strip, the engine roared and we bumped along and into the air with barely a foot to spare. The next call was no more than ten minutes away, but again we were spiralling up the valleys and around the craggy peaks; another strip, roughly hewn into the mountain side, another dive, the rattling over rough ground and I wondered how the plane held together. Not a hut was to be seen or other sign of life, apart from a man who stood waiting on the strip to haul out the packing cases. Then away, climbing, climbing. Deeper into the mountain range we penetrated until, from a valley, a small plateau opened up beneath us; from no more than 300 feet above it I could see clusters of what appeared to be tents and people, hundreds of them, milling around. From the far side of the plateau where the mountains rose again came a continuous stream of more people, animals and small carts. But then we were diving again, this time on to a landing strip longer than the others but no less bumpy and pock-marked with holes. People were running from all directions towards us and the pilot stopped the engine as we came to a halt, 'This is as far as I am going,' he announced and I was out of the plane to see a score of hands passing the main load out of the plane – blankets, tinned milk and sacks of flour – along a line of eager helpers, men, women and children working together.

The plane was returning to Vientiane, but for me this was the beginning of the road and from the pilot I gathered that one plane should be calling later from the north and another should arrive, flying in that direction, at around eight o'clock in the morning. The one going south did not interest me; it was still another hour of mountain flying to get anywhere near the Plain of Jars, I was told, so here I was for the night. Looking around at the sparse and course grass, the dusty tracks and the rough tents in the distance it did not look inviting. But then, I had not expected to find a Hilton hotel up in those mountains.

He was some sort of camp supervisor and his French was appalling, but the little man, barely reaching my shoulders, greeted me as a friend and became my guide, my interpreter and my only source of comfort for the next sixteen hours or so. I was in a refugee transit camp from where the poor wretches were passed on down the mountains to Vientiane; after weeks of fleeing from the north they arrived here, hundreds every day, starving, exhausted to the point of dropping, and many of those who had not died on the way were sick and suffering from all the ravages of hunger, exposure, disease and fear.

A camp it was in name only; sheets of canvas, wood and nails had somehow been flown up to the plateau, attempts had been made with it to provide some kind of shelter, but the supplies were hopelessly inadequate. Those who felt lucky enough to grab any part of the shelter were crammed together with not an inch to move whilst most stayed in the open or slept under roughly made bivouacs from the few belongings they still had with them. If the supervisor was small these people from across the mountains were minute; few of them were much more than four feet high. They were filthy and they were covered in rags which did nothing to keep out the freezing night mountain air and they were petrified at the sight of a stranger. To them I appeared as a giant and they shrank or ran screaming before me as I approached, driving their chickens, pigs, their dogs and perhaps a calf, before them. The children were covered with flesh sores and the old among those who had got this far lay groaning and tightly packed among the rest of the human misery. That evening I saw two old and shrivelled wrecks lifted out from the fear-deadened lines, to be carried a hundred yards or so away and put into quickly dug and shallow graves; no one mourned them and there were no rites, no ceremony; they may have been the last survivors of families which fled before the Pathet Lao from two, three or more hundreds of miles away. I saw no tears, I doubt if anyone in that camp was capable of crying ever again.

The arrival of my plane had meant another pitiful ration of food and the younger and fitter among the refugees began to prepare it from the flour and milk and green leaves they had gathered, in battered cans over fires built from bracken and dried grass gathered by the children. It was they and the old ones who were served first, leaving the others with no more nutriment than the chickens were scratching out of the ground; but there were no arguments and no cries for more, it was a question of keeping the children and the weakest alive until the day which became journey's end, if ever that was to come. Blankets which had arrived on the plane were distributed in utmost fairness to those who had no covering of their own, but I could see that fifty such deliveries each day could never be enough to give just that small piece of warmth to everyone in such a place, where the numbers grew hourly and alarmingly under my very eyes. Doctors and medicines – this small plateau was crying out for them, and the small supplies of bandages, iodine and aspirin could do nothing to alleviate the ills which sprawled upon it. Down in Vientiane the generals, sergeants and privates grew fat without a thought for these poor souls; they were refugees weren't they? And that term already meant some other form of life, something to be treated as animal, or disregarded completely.

Along the trail and across the plateau I walked as the

refugees continued to arrive. They came in groups of fifty, as families or singly. There had been a break for a while, but now a figure on the horizon was signalling that more were but a mile or two away. I watched it as it grew larger and proceeded smoothly as though on wheels, leaving a cloud of dust behind it; closer it came until I made it out as a man on a horse, but never had I seen a horse, or pony, of this size. Like its rider it was tiny and it came along at a trot, with its hooves working at such an incredible speed that it produced the effect of locomotion; it passed, seemingly with no greater movement than the dust behind, and its rider wafted along with it. He was the scout, the one going ahead, searching for any shelter, resting-place, water or even a berry to be plucked from a bush. Behind straggled the main caravan, sometimes a hand-cart pulled by two or three, piled high with bundles and pots and a goat, a pig or chickens being either led or kept on the trail with sticks wielded by the children. Men supported women and women carried children who could struggle along no more; those with any strength left had weighed themselves down with possessions. Not a word passed between them and their mongolian features were completely expressionless; they walked or staggered as if in a dream. Their movement was automatic until the flesh gave up, the same as it had been the day, the week, the month before.

Away from the trail I stood and watched, not going close for fear of startling this human train of despair. From the distance I heard the noise of planes and as they came nearer from the south I made them out as a flight of six T-28s of the Rightist forces, on their way, I presumed, to attack the Pathet Lao on the Plain of Jars. Again I was admiring their close formation flying and they were almost above us; then I saw the formation break and they circled in line astern, a preparation for action. Good God, it could not be! But even as the incredible thought flashed through my brain that we were about to be attacked, the leader put his plane into a dive and the first bombs crashed into the mountainside on the southern edge of the plateau and not more than a quarter of a mile away.

In an instant there was pandemonium; the people on the trail turned and fled back the way they had come, dropping their bundles, abandoning their handcarts and leaving their animals and chickens to scatter in all directions. Dogs were barking, pigs snorted and the chickens clucked in fear as they opened their wings to speed their flight. From the refugees rose a high-pitched screaming as chaos hit the camp. They ran in their hundreds away from the falling bombs, but already the second plane had released its cargo, adding to the wild cacophony of screams, wails, diving planes, the roar of engines as the planes pulled out of their dives, and the explosions which shook the mountain and reverberated back and forth across the valley.

The next two bombs landed on the plateau itself, but mercifully near the edge. In came the next four planes; two of them were no better in their aim and the others were even worse, hitting nothing but the mountainside. Then they formed up again as a flight and turned southwards and back to their base. By now the camp was a wreck; the wood and canvas shelters had collapsed in the mad scramble and dozens of those too weak to move were still beneath wreckage, moaning and screaming until we pulled the coverings and broken supports away. Gradually the men led their womenfolk back to the camp, but now the frenzied hunt was on for all the animals and chickens; it was two hours or more before calm came again to the plateau and the shelters were got up again for the night.

As I and many others had suspected, this was the bravery and the strength reported by the T-28 pilots every day back in Vientiane. The Plain of Jars was a full fifty miles to the north across more mountains, and they had no intention of facing the Pathet Lao guns. I had several reports eventually of the pilots dumping their bombs anywhere around the mountains, but nowhere near a battle; today they had found a target on which to practise. What did it matter who those on the ground were and what were they doing in the mountains anyway? We will never know if the raid was intentional and ordered from Vientiane; the attitude towards the refugees was such that a few thousand less to think about would have been welcome among the so-called leaders there. Only a miracle – the atrocious bomb-aiming of the pilots – had saved these wretched and homeless wanderers and someone had to be told that there had been a witness to the devilish attack. I was on the airstrip as the Air America plane landed and gave the pilot my message, 'For God's sake, see that it gets to the American Ambassador and is passed on to Souvanna Phouma and those bloody generals', I told him.

The night was freezing and I shared a tiny bivouac with the camp superintendant. He had offered me a blanket, but as I listened to the moaning coming from the nearby canvas shelter I felt sickened and refused it, telling the superintendant to give it to someone else. I slept fitfully and several times walked up and down the trail in an effort to keep warm. I was out there when the first shots of colour came over the mountain tops and burst into a sunrise of unequalled glory. It was only afterwards that I recalled the beauty of the scene; now I was numb and it was the sudden warmth which I needed more than anything else. In the first rays of light I ran up and down the trail until the blood coursed through my veins and brought me back into some state of normality. Then I ate the second of the thick sandwiches I had brought from the canteen in Vientiane. It was another day and one in which there was much to be done.

The numbers in the camp had risen to over 8,000 before the tiny plane dropped onto the airstrip with more, but meagre supplies of food. I was on the strip ready to leave as the pilot opened the cockpit door and shouted, 'Hi, get in, heard you might be around.' He had some ammunition and would try to get onto a strip near General Kong Le's new headquarters at San Tong. 'We made it yesterday,' the pilot told me. 'Might get in again today, but I won't guarantee it.' Then we were in the air, climbing and heading north around the mountains once more and the pilot knowing every peak, pass and valley.

It was superb flying in wondrous surroundings, keeping below the tops of the mountains and sometimes flying through gaps with no more than twenty yards to spare on either side. After forty minutes the great Plain of Jars opened up before us in the distance and as far as the eye could see, dotted with scrubland. But we went no nearer, for down on the mountainside just below I could see the landing patch, cleared of trees and bushes. It did not seem possible that anything could land on it, but men were there, waving white sheets. 'We're in luck,' shouted the pilot and down we went in the familiar spiral, dive, nose up and grinding to a halt.

The men were Kong Le's troops and they were strung out in a line with the ammunition boxes tied on to their backs as they made for a rough path up the mountainside. 'Best of luck,' the pilot called and told me that a plane should be in that evening. He grinned as he said another should be around at the same time tomorrow morning and added: 'That depends on the situation around here. If not you have a long walk.' He passed some chocolate bars down to me and was off with a quick wave, rose from the runway and then pointed the plane's nose downwards along the valley.

Winding upwards through the trees the path led to a cluster of seven or eight wooden huts, and after forty or so minutes of climbing I sank to the ground with the troops for a rest and the water they passed around. As far a I knew they had no idea who I might be, but that did not matter. The fact that I had arrived on the plane was enough. Not one of them spoke anything I could understand, but these short and wiry men made up for that with smiles, especially when we moved on and they pointed their fingers above their heads.

I soon found out what they had tried to convey: the climb was gruelling and painfully slow; for another hour I struggled upwards, my heart pounding, until the ground began to level out. The tall trees thinned out into bush and scrubland and we took another rest and a drink before continuing. Then, and after twenty minutes or so, we came into a clearing dotted with tents and filled with troops; from the main tent stepped the small but stocky figure dressed in jungle green like the rest, a pistol hanging at each hip on an ammunition belt. Soldiers who had been sitting were on their feet at once and I saw the gold stars on the little man's soft and long-peaked cap. This was Kong Le, the man who had no time for the Vientiane generals or government and was prepared to fight the Pathet Lao, prepared to go it alone as he was doing now and to the last round of ammunition. He came forward and greeted me in good French, then he led me into his headquarters tent, bade me take one of the two wooden chairs at the trestle table and pushed across his water bottle.

Kong Le was in a desperate position and with a map he explained it; the main body of his Neutralist army was cut off by the Pathet Lao fifteen miles away across the plain at Muong Kheung, a small village, and was completely out of ammunition. Most of his heavy guns had been lost and with the few he had been able to haul out he had set up a defence line across the outskirts of the plain around us and under cover of the bushes and scrub. The fighting force he had now was no more than a few hundred; shells for the big guns were almost exhausted and his men were relying for ammunition on the Air America planes which came up twice, or sometimes once, a day. Bitterly, Kong Le told me how he had called repeatedly for air attacks on the advancing Pathet Lao infantry, only to see the T-28s – and then only occasionally – wheel away in the distance and head back south when they spotted smoke from the big guns. His men were reduced to operating in groups, attacking the Pathet Lao lines as they slowly but surely advanced and then retreating to safety. How long they could hold out from where we were it was impossible to say, but the general, despite his great courage, was pessimistic. He needed men and supplies from Vientiane if he were ever to attempt a breakthrough to his main army, but from what I had seen of the Rightist forces, who should have been fighting the common enemy, Kong Le agreed with me that help from that direction was an improbability. It never did arrive; Kong Le's forces were all but decimated, and it was decisively hammered home to the Americans that they had made a stupid but ghastly mistake. By then it was too late and the Pathet Lao went as far as they needed; they controlled the vital areas of east Laos through which went the Ho Chi Min Trail – the supply lines from North Vietnam to the Vietcong, and later North Vietnamese troops, in South Vietnam.

The Pathet Lao had been quiet since the evening before and it was after two in the afternoon when their guns opened up to signal that another advance was on the way. Kong Le estimated that the firing was from something like five miles away and the first shells were dropping two miles or so from his headquarters, where he had deployed the remains of his sadly depleted forces. His own guns remained silent, saving their precious shells for the right moment, but then the Pathet Lao guns extended their range and their barrage crept systematically forward until the explosions were no more than a quarter of a mile away and spread along a front of less than two miles. There was no doubt that the Pathet Lao knew exactly where Kong Le's men were and were slowly forcing them into a corner of the plain from where the only retreat could be down the mountains.

The troops who had been in the headquarters clearing when I arrived were somewhere out among the scrub after their brief rest, and Kong Le was working furiously at his radio; there were still a few sets left among his troops and he was directing the operation as best he could. The barrage came even nearer, indicating that the Pathet Lao were no more than a mile or two away, and the ground around the headquarters shook several times before Kong Le gave the radio order to one of his guns; it opened up and was followed immediately by the others, but in ten minutes Kong Le gave orders to stop the firing. Later he told me that he could not sustain an artillery duel for more than another hour, but those ten minutes, it appeared, had had an effect; the fire from the other side died down considerably, and as the chattering of machine guns and muffled grenade explosions rose across the plain they shortened their range.

For another two hours the noise of fighting came in fits and starts, but it became evident that the Pathet Lao were not in sufficient strength yet for their grand onslaught; large numbers must still have been deployed around Muong Kheung. 'Tomorrow, the next day or maybe a week,' said Kong Le, as he shrugged his shoulders. With a force as small as his now was, he knew the end must come soon, but he still had no intention of giving up, neither had his troops. He was outside his tent giving instructions to the twenty or so men there to get down to the airstrip, there might be more ammunition on the plane which would allow him to stay in battle for an extra hour or two. My despatch went with the leader of the supply bearers and was given to the pilot, yet another link in the chain on the way to London.

Also with the bearers had gone the message that Kong Le wanted another supply plane next morning and it was his confidence that he would still have a headquarters that made me decide to stay. Unless the Pathet Lao mounted their main attack during the night, which Kong Le doubted – he was right, it did not come for three days – we were reasonably safe and there was the great fascination of seeing this man in action. Not that I expected any sleep; no one got any that night and the only time that Kong Le sat down was to pore over his maps with a shaded torch. The Pathet Lao opened up again at nine o'clock; many shells came dangerously close and twice we took to slit trenches around the clearing. It was as though the enemy were warning Kong Le that the end was nigh, for they kept it up until dawn; their troops carried on small battles with the Neutralists and flashes from grenades lit the sky a mile away. But the Pathet Lao were not quite ready to sweep the plain completely clear, although, as the sun came up and the fighting gradually stopped, we had to agree that we had just come through the prelude. Kong Le gave me a big grin. 'It's better if you go,' he said. 'We may not be here tomorrow.' I was sorry to leave as I shook his hand and went off on the trail with the bearers, I was saying goodbye to one of the bravest men in Asia.

The flight back to Vientiane was uneventful, except that every mountain landing is an event in itself. There were three calls to make, but now I was on a different route and I did not see the refugee camp again. Simon was at the Air America building when the pilot and I walked in, faithfully awaiting another possible despatch. He looked at my filthy clothes and my third day's growth of beard. 'Christ,' he said, his eyes open wide. 'I didn't think I'd see you again. The radio has been saying this morning that Kong Le is surrounded and finished.'

I stayed on in Vientiane for a few more days, as the news was expected hourly that Kong Le was, in fact, off the Plain of Jars and his army liquidated. When the news came it was a sad moment, but I saw no signs of the Rightist forces taking up any positions of defence or making the slightest move which might suggest they would now take up Kong Le's fight. An Air America pilot told us that it was over; the morning plane had dropped as usual on the mountain airstrip, but only six bearers awaited him. When he circled it that evening, there was no sign of life. If the Americans had begun to airlift supplies just two or three weeks before they at last realized their great blunder, it could have been a different story.

Whatever the importance of any world situation, it has to be weighed in comparison with events elsewhere, and when the news came over the radio that India's Prime Minister Nehru had died the decision that I should be in New Delhi was immediate. I had known Nehru well, and knew the dangers and political scrambling which could so easily follow his death and the dangers they could entail. India was in my territory and normally I would have been on a plane for the Indian capital within hours. From Singapore, Bangkok, Hong Kong or practically any other place in Asia I could have reached New Delhi the same night or, at the latest, in the early hours of the morning. Now, and for the first time in years, I quickly realized I was trapped in Vientiane and I was not alone.

Six of us were trying to get out and every means was explored before we got together at the hotel, fuming and admitting that we were defeated. No regular plane was flying to Bangkok until the following afternoon and no other plane was expected that day going in any direction. Air America had nothing we could charter, even if we had permission, and a telephone call to Bangkok – miraculously the Vientiane operators realized the urgency and were willing to help – shattered our last hope; nothing was available for charter there. The only way left open was overland, across the River Mekong, with the chance of finding a car which would drive us to Bangkok – an operation which, with all possible luck, would take anything up to eighteen hours. We discussed it as we had discussed half a dozen possibilities, but then the radio news finally showed us that this was one assignment we would not be covering: Nehru's body was to be burned with all its funeral rites and before hundreds of thousands of Indians the following morning. Whatever we did we would miss this, the most important thing India had seen since the death of Gandhi; I sent off an urgent cable which, again miraculously, reached London in time for a journalist to be sent from there on the overnight plane, landing in New Delhi just in time for the funeral.

Estelle Holt was sitting with me in the hotel that evening. Nehru's death did not affect her movements; she seldom left Vientiane, but she understood and sympathized with me in this stupid predicament. It was the first time we had spent any time together and I was intrigued to know how this English woman came to be in Vientiane or why she stayed there, to rot as far as I would have imagined, in this decayed, corrupt and depressing corner of the world. We talked for hours and gradually Estelle's story unfolded.

She was the widow of a London journalist who had died tragically; she had left the England which had so many memories for her and wandered eastwards across the world until she finally came to rest in Vientiane. She mentioned a London newspaper which accepted her news stories and articles, out of gratitude for the fine writing her husband had given it in the years before. Suddenly it all became clear to me and I stared at the face of Estelle, the lines in it which the years had brought, and the tragedy and worry which had changed it from a face I had looked at years before. Then I asked her, 'Was your husband's name Paul?', and she looked at me for seconds before she closed her eyes. I could see the slight trickle of tears. 'Yes', she answered, but her eyes stayed closed. 'Did you know him?' Her hand, resting on the table, quivered slightly and I placed mine upon it and held it still.

'Estelle,' I said, 'one day in 1944, it was in Brussels and near Christmas, Paul came to a war correspondents' briefing I gave on an air operation in which I had flown that morning. We had not seen each other for over four years, since we had been friends together on the newspaper, and Paul said, "I must take you to see the most wonderful girl in the world. I am going to marry her".' Estelle's eyes opened. 'Please, tell me more,' she said and her head bowed as the tears flowed. I continued. 'Paul took me to the Canterbury Hotel and there I met this wonderful person; she had dark hair, cut short, she was dressed in khaki, a battledress as far as I can remember, and on the shoulders were tabs with the letters E.N.S.A. She was a public relations officer. Paul married her a month later.'

As though it had been yesterday it had all come back, the little alcove in the Canterbury Hotel in Brussels where Paul had introduced us only a few months short of twenty years before. The dark and classic beauty of the girl Paul was to marry, the gay smile and the bubbling happiness of a girl in love with the only man in her life. She looked up and I saw the smile again. She pressed my hand and blinked the tears away. 'Yes,' she said, 'I do remember. I think we should celebrate with a drink – one for Paul.' She looked at me again, scanning my face as that Brussels scene came to life. 'But you had a moustache then,' said Estelle.

Chapter 5

UNPEACEFUL TEMPLES

The old and the new, they are thrown together all over the world, but seldom have I seen them in such profusion or in such close proximity as in Bangkok. Arrival at the airport gives the immediate impression that one has come to the most sophisticated city in South-East Asia and, up to a point, that is so. As one of the major air junctions it hums with activity. The staff are efficient and smartly dressed for the continuous, humid heat; the airport buildings glisten white and in the sunshine, housing the large and comfortable restaurant, the bars, the banks, a multiplicity of attractive tourist shops, lounges and endless lines of air company counters. Long ranks of modern taxis stand on the clean and concrete forecourts, their uniformed drivers ready to whisk one into the city with the utmost courtesy and at breakneck speed along the straight and flat dual carriageways.

All is neat and new and then, suddenly, and no more than a hundred yards or so from the road, there is the small collection of life which has stood there for centuries: tiny, wooden and thatched houses perched on stilts beside a canal. Among them, and in the nearby paddyfield, live and work the people who have been passed by and are completely oblivious to the rush of progress and construction around them. They dress in the only way they and their forefathers have known – long, baggy black pants and short-sleeved blouses with huge umbrella-shaped bamboo hats to shelter them from the sun or the rain. If the ever-growing network of roads and factories does not engulf them, they will not change in another hundred years; if it does, they will move away and set up a similar life elsewhere, living in the same simple way and wearing the same clothes.

All around the countryside is flat, with not a trace of a hill to break the skyline; nearer the city which never ceases to creep outwards, there are the bulldozers, earthmovers and demolition squads in action. More of the old is being swept away to make way for the new, but the old is endless. New houses, flats, shops, restaurants and office blocks rise from its midst, but it is still there. From this point forwards it is stop, start, rush and squeeze through the crazily congested streets, built wide enough for six lanes of traffic, but a mad jumble of trucks, buses, cars and thousands of motor trishaws which dart hither and thither, their two-stroke engines crackling away and belching black smoke. Concrete creations line the sides, festooned with neon designs; here at a junction a flyover road is being built to ease the crush of vehicles and the steel reinforced shell of yet another giant edifice is rising. Just a glance down the countless dusty, narrow lanes reveals that this is a massive façade which can never completely obliterate the age-old Bangkok or Thailand. On the new boulevards they walk in well cut, western clothes, the men in suits and ties convincing themselves they can endure the ever-present and oppressive heat until they take refuge in freezing air-conditioning. At the end of the lanes there is the canal, its stilted, thatched and wooden huts and its ordinary people in their baggy pants, blouses and bamboo hats: the simple and proven dress which, for them, time does not change.

Farther into the city the late twentieth century has gained a stronger hold and brought its criss-cross of new streets, its new and flat-fronted, uninteresting hotels and office blocks. But walk outwards in any direction for ten minutes or so and one comes across the old again. A large part of the city near the river has still escaped the demolition squads and this is the real Bangkok – tumbledown buildings, nightclubs with oriental dancers, dingy and dust-ridden shops selling the intricate Thai silverware, the gaudy jewellery set with amethysts, rubies and emeralds, mostly ersatz, the Thai silk in all its brilliant hues, the pots and pans and the sticky and sweet cake and confectionery.

It is from there that one takes the boat in the early hours of the morning on the broad and busy river where tugs haul long lines of timber-laden barges; from the main stream a turn into a maze of creeks takes one to the never-to-be-forgotten floating market. Hundreds of small and roughly made boats ply their trade, loaded until they are almost sinking with fruit, vegetables, earthenware, laces and lengths of cotton – and hundreds more boats bearing the shoppers from their houses, raised above the mud and low water, come to buy and bargain. The small craft tip alarmingly as scales are held high and goods passed from one to the other; the air is filled with the cries of the vendors and the calls of the customers; wooden huts are perched above the water's edge where they sit and sip sweet tea and the only western dress to be seen is worn by the tourists who goggle with fascination, not knowing where to turn their cameras next. The crush of the boats equals that made by the conglomeration of vehicles in the city close by, but there are hundreds of years between. Most of these people have never been into that other and strange world; it was here on the river banks that they were born and here that they will die.

Bangkok has its fabulous Buddhist temples, of course, but I must confess that I am a bad tourist and I have never taken more than a passing glance at the gilded domes, the marble and mosaics and the old Siamese carvings from which charcoal rubbings on rice paper decorate the homes of so many friends and acquaintances, proving that they have 'done' Bangkok. That was a word I have heard countless times and in a hundred places around the world from the hordes of American tourists who swarm in organized groups rushing from airport to airport, city to city, and hotel to hotel, mostly praying for something called in the itineraries 'free periods', so that at last they can sink into a chair or on to a bed to rest their weary bones for half and hour before the official guide herds them into the next bus.

Once when I flew out of Saigon I found myself in a plane practically filled with an American tour and the woman beside me was instantly ready for conversation. 'Have you really been in the city?' she asked incredulously, and then turned to her friends to announce, 'Gee, this gentleman has been right in that city of Saigon.' She told me the group had not been allowed to leave the airport. 'Our tour guide said it was much too dangerous,' she said and repeated again, 'but gee, you really went in there!' She thought this over for a while and I did not enlighten her that I had been in Saigon for weeks, and so had a couple of million others. After a while she turned to me again, 'Would you have a Vietnamese coin you don't need?' she asked and I handed her a tiny piece of metal, worth less than a farthing. The woman was delighted and handed it round for all to see; then she pressed a dollar bill into my hand, asking, 'Will that be enough?' I handed back the note, but the woman was disappointed. 'Gee,' she said, 'when I get back home with this I can't really say I've "done" Saigon if I haven't paid for it.' It could have been a profitable transaction; instead I emptied my pocket of another dozen Vietnamese coins and passed them round among the other members of the tour.

As headquarters of the South-East Asia Treaty Organization, Bangkok already had its foreign military missions and the city provided a large number of 'diversions' which it thought they might require. Seamy clubs, hostesses and brothels had always been in abundance and Bangkok's reputation for 'vice' far exceeded those of other eastern capitals long before the advent of the S.E.A.T.O. personnel or when I first began to know the city well in early 1964. But then came the Americans; G.Is were sent there in their droves on 'Rest and recuperation' leave from Vietnam; and finally, when America set up bases in Thailand to hit at North Vietnam, the vice kings and their prostitutes, pimps, female impersonators and every known purveyor of sex, to animals as well as humans, had moved in to make Bangkok the filthiest city on earth. It was annoying, at two o'clock one Sunday afternoon, after spending the morning writing a particularly deep and complicated political article, to take a taxi from the hotel to the cable office and then find that the driver, unasked, had turned off a main road and down a dusty lane, where I was surrounded by twenty clawing girls from a large wooden and thatched brothel.

That, however, was only a mild case on one of my early visits, for within two years I saw Bangkok transformed into a place where it was unsafe for a man or woman to walk the streets after dark, even near the fashionable hotels or the Sporting Club. Hardly a taxi driver could be trusted and many, in uniform, spent their working hours driving prostitutes around for kerbside pickups. True, most of them were beautiful; they had descended on this goldmine from far and wide, and could be dealt with during all the hours of daylight in which they operated. After dark it was a different story; to enter a taxi was to enter the unknown. If it were one girl inside 'she' might be female or could just as well be male; (oriental youths with their smooth features are hardly distinguishable from their sisters when dressed and painted the same) and the object was normally robbery in some way. If there were two 'girls' in the taxi, and this became the more usual pattern at night, it was robbery with any violence necessary. If the first invitations from the taxi were not answered, the 'girls' would leave it whenever the street was reasonably deserted and it was only my size and aggressiveness which, on more than one occasion, safeguarded me from attacks which eventually were commonplace. By then whole streets of new buildings were lined with clubs and dives of every variety; fortunes were being made and there was a currency crisis – the America dollar took over and the green-backs flooded the country. If one offered local money for anything it was more than likely that any change would come in dollars.

I was in Singapore when the Malaysian and Indonesian governments announced that, at foreign minister level only, they would hold a preliminary round of 'peace' talks in Bangkok. It was the first of such abortive meetings, in February 1964, and was doomed before it began, as were the others which came up spasmodically for another two years. And, as on most other occasions in a correspondent's life, it meant a swift move, for with the announcement it was said that the separate delegations would be travelling to Bangkok the following day.

The daily Comet, starting from Singapore, calling at Kuala Lumpur and then, unlike other and slower planes, flying direct to Bangkok, seemed to be the obvious choice and I was surprised when I telephoned the airline for a first-class seat that I could have had as many as I wished. Whoever in Kuala Lumpur was responsible for travel arrangements had (typically) not worked very fast; but as I had surmised, I travelled in solitary state to Kuala Lumpur, where the delegation piled into the first class cabin and took every other seat, the overflow going into tourist class.

They were a jolly crowd, on a trip at government expense and led by Abdul Razak, the Deputy Prime Minister, the Foreign Minister and the 'strong man' behind the scenes in Malaysian politics, so I had often been told. I introduced myself and Razak, with a large and confident smile, assured me that he had 'the match of the Indonesians' and would 'sort out this trouble with no difficulty whatsoever'. But now they must begin to enjoy themselves, and if the Koran told these Moslems that they must not drink wine, they chose the next best thing from the grape, champagne. My companion in the next seat, a bald Malay in civilian clothes, with a neatly clipped moustache, had no better ideas, so we shared a bottle as we chatted. I had seen him before but his face was connected with uniform; where was it and under what circumstances, we wracked our brains nearly all the way to Bangkok to discover. Then I knew: he had led the Malayan contingent to the United Nations Force in the Congo at the beginning of 1961. The recognition called for another glass of champagne. My companion was now military adviser to the Malaysian delegation and he grinned as we touched glasses. 'I was a major in those days, now I'm a major-general,' he said as he emptied his glass and turned to me again. 'Not bad in three years, eh?' he asked.

The true background and experience of the major-general for such a high rank, I was soon to find, was matched by the rest of the delegation, 'strong man' Abdul Razak included. Only one, Jack da Silva, who was a Malaysian of Indian descent, could be considered capable in the slightest way; the others were all Malay, and in their eyes the fact that they had rank, whether political or otherwise, sufficed. Like the majority of their race they floundered along on their own conceit and all was well until difficulties were encountered – then they collapsed like a pack of cards. Jack I had met before and had found him an amiable character and, as journalists were not allowed into the talks themselves, he had promised to keep me supplied with details on an off-record basis. The night before the talks opened we were all together in the Erawan Hotel, where I was staying and the spirits were still high. Success was already in sight, according to the Malaysians, and all they had to do was put forward their prepared speeches, which would show that Malaysia was in the right and Indonesia was in the wrong. Simple enough, but that is the way the Malay mind works. Da Silva made a rendezvous to meet me at six o'clock the following evening; he, of all the happy band, might have known that it was not all to be as plain sailing as they imagined; they had not come up against President Sukarno's Foreign Minister Subandrio yet, and from the little I had seen so far of Abdul Razak I would have backed the supercilious, wily and fox-like Subandrio any day.

There would have been plenty to discuss; Indonesia's confrontation was by now well under way, with all its psychological, political and actual military warfare, as well as the subversion, sabotage and arson which Sukarno had unleashed throughout the whole of the new federation. The talks were opened in one of Bangkok's several palaces by the Thai Foreign Minister and Chairman, Thanat Khoman, with all the usual blinding lights and cameras, the smiles and handshakes and the platitudes of confidence and bonhommie in speeches which politicians the world over adore as they envisage their pictures and wise words flashed on screens or across newspapers. To me it was a bore, and when I caught sight of Tony Lawrence, the BBC's Far East correspondent, we ducked out of the palace as one. We had not seen each other for weeks, and then in Saigon, and we were both hardened to these preliminary rigmaroles. It was the end result which mattered and Tony and I had much more interesting things to discuss for the moment. I told him of the rendezvous at six o'clock and Tony was more than welcome; in the meantime there were eight hours in which Razak, Subandrio and Khoman could go to hell if they wished. We lunched on the shaded terrace at the Sporting Club, whilst the miniature racehorses raced around the track with their miniature jockeys. But we placed no bets; racing in Bangkok was no less corrupt than in most places around the Middle and Far East and we were hardened to that too.

All was expensively serene in the Erawan Hotel. A few younger guests were showing off their figures and muscles in the pool and waiters were clearing the tables on the surrounding terrace as a palm court orchestra softly played through the short transition period from tea to cocktails. Tony and I sat comfortably in the huge lounge, from where we could see the high, carved, mahogany doors of the entrance and the group of American tourists had not yet arrived from their labours of sightseeing to shatter the atmosphere of quiet well-being for all and sundry. It was well past six o'clock, as we could see from the gilded figures which adorned the marble walls of the reception hall, but there was no da Silva. Six-thirty and we strolled through the bar and around the pool in case we had missed him. We would give him until seven o'clock, but no later, Tony and I decided, and would then think of looking elsewhere. Six forty-five and we ordered a drink; we studied our watches and the clock in the hall again until the hand came up to the hour. A little worrying, for I had invited Tony to meet what I had taken to be a good contact and now he was nowhere to be seen, wasting what was now beginning to be precious time. We rose to go, but even before we reached the entrance the four dejected figures came in, Jack da Silva, the major-general and two other members of the delegation, and there was no need to ask if they had had a bad day. 'Thank God you are still here!' said Jack. 'Razak has sent us to find you. You must help us; we are finished!'

We adjourned to a quiet alcove in the almost deserted bar, but the drinks did nothing to brighten the mournful faces as Jack and the others poured out the story of the 'conference' between them. It had broken up before lunch and since then the delegation had been closeted together wondering what they should do and failing to find a solution to their next move. Razak had opened with a speech accusing Indonesia of one wrongdoing after another, only to be interrupted by Subandrio with a question, one which he repeated continuously as Razak, completely off guard, attempted to continue. Sukarno, through the evil Subandrio, had not intended to budge an inch, but now he was going to use the words of that young and naïve American emissary who had so recently bumbled his way around the eastern capitals.

'Do you agree,' asked Subandrio, 'with Mr Robert Kennedy, the American Attorney-General, that the issue is an Asian one to be settled by Asians alone?' Razak had tried to disregard the question, but it came at him time and again until he cracked. The 'strong man' had collapsed under the first onslaught and he had no answer. If he agreed with Kennedy's words, then Malaysia should withdraw its defending British troops; if he did not, then he could expect only one answer from Subandrio, escalation. Either way it appeared to be dismal and abject failure for Razak, who had set off from Kuala Lumpur only the day before in a blaze of glory.

Tony and I listened carefully, injecting a question here or a question there. No way out was the attitude of the Malaysians, absolutely none, and the misery of Razak was plain to see, if he had sunk so low in his pride that he had sent these four to me in the hope of grasping the tiniest straw. We talked it over, then Tony and I came up with an answer and its simplicity left looks of wonderment, then joy on the faces of da Silva and his colleagues. 'Tell Razak to go in there fighting tomorrow,' we said. 'Whatever Subandrio says, Razak must insist that every Indonesian soldier and saboteur must be off Malaysian territory before it can be considered an Asian affair.'

It was as though a dark and forbidding monsoon cloud had passed away. More drinks were ordered and the Malaysians, as the sun came through, slapped each other's shoulders with such words as, 'That's it, we've got him. Subandrio can have no answer to it.' They left, delighted and with promises to meet again the following day with news of the outcome. But not before I had said quietly to da Silva: 'Tell Razak from me that he must stand firm on this and not weaken for a moment. Whatever Subandrio says, Razak has the reply, even if he repeats it a thousand times.'

I am not sure if Tony and I should accept the praise which was showered on us when da Silva rushed to see us after the next conference session with the jubilant words. 'We've won. Razak did as you said at least ten times today and Subandrio has no answer.' It could be that we should take some of the blame for the fact that the conference broke up two days later; but at least we had spiked Sukarno's guns and by then it was clearly evident that he had never had any intention of dropping his confrontation. Subandrio was reduced almost to an appeal:

'You must help us.' Indonesia had internal difficulties, he said, and the people would not accept Malaysia in its present form as a British imperialist project. However right he may have been that the federation was a British project, the Malaysians in their conceit now proudly took it as their own; imperialism, as Sukarno chose to call it, was most decidedly not the object. Britain had given away another part of her valuable possessions gladly; another step on the road which was to take the Great out of Great Britain and reduce her to a minor role among what were so loosely called 'Great Powers'. However, there was no reason why Malaysia should not have had the last word at this Bangkok conference and my last spot of advice to Razak was conveyed officially to Subandrio. 'Your internal difficulties are your own affair,' said Razak. 'They are your responsibility and you must deal with them.'

It is strange how short memory can be and how past help can be conveniently forgotten. Within eighteen months Razak, the Tunku, every other Malay politician and every Malay newspaper was attacking me as an 'enemy of Malaysia'.

Chapter 6

THE INNOCENTS

War weary, those were the words the South Vietnamese were using to describe themselves at the beginning of 1964, and that was the year in which they made frantic and desperate bids to settle their own affairs. Many sections of the community tried at different times – the students, politicians who were grudgingly allowed a short run of government, the Buddhists, peasants who co-operated with the Vietcong and, of course, the Vietcong themselves. The one exception was the Catholic minority; they saw little chance for themselves whichever way the tide might turn and made vain appeals to be allowed to emigrate to such countries as Australia. It was also the year in which America, or at least her generals, decided to prove her or their might against anything labelled 'communist'. With the able assistance of Defence Secretary Robert McNamara, she made a great play of cajoling and threatening the South Vietnamese military into greater action; she stepped up the dollar aid from a million a day to a million every nine hours and then said she would take it all way as the troops wearied of the war.

Later in the year, America did give a glimpse of what was already predestined when, it was said, her naval force in the Gulf of Tonkin was attacked by North Vietnamese gunboats; she immediately retaliated by bombarding 'targets' on the North Vietnamese mainland. But only God and a few others know the real truth of all that. I was certainly not in the Gulf at the time; I could only wait and watch for the real fray to begin. By February 1964 the first planes bombed the north in the vast air assault against the 'real enemy', and at the same time American troops began to pile into South Vietnam. It was no surprise, for exactly one year earlier I had written . . . 'The United States Government will have to make up its mind to get out of South Vietnam or take over altogether. I am certain they cannot and will not pull out.'

The meantime had been dangerous, interesting but tragic. Each week brought a new angle into the chaos and dilemma in which this half a country had found itself and it was impossible to forecast from where the next bullets, bombs or grenades were to come – from so-called friend or recognized foe. The year 1964 had opened with panic rapidly setting in among the American families in Saigon as the Vietcong sailed into a terror campaign against them. Trusted Vietnamese came out in their true colours and planted bombs in a cinema and at the American sports ground on the Saigon outskirts, killing Americans in their leisure hours. Marines went on guard at American houses, offices and the school, and eventually this was to close, leaving hundreds of young Vietnamese with no means of carrying on their English education. Any gathering which might include Americans was shunned. For an American to walk into a restaurant or café was the quickest way to clear it – a Vietcong grenade or bomb could be expected at any moment.

The South Vietnamese army had lost its will to fight and suffered reverse after reverse until it was unsafe to use any road out of Saigon with the exception of the main one south into the Delta area, and that only during the hours of daylight. Casualties among American advisers, pilots and helicopter crews rose alarmingly in the rapidly deteriorating situation, but for some reason best known to himself General Khan appeared to have no intention of arresting it and, it was said, refused to accept any advice from the American Military Assistance Command – MACVI. Incredibly, General Paul D. Harkins kept up a steady line of optimism until he was relieved of his post; but by then it was difficult to believe anything which emanated from his headquarters.

Many were the changes I saw in that year of 1964 and not least did they come among the American diplomatic set-up; the old hands at the Embassy were viewing things with more realism and did not like what they saw, so they had to be replaced by others dedicated to the Washington line. At the USIS came a complete turnover of personnel as disillusioned information officers gave way to others who could be guaranteed in their thoughts of 'America is right, whatever she does and whatever the cost'. Ambassador Henry Cabot Lodge – a Republican conveniently appointed by a Democrat President Kennedy – had to go; he was replaced by a military man, General Maxwell Taylor, although I am sure it was a happy release at the time for Lodge, who became progressively more testy as he lost contact with the South Vietnamese. He was lucky to get away with his life; the Vietcong made him their main target and he narrowly missed grenades on more than one occasion.

Gradually the scene was set for the coming grand plan and nothing the people did could thwart it. Khan ostensibly bowed to American pressure and allowed in a civilian government – the full process of democracy had to be gone through – but the moment it was seen that the meek and mild Premier Tran Van Huong was coming under the American thumb the students rioted in their thousands. For me it was yet another quick dash into Saigon; now, at the end of 1964, it was the ugly sight of South Vietnamese fighting South Vietnamese for peace; Maxwell Taylor added to the flames by flying off to Washington, making it known that he was pressing for an extension of the war by full-scale bombing of the North. Four years had passed and the South Vietnamese were saying they had had enough, the year was drawing to a close and it had claimed tens of thousands in dead, wounded and maimed. Nearly every western embassy in Saigon had warned Taylor that he was heading for further failure, but did he or the Pentagon need advice? The die was already cast, the plan was in being and now it was only a question of fixing the date to implement it. The rioting students could have saved themselves the beatings, the injuries and the deaths they suffered. Nothing was going to be allowed to stand in the way of the Pentagon, and most of them were to die eventually anyway.

It was a city under siege I arrived in, but the Vietcong were playing little part in it. Tran Van Huong had proclaimed martial law, but as I got near the university nothing could have been more evident than that the students had prepared to fight to the finish. With nothing but clubs, rocks, pieces of broken furniture and even school blackboards, they hurled themselves

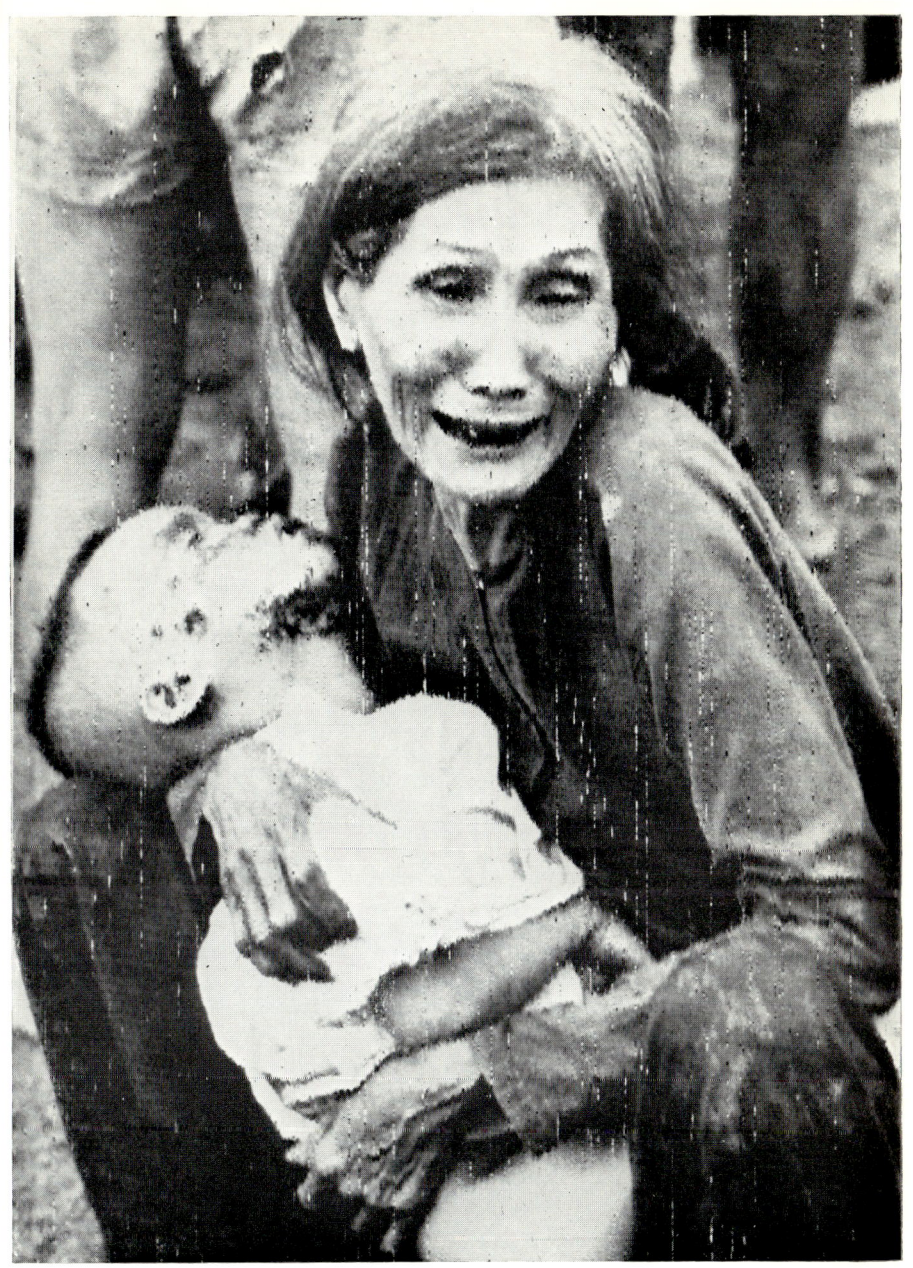

7. Vietnamese mother with dead child after the storming of Dong Xoai by U.S. troops. The child had been killed during an airstrike. (Photo: Assoc. Press)

8.

Right: Old Vietnamese man turns to leave the body of a girl killed during an airstrike. *Bottom:* Two Vietnamese farmers wounded during a South Vietnamese attack on Vietcong positions (Photo: Assoc. Press)

against riot police; fighting spread from street to street, pavements were torn up, shops and houses were smashed and students, young men and women, were dragged away, bleeding and unconscious, in their dozens. A quarter of a mile away two thousand or more students made an assault on the Presidential Palace, their posters held high, demanding the resignation of Tran Van Huong, the 'Stooge of America'. Bayonets flashed again and vicious rifle butts clubbed the students to the ground as sirens wailed and more reinforcements rushed in; then came the tear gas, the one weapon the students could not combat, for this day the rioting was to end, but only until the following morning and every morning for a week, when the battles broke out again. Civilians joined the students and several were the army officers I saw among the crowds fighting the riot police; but the cause was lost, every school in Saigon was closed, censorship was clamped on the newspapers and Tran Van Huong declared that every 'terrorist and saboteur' would be tried and executed.

It was on the Sunday, at the end of the week's rioting, that the students – and they now included every schoolchild in the city – made their last demonstration against the war they hated. One of their victims, a boy of fifteen, was to be buried and from the early hours the silent processions formed all over Saigon and converged on the boy's house where the hearse, drawn by four black horses, awaited. Also waiting were the riot squads and I could see them in their trucks, moving along adjoining streets with the procession as it moved off; never before had I seen such a display of force and if there were 5,000 following the hearse eventually there must have been at least half that number of steel helmeted police stalking them, bayonets at the ready. For three hours the great file wound its way around the city for all to see until the police put up a barricade to stop it. The students refused to be diverted; they sat down in the broad and dusty street in their hundreds and defied every order to move. Hour after hour they sat there, completely surrounded; the riot squads put on gasmasks, but this was greeted with howls of abuse from the students. In the middle of the squatting mass a girl was using a loud hailer to great advantage and the crowds came from all directions. It was an impasse and the riot police did not like it; they held roadside conferences continually, but I could see they could not agree on the next move and some of the police took off their masks and walked away.

By now the procession had been on the roads for seven hours and the sun still blazed down unmercifully; not for a moment had the wailing stopped from the dead boy's family and friends who stood around the hearse, and the police made no move. Then down the road came the trucks loaded with paratroops; the police were pushed aside and the toughest of all the troops formed in ranks around the students. Something had to break, but if the danger was staring them in the face the students disregarded it and three times refused the orders to move before a colonel gave the command.

In an instant blood was flowing. It poured upon the scorched earth as the paratroops rushed into the squatting mass, wielding rifles like clubs and bludgeoning students into unconsciousness. Male or female, it did not matter; few escaped without a thrashing as they scrambled from where they sat and the battleground spread to surrounding houses, shops and waste ground. Through the dust they were dragged and beaten, and by the score they were thrown into army trucks. Anyone not in uniform automatically became the enemy and onlookers fled.

I could easily have been one of the casualties filling the Saigon hospitals that night. A few yards from me a student was struck down and a paratrooper swung round, looking for his next victim. Don Wise, a colleague in many scrapes throughout the world, saw it first: the paratrooper raised an ugly knife, his teeth were bared and his eyes were those of a madman. Don shouted and dragged me clear as the paratrooper came at me. We ran. We continued running as in the distance we saw more troops dragging away the hearse to which clung twenty or more screaming women. For a mile we followed on foot until we found a tricycle rickshaw, trailing the hearse to the graveyard. There the dead student was buried to the wailing and sobbing of the women and against a background of tommyguns which covered every approach.

It was now December and military ambassador Maxwell Taylor returned from Washington, tightlipped about the decisions which had been taken there. Not that they would have been changed, whatever he may have said. Democracy had been offered to the people, but it had failed and changes had to be made once again. Too many factions in the civilian government had demanded and were working for peace.

Four days before Christmas a group of officers calling themselves 'The Young Turks' threw most of the politicians into jail and announced that the war would go on, in their way. Carefully worded hints were dropped by the USIS that America would have to reconsider its aid to South Vietnam if there was any more political chaos, but politics were now a thing of the past. The Pentagon was now in command of Vietnam's destiny and it had the South Vietnamese officers who, despite the smokescreens of words that they were carrying out their own policies, would dance to the Pentagon tune. General Khan went into the background and was soon to make his millionaire's exit, while into the foreground came generals Thieu and Ky, and strangely they held their posts at the head of a military government throughout the coming years of death and destruction.

Within weeks, American jet planes were pounding at the Vietcong, and on February 8, 1965, they began the bombing of North Vietnam; the raids had been requested by the South Vietnamese, it was said, and as if to prove to an angry world that this was so the Americans allowed General Nguyen Cao Ky, a mere major in the air force a year before, to lead a flight of twenty-four antiquated Skyraiders over the border in his scarlet flying suit and wearing an ivory-handled pistol at his hip. Preparing a gullible nation for the horrors which awaited its young men, President Johnson in Washington addressed a gathering of Boy Scouts in a well-reported speech which warned the world not to miscalculate the character and strength of America's youth. 'We love peace,' said Johnson, 'but we love liberty more, and we shall take up any challenge, answer any threat, pay any price to make certain that freedom shall not perish from the earth.' Then he gave the order to evacuate all American wives and children from Saigon and the last of nearly 2,000 were out within a week.

The decks were cleared. One of the most powerful nations on

earth was now in the inescapable clutches of its warlords, while its president, unfortunately for another four years, was to act as little more than their mouthpiece. Another hundred thousand youngsters in South Vietnam were immediately drafted into the forces on American instructions and under the promise that the sky was the limit for those lovely American dollars. On February 25th the call for peace by South Vietnam's president, Dr Phan Huy Quat, was brushed aside: 'My country is suffering too much; we want to end the war with honour,' were his words, but they fell on deaf ears in Washington. The battleground had been chosen, now the curtain was to rise on one of the greater follies of this century.

This is not the first time I have used those words. On countless occasions I have said that America can never win a military victory in Vietnam. She misjudged the people and the situation from the beginning; she was wrong. Not that my judgment has gained me popularity in many quarters, and what did it count against the view of Harold Wilson, a British Premier whose mind travelled no farther than the shores of his Little England? Whatever Big Brother America did must be right was as far as Wilson's knowledge of the world went, and in one of his more shameful utterings he could not wait to tell Parliament and the world that Britain backed America's policy of bombing North Vietnam. Although it was of minor consequence, one of my plans was completely ruined within hours of Wilson's declaration; for three weeks one of my passports had been in Hanoi, quietly taken there by a Canadian member of the International Control Commission for Vietnam – soon to be defunct. Ho Chi Min had looked favourably on a visit by a British journalist and had authorized a visa, the British representative in Hanoi had told the Saigon embassy. Ho Chi Min quickly changed his mind; the passport was returned – empty.

Wilson, once again, had gone completely against the advice of his experts. Britain had three excellent men in Vietnam who had been consistently against an American military onslaught. Tucked away in a quiet Saigon street for nearly four years had been Bob Thompson and his ten-man team of advisers, working on a programme to organize South Vietnam into new and protected communities, assist them in agriculture, welfare, education and administration. Behind them, and with the same scheme, lay success in Malaya, where they had finally defeated the communist uprising. But Bob and his men were to leave Vietnam in disgust, their plans in ruins, when it became apparent that nothing could stop all-out war. Strange that Wilson agreed to a well-deserved knighthood for Bob, who became Sir Robert Thompson; even stranger that the Americans – but only when they were inextricably involved in nothing but slaughter and destruction – should eventually call on Bob for advice on how to get them out of their self-imposed agonies. By then it was too late.

On a broad and treelined avenue in Saigon lay the British Embassy, built to the same neat and efficient plan as that used for the now burned-out wreck in Sukarno's Jakarta; and it housed the offices of the two other men whose advice, with Thompson's, might have averted the tragedy if it had been accepted or taken timely. Odd, perhaps, for a soldier, but the military attaché, Colonel Charles Napier, had advocated anything but the crazed action taken by America; a decorated veteran of war and colonel of his Highland regiment, it could be imagined that there would have been much hand rubbing at the prospect of bloody battles. In fact, Charles Napier took an entirely different view and never spared his words whenever he was with his American colleagues. Start all over again, he advocated; the concept has been wrong; it is a question of gradually wooing the people back from the Vietcong and to bring war to their villages is to force them in the wrong direction.

John Morley, First Secretary in the political section of the Embassy, was the third of the trio; his political insight far surpassed that of other diplomats in Saigon at the time and his views fitted perfectly into those of the other two. There could have been time, much of it before North Vietnam was forced into the conflict. Some American advisers and diplomats agreed that the three Britishers had the only concrete plans to defeat the Vietcong, and they even suggested that Colonel Napier should go to Washington to explain them. But General Maxwell Taylor and his Pentagon bosses were in no mood for any solution other than their own. Thompson left and the Foreign Office posted Morley from Saigon at a crucial moment, when his knowledge would have been invaluable. Someone in the Defence Ministry in London obviously disagreed that there should be political overtones to reports from a military attaché and the brilliant brain of Charles Napier was set to work on the more mundane sides of army life at a command headquarters in Scotland – counting knives and forks, as it is sometimes referred to in military circles.

I was to see little of my home in Singapore for the next six months. Into Saigon flew the advance parties of American Marines, conveniently and already placed strategically in Pacific bases. Overnight the city lost its last vestiges of charm; rubbish began to pile up in the streets until it became rotting mountains – nobody could be found for the lowly-paid task of collection as American contracting companies moved in to build hotels and barracks for the coming hordes, paying rates whereby ten-year-old boys carrying bricks earned twenty times more than their fathers had ever known before. The USIS swung into action and built up a huge staff to deal with the correspondents who were being drawn to the obvious flashpoint from all over the world. No longer was the office large enough for the sixteen or eighteen of us who had gathered daily to discuss the worsening situation. We were moved into a theatre and I was to see the number of correspondents, radio and television men rise to three and then five hundred at afternoon 'briefings'.

In March 1965 we were to see the first Hollywood spectacular, designed to strike fear into the hearts of the Vietcong, the North Vietnamese and, I suppose, the whole communist world. Sixty of us were flown north to Da Nang, from where American jet planes dealt out their rockets and bombs around the countryside with orders not to bring any back. Just eighty miles from the border with North Vietnam and in a bay not far from the airfield, 1,400 American marines were disgorged from landing craft and splashed up the beaches yelling their warcrys and ready to take on anybody's army. No Vietcong put in an appearance, but we were there, of course, and so were a couple of hundred Vietnamese girls, herded together for the occasion. The cameras whirred to take in the bloodthirsty scene and then showed the garlands as they were placed around the necks of the marines; they panned onto the banners, all in English, which had been strung across the road, all the way into the base. 'The Vietnamese people welcome the Marine Corps,' they proclaimed and the young liberators loved it. They believed it. Long before they set foot on that beach they had been prepared, and they believed in the justness of their cause. It was not to be long before the wild whoopings gave way to the unrehearsed groans and screams of men in agony, men dying. However, the invasion film went well in America. Was it not there, thousands of miles away, that more young men like these marines, millions of them, must now be fed with the idea that this was the fight for freedom? That night I watched the Vietnamese faces in the small town of Da Nang; they were sullen and full of foreboding. Whose freedom? – they might have been asking.

Easter I spent with the marines in the Da Nang bridgehead, but by then they numbered thousands. Hill 327 overlooked the airfield from where the Starfighters, Phantoms and Thunderchiefs worked round the clock delivering their deadly loads, and the hilltop was festooned with Hawk missiles and all the electronics which went with them, ready to blast off to intercept any air attacker from the north. Roads torn out of the thousand-feet-high hill filled the air with choking red dust and the valleys and hills beyond did not respond to the probing patrols we made in search of the Vietcong who were known to infest them. It is as well that they did not, for the marines were absolutely green in guerilla warfare, despite their attitude of 'let's get at them'. Their movements on the slopes and in the valleys invited sudden death if the Vietcong had chosen to act, and I quickly decided that my visits to their forward slit-trench positions would be brief and unaccompanied. They had their tanks, their anti-aircraft guns and all the sophisticated equipment of modern warfare, but I wondered if their type of fighting could match that which suited the Vietcong; the marine training had left no room for individual strategic command beneath company level. But the marines were expecting a short and swift victory – 'We don't want to be here forever; they must look after themselves once we have won the war,' their commander told me. So soon the attitude towards the

STORY UNUSED

South Vietnamese was one of contempt and they were all 'gooks', whichever side they were on.

On the Good Friday I sat among the rockets on the hillside with an American major as he outlined the American plan. 'We're going to blast this lot out of existence and any others who might be thinking of interfering,' the major said, 'and we've thirty thousand more marines in Okinawa waiting to come in.' Despite their inexperience, it did not appear that, at that time, American casualties had been given any serious consideration, for the major went on, 'We'll make these goddammed southern gooks fight for themselves, even if we stand behind them with guns and shoot those who turn back.' I had heard enough. Going down the hill I passed a group of marines, bareheaded and in prayer, standing beside their slit trenches and weapons – a Protestant padre was trying to bring a little holiness to the Easter scene.

Da Nang had hardly been touched by the war until the death-dealing jetplanes came, but nobody would have expected the Vietcong to disregard the base now. To the north and to the south ran the railway tracks and each night we could hear the explosions in the distance as the guerillas systematically blew up the lines or wrecked railway bridges over which came supplies, including the bombs. Eventually the fight to keep open the rail links was given up and everything had to be landed direct from supply ships; but this weekend, as I sat with the French proprietor in his small café and hotel (later he leased it to the Americans and retired on the proceeds) it was natural that the conversation should focus on the bombs, and the bombs alone. Every few minutes the jets took off with deafening roars and flames belching from their tailpipes and so close were they that we could read the numbers on their sides. We fell to timing them out and in and found that the average flight was between twenty and thirty minutes – and they all came back from the south. Quang Ngai, on the coast, was too near, according to my timing, south of it lay Qui Nhon, but there were no reports of major battles anywhere down this eastern coastline. So what were the targets on to which the bombs were being poured by the tens and hundreds of tons, who were on the receiving end of these raids – were they all Vietcong as the daily communiques claimed? It was a subject carefully avoided in all official circles and certainly it was never admitted, but for months evidence had been building, convincing evidence that more civilians were suffering than the total of military casualties of both sides, claimed or real. Only two weeks before, the Frenchman was telling me, forty-five small coffins had been carried into Da Nang from a village to the south. The bodies were of children, victims of an air raid as they sat in their village school; the tragedy had never been reported, unless the deaths had been included in a report which would have read, as did so many others, 'Forty-five Vietcong were killed in the attack.' A transport plane was leaving Da Nang the next morning for Qui Nhon and my companion knew of a hotel. 'Go,' he said, 'you may learn more of the truth in Qui Nhon than we are allowed to know here.'

What a wonderful and beautiful country this could have been. From the plane I looked down on one of the most awe-striking coastlines in the world. Great sweeping bays with palm-fringed beaches, gentle hills rising from them into mountains, forest covered slopes and valleys of emerald green. Clusters of thatched huts and here the straggling town of Quang Ngai with the French-built Highway One running parallel with the coast, its fascinating coves and majestic rocks jutting out into the South China Sea. Every view a perfect picture postcard setting. Could this really be a country at war and facing its complete and inevitable rape? It was difficult to imagine, for height hid what horrors might lie below.

An American Air Force jeep dropped me into the town from the airstrip. It was lunchtime and the streets were quiet. Qui Nhon was at rest. I found the hotel, although there was little to distinguish it in a line of low and shabby buildings showing the deterioration and decay of all the troubled years. Nguyen Co, too, I found; his sleepy eyes regarded me with astonishment as he came from a back room. I was probably the first or second visitor he had had in all the months since the French owner left, leaving the place in Nguyen Co's care. The dust-covered dining room betrayed the fact that it had not been used for many a long day and Nguyen Co shook his head apologetically. But there was a café nearby, he said, and I realized that his French was extremely good. He led me to it along the broken street; he ordered rice and hot-spiced fish and, when I was comfortably set at the table, produced a bottle of excellent brandy. It was all an event for Nguyen Co and one which grew in importance when he understood why I was there and acted as interpreter to my questions. This was going to be no wasted journey, I decided, as soon as the men in the café began to talk; they pointed to the sky and to the hills beyond, they talked of the camps and the hospital. 'Take him,' they told Nguyen Co and the little man nodded his grey head – he would do so, he told me, that very afternoon.

My room was some kind of attic and we reached it by climbing the metal staircase attached to the back of the hotel; it had a misshapen iron bed and a rough wooden chest, ab olutely nothing else, and I saw that there was no water. Nguyen Co, however, showed no embarrassment; it would be very comfortable, he promised, and went off to get two buckets of water and an electric table lamp which miraculously worked. In two minutes he was back again, a huge grin on his face; on the chest and beside the lamp he placed it and he' had not forgotten the glass – it was the bottle of brandy from the café. But now we must go, said Nguyen Co, and he led me down to where two tricycle rickshaws stood, our transport. Side by side we rode in style through the town with Nguyen Co pointing out what he thought might be of interest to me but especially anything of which he could say, 'The French built that.' He loved the French and had worked for them most of his life and he talked as though he were welcoming back one of those, he said, who never should have left. Nguyen Co was enjoying this surprise visit, but he was not preparing me for what was to come.

Through the hospital gates we swung and up the sloped drive to the main building; inside Nguyen Co spoke to a nurse who looked at me and nodded. Then my arm was taken and I was led through a door and I remembered the words I had heard in Da Nang – 'You may learn more of the truth in Qui Nhon.' It was a ward and forty beds lined the two long walls. Each bed was occupied, but here were not forty injured and broken bodies; each narrow bed had two and three people somehow lying on it, plastered legs hung high above them. Limbs were missing, bandages half-covered burned and hideous faces, and over all hung the revolting stench of gangrene and human rot. Between the beds on the floor squatted silent groups of women and children and they filled the corridors through which I was taken to the other and similar wards, packed and stinking like the first. Seven hundred victims of American bombs were sardined into this hospital of little over 200 beds, but the only men I saw were those who had been carried there, mangled and maimed.

I stopped at a bed on which lay a woman and two children, all three of them burned, crippled and minus a hand, a leg or an arm; around the bed sat more of the family, but all female, and Nguyen Co asked the questions for me. Their village had been bombed and they had been two weeks getting to Qui Nhon. Where was the father? The reply came from the woman: 'The birds and the dogs have him.' Where were her sons? Nguyen Co translated: 'They have gone to the Vietcong, they are not communists, but where else could they go?'

There were four doctors, all Austrians, doing their utmost to keep these miserable wrecks alive, but daily the number of new arrivals was greater than those who died or survived to be taken into a refugee camp. Without the fit and capable members of the families who had moved into the hospital it could not have carried on; these were the nurses. One of the doctors was bitter. 'We are almost forgotten here,' he told me. 'Daily we ask the government for more help, more medical and surgical supplies, but never do we receive enough. Some refugees are past help when they arrive, but many die needlessly.' He turned away. Another pitiful group had arrived; a mother carried her small child, but it could have been too late. The body looked lifeless. The doctor shook his head. 'This is only the beginning of the war,' he said.

The café where I dined on a noodle dish that evening was full. News of my arrival had spread throughout Qui Nhon and many were those who, talking through Nguyen Co, viewed me as some sort of magician who could tell the Americans to stop the bombing and go away. The valley had been peaceful until the planes came, they said, but soon not a soul would be alive in the green and lush lowlands or in the hillside villages if the bombing went on. They insisted that the bombing was indiscriminate; never had the countryside been Vietcong territory and only occasionally had the Vietcong operated in the area – against communications leading north to the Da Nang base and Highway Nineteen, leading westwards from Qui Nhon across the country to the base at Pleiku. When death-dealing planes came from these bases these people saw no wrong in the Vietcong attacks, but now food supplies from the valley had been all but cut off and those who had tended the land now flocked into Qui Nhon as refugees. There was not enough to eat for the townsfolk themselves, they told me, but by no means was this the full extent of the tragedy which had hit this once lovely land. That did not become clear until the following morning.

It was impossible for these simple people to understand all the ramifications of this war in which they had been caught up. Pleiku was many miles away. They had probably never heard of it and certainly they would not know that large numbers of South Vietnamese forces had been massed there. Pleiku, it had been planned, was to become one of the main American helicopter strike bases and for weeks now convoys taking supplies along Highway Nineteen had been attacked by the Vietcong and sometimes wiped out. Time after time the convoys fell into the same ambush traps by failing to send scouting parties ahead, but the American reply was to call in the jets to strike at anything which could give the Vietcong any type of shelter. Never were ground reconnaissances made before the bombs rained down; these would have been considered far too dangerous by the army commanders and their American advisers. It was simple to create a valley of death from which no interference of any kind could come and this is what the people of Qui Nhon saw and understood. But that morning, at his headquarters just outside the town, an American major had proclaimed that the 'battle' of Highway Nineteen had been won – a convoy had just got through unmolested, he told me.

What a bitter-sweet scent his 'victory' had was of no concern to the major. Soon Highway Nineteen was closed again, permanently, and no doubt by the countless youths from the valley who had seen their homes destroyed and their families maimed and killed. Innocent civilians, dead, wounded or now refugees – they did not come into the major's range of thinking. 'Hell,' he said, 'you're bound to get a few refugees in any war.' I wonder if a visit to the hospital could have changed his reasoning, I wonder if his heart may have softened, just for a moment, if he had followed me when I left him shouting over a telephone, 'Get those planes south of here.' He gave a map reference and continued, 'Sure, west of Highway One, two miles at my reckoning. Just get in and knock hell out of them.'

The faithful Nguyen Co was there to lead me in the trishaws to the first of two refugee camps – there was one for Buddhists and the other for Catholics, he explained. The Buddhist camp was the nearest but there was no room for the trishaws to enter and Nguyen Co lead me up the narrow path on foot. He pushed open a gate in the high bamboo fence but already the stale and awful human smells had reached me. Behind that fence stretched endlessly the rows and rows of minute hovels, ten, twelve and fifteen excuses for humanity crammed into each. Sacking, flattened tincans, odd scraps of wood, and here or there bits of corrugated iron sheeting – scrounged, stolen or acquired from God knows where – formed the main construction and there was no more than five feet between the rows in which filthy children crawled or stumbled through the litter-covered dust. Among all this the women – for again not one man under forty or so could be seen – knelt or squatted over earthen pots, mixing some kind of hash, maybe enough to keep two alive but which had to be shared among six times that number. Inside the hovels, as I went from one to the other, lay the old ones, too weak to move outside, motionless; and if the smell of death was not already there from the day before it was soon to come. Eyes stared at me, but I could not see a tear among all the misery and degradation; the last tears had long been shed and there were no more. Fifty thousand crushed and mute souls were awaiting their release, whichever way it might come – and hourly the numbers were growing.

From the Buddhist camp we made our way to the Catholics, a mile away and on the other side of the town; here were

30,000 more, living from one handful of soggy food to the next, emaciated and with the same staring, fear-deadened eyes. Packed together as I had seen before, women, children and the old who had kept their strength to reach here and had no more. But strangely, and if the term can be used, better housed: the hovels had more corrugated iron sheets, more and better wood than had the Buddhists and palm leaves made up many of the walls. Why this religious difference? Nobody could explain. I could only imagine that what minute relief was reaching the refugees had mostly come from predominantly Christian organizations. But did it matter? There was so little for anyone. That day I had seen 80,000 refugees from the American concept of making war. These were among the first. As the Austrian doctor had said, 'This is only the beginning.'

That evening I sat in the quiet courtyard of a temple with Nguyen Co and a Buddhist priest. 'We don't want Chinese in Vietnam,' the priest was saying, 'and we don't want Russians.' The stillness was shattered by the noise of jets flying just west of Qui Nhon and the priest turned his shaven head to the sky. 'And we don't want Americans,' he added. 'Why can't we be left in peace?'

A thousand times it has been argued and I have no reason to doubt that the controversy will continue for many years and long after America has, perhaps, retreated once again into isolationism and drawn a curtain tightly around herself. Would South Vietnam – or a united Vietnam, for this is still the ultimate possibility – have been better off under its own style of communism than the ism America imagined she could impose on her? I can only form my own opinion – many have disagreed and will continue to disagree – on what I saw, my eventual knowledge of the people and the country, and I believe that it would, had it been left to iself. Saigon is not South Vietnam and if ever there were similarities, its ways and life, as the Americans changed it, bore not the slightest resemblance to those in the rest of the country. Not far from Saigon, in the Delta area to the south, one could see the real Vietnam. Agriculture was its main reason for existence and it was the peasants on its land on whom it relied for survival. But rapidly, and as the American offensive mounted, the Delta, the whole of

South Vietnam, lost its internal links with itself; government or American-controlled areas became pockets entirely surrounded by hostile country and with no land links between them – the only way to travel one to another was by air, and government claims of control became so many myths.

One of the myths was Long An province, 1,000 square miles and linked with Saigon by the Highway Four. To see the government troops ploughing across the hard and parched paddyfields, as I drove down the highway, could have given the impression that they were in control. But this was daylight, they were careful not to stray more than 500 yards either side of the road and dusk would see them going just as fast in the opposite direction and back to their fortified bases. At night it was Vietcong land and they moved their columns as they wished. If the Government was claiming forty per cent control I would have assessed it as nil by the time I made my way back to Saigon three days later.

The provincial capital itself was 'free', if it were realized that this was but one half of its double life. Not that it appeared to be anything apart from normal as I drove in; the market was full of the fresh foods brought in by the farmers from miles around, shops and whatever small businesses there were seemed to be functioning well and the military base was just far enough away to allow one, most of the time, to forget the war.

That is as it could have been, and could have remained, but history did not shape that way. The Vietcong plan for Long An province in 1965 was well under way and under the administration food production was already rising. They were imposing their taxes and everyone paid, even if he worked for the Saigon Government. Naturally the Vietcong needed much of the tax money at that stage to buy arms to continue their revolution, but most considered the tax scales fair when they were compared with the extortionate demands of provincial chiefs who, hitherto, had made themselves and their Saigon masters rich.

It was one of the town's grocers who was able to give me the details as I sat with him in his house that evening. He was the local tax collector for the Vietcong and my introduction from a Saigon contact had been well received. Poor farmers now paid a flat tax of two pounds a year and for the first time they had the assurance that all the crops they grew remained theirs. Paddy tax rose in accordance with the rice yield and not to the sum demanded by the provincial chief, which took no account of the crop. Richer farmers paid two pounds per year each acre and no more and landless peasant families paid one and a half pounds per year, if they had not been prevented from working. Property owners paid a set tax, and income tax for those who were not on the land was collected at the rate of ten per cent of earnings – and that meant for everyone, including those in 'free' towns. But perhaps the most impressive thing was that the Vietcong had their own local governments operating throughout most of the province; they organized collection from the farms and deliveries to markets, kept the roads open and protected the farmers and peasants. I found it all most interesting, but wanted to know what tax scales might operate if ever peace came with a Vietcong victory. Without the drain on revenue for troops and arms they would be halved, then quartered and in some cases cut completely, my Vietcong grocer informed me. The organization was there and was showing results in Long An as elsewhere, he said, but they needed the chance to prove that theirs was the only way for South Vietnam in the long run.

Needless to say, this orderly and seemingly equitable state of affairs never could have suited the monetary machinations of the Diem regime, and all the tyranny and oppression which went with it. And, among all the smokescreens which have been drawn across the South Vietnamese picture, it can all too easily be forgotten that it was against Diem that the Vietcong resistance rose and took shape. How different might history have been if, somehow, American 'aid' had been spread among the people and not given to one corrupt group; if the money and effort which had gone into building armies had been funnelled into agriculture and development – fertilizers, modern farm equipment and methods, communications, education and health services. How different it might have been if President Kennedy's faithful promises to help under-developed countries by peaceful means had stretched as far as South Vietnam and America had not blatantly gone against all that was hoped for the country under the Geneva agreement. Then America's assistance, given as a friend, might have gently led South

Vietnam forward over the years – the wasted years – until her own brand of communism became the envy of the north. America might have been regarded as the great benefactor and South Vietnam, maybe the whole of Vietnam, could and would have shunned any interest shown in her affairs by Communist China, Russia or anyone else if it were thought that they might interfere with her right to live her own life. Over simplification of the problem? – it was never tried, never given a chance to succeed or otherwise. But rather would I have seen an attempt at that approach than the club and bomb policy. Once Vietnam had split into two countries South Vietnam had little hope, a new set of politics were forced on her by Washington and Diem, and they added up to the one thing – you are for us or against us.

Mine was no preoccupation with one set of ideas or another when I first went to Vietnam; I was biased towards neither the right nor the left. I have had to agree that, on occasions in the past, war has been justified although that has not changed my deep-rooted hatred of war as such. In South Vietnam I considered that the actions leading up to the war were completely unjustified.

I listened to the Vietcong tax collector but here was no proof, and I told him, quite bluntly it was the proof I sought, if that were possible to find. It was possible, he assured me; he was willing, even anxious to help in providing it, and early next morning we set off in his truck on what might, ostensibly, have been another buying expedition to restock his store. The grocer was under no suspicion from the military but he did make some purchases at recognized places where he would have been noticed; then, and only ten minutes from the town, he suddenly branched off the main highway and soon we were in country where government troops would never dare to stray. Rounding a bend in the narrow road the car slowed; ahead of us tree trunks were stretched on oilcans across the road and I came face to face with Vietcong guerillas for the first time. Not that I could see them now. The grocer stopped at the road-block and waited until from the bushes around rose the tiny figures. Dressed in long black pants and black blouses, two of them came to the side of the truck smiling, their automatic guns hanging loosely at their sides. They nodded to me cheerfully as they carried on a conversation with the grocer, and when it was finished they raised a treetrunk and we passed through. Our approach had been watched; they had checked the truck before rising from their hiding places. Any government troops attempting to use the road would have driven into certain and deadly ambush. I would never have gone through alone.

For several hours we visited villages and farms, at intervals being passed through roadblocks as before. Everywhere farmers and peasants were about their work, busily and normally; old trucks and bullock carts were being loaded with produce and these were passed back along the roads onto the main highway and into the market towns. From there much of the produce went to Saigon. The Vietcong had no wish to cut off supplies at that time; they needed to show the people that life could be good and fair under their direction. And they needed the money from taxes, and this could not have been collected if the produce had not got through. Nowhere, apart from those at the roadblocks, did I see armed men, but many were the young ones I saw working in the villages and fields and I asked the tax collector for an explanation.

'An army is not needed among people working and living at peace with each other,' he said, 'but every one of the men you see has been trained and is ready to fight the enemy when he is needed.' Quietly and efficiently, as far as I could see, life was going on in the way into which the Vietnamese were born, lived and died. They were hard workers and each, from a child, had his or her allotted task. Long An was but one of eighteen provinces in the rice bowl Delta over which the Vietcong exercised two-thirds control and the rest they controlled partially. But it was not to continue in the way I saw that day, and that was all they asked; all out war had been decreed and the men I had seen working were forced to leave their fields and villages for another permanent job, with guns.

The following day an official of the American Aid programme, just getting under way in Long An province in some vague attempt to convince the people that they came as friends, drove me around to see the projects he was trying to organize. Two villages along the highway – 'pacified', they were labelled

– had been supplied with fertilizers, tool kits, cooking oil and clothes; peasants were being taught pest control, animal husbandry and new farming methods, but all the time they stayed in their compounds, surrounded with barbed wire. A dedicated man, as were many others who volunteered for this 'Hearts and Minds' operation, the AID official was already feeling the frustrations of trying to do good whilst his brothers rained death from above. 'What is the use of teaching them modern farming when we can give them no land?' he asked. 'We get them in the pacified hamlets for a while and then they disappear, back to Vietcong territory where they can work and live the life they know.' We passed a wooden and tin roofed schoolroom built by AID as the children were leaving after their lessons; when they recognized the truck they stood in sullen lines on either side of the road to allow us through, without a wave or a sign of recognition. A young woman teacher stood at the schoolroom door, but she bent her head, looking at the ground. 'We build them schools and give them books,' said the American, 'but all the teachers are in sympathy with the Vietcong and we cannot control what they teach.'

Later that day and in the AID villa I saw another reason why, perhaps, these people would never be accepted. Two bullet-headed Americans introduced themselves as 'Security'; they were tough policemen, seconded from the Chicago force, and over cans of beer I heard some of the lastest methods of making Vietcong suspects talk. With 'Hearts and Minds' had come a gestapo, and with all the brutality practised by the nazis.

I thought of the 'pacified' hamlet I had visited earlier in the day. True, there was more room for its occupants than in the refugee camps of Qui Nhon, but beside every straw bed in every hut there was the slit trench, a funk hole against badly aimed American bombs or the mortars which came for being under government 'protection'. On an arch over the hamlet entrance, in big letters, were painted the words 'Ap Tan Singh' – in plain English, 'Hamlet of New Life'.

The same week found me 500 miles away, in the Gulf of Tonkin and aboard the US aircraft carrier *Midway*. That the raids on North Vietnam would soon bring violent reaction from Hanoi was a foregone conclusion, and maybe that was the way

STORY UNUSED

the Pentagon had planned it. But how fierce were the raids, how strong? We knew from the daily communiques that both the American navy and airforce were engaged; the B52s were making the long haul from the Philippines and from Guam, in the Pacific, but my applications to fly to either place and join them had been met with a flat refusal. The navy, however, had been much more receptive to my suggestions and it may have helped that the chief of the services facilities branch at the USIS in Saigon was a naval commander. He was proud to assist a British correspondent see his service in action. In three hours of back and forth signalling Rear Admiral William Floyd Bringle, Commander of Task Force 77, sent the message, 'Welcome aboard'. From then it was simple: 'Stand by at zero-four hours tomorrow for collection'.

The sun was just rising as we took off from Tan Son Nhut and the twin-engined, naval communications plane climbed for the east coast, now to be seen in all the yellows and golds of the first daylight hours. North past Nha Trang, Qui Nhon and to Da Nang, where the jets were eternally busy, out across the Gulf with the Chinese island of Hainan somewhere out of sight to the right and, hidden in the haze, North Vietnam to the left. It was almost eight o'clock and the pilot reduced height; 2000 feet below us was the massive structure of the *Midway* at full steam ahead and the creamy wake stretched in a perfectly straight line behind her as far as the eye could see. On her decks were assembled the warplanes and for fifteen minutes we circled, watching them as they catapulted into the air. Then it was down in a perfect approach to be caught by the arrester wires stretched across the deck and a sudden halt which almost sent the flight straps through my ribs. The Admiral was there to welcome me, standing below the bridge, and so was Captain James O'Brien of the *Midway*, and the hustle with which I was hurried off to the operations room left hardly a moment for introductions or a handshake. But that was life on the *Midway*; round the clock planes were landing or planes were taking off, with briefings on the next targets and studying photographs of the damage – or the lack of it – quick meals and almost as quick naps.

At the sides of the flight deck some lay sleeping whilst others scurried around preparing planes for the next raid and until it was their own turn to sleep. In the hangar it was the same; one shift at rest but no time to get to their bunks, and another shift loading cannon shells, rockets, bombs or the Sidewinder, Hawk and Bullpup missiles according to the tasks of the planes – bomber or fighter cover. Every forty-five minutes the steam catapults, two of them, were in action and off went the Skyhawks, the deadly looking Phantoms and the 1,600 m.p.h. Crusaders. When the catapults were not working the planes were returning to crash onto the deck, caught by the wires, or to go round again if they missed.

Today the raids were against the Dong Hoi and Vinh areas of North Vietnam and Admiral Bringle showed me the photographs, as he studied them, of bridges attacked, roads, transport and anything else found moving. One bridge was still standing and a flight was sent off to finish off the job. Every target had to be shown as destroyed before the evening raids began on the port of Haiphong. There was no need for me to be in doubt about the scale of the battering North Vietnam was getting; the *Midway* was not the only carrier operating in the Gulf that day and she was launching an average of around thirty planes an hour – two thirds of them carrying bombs. Even the old, propeller-driven Skyraiders were in the queues on the decks with their thousand-pounders, and the bomb loaders were making sure that their part of this undeclared war was duly registered. On the bombs they were chalking their messages: 'From Midway, With Love', or 'Pleasant Dreams'. He hoped I had enjoyed my stay, the Admiral said as we climbed into the plane to be catapulted off the *Midway*; and into my hand he pressed a memento to remind me of the visit – a crested cigarette lighter designed to keep the flame burning whatever the winds were which blew against it.

Soon afterwards, the first three months of the bombing of North Vietnam drew to a close; it was estimated that over 5,000 tons had been dropped; supply depots and barracks had been destroyed, countless railway wagons, convoys, river ferries and radar posts had been hit and twenty-seven road and rail bridges had been put out of action. But supplies from the north to the Vietcong were mounting daily and their army

STORY UNUSED

became larger and better organized. In Washington an appraisal was made. Had the bombing been a success and had the North Vietnamese been taught a lesson they would never forget? Of course they had not; the bombings had hardened them and determined them to get into the war on the side of the Vietcong. Which was, apparently, just what the Pentagon was reckoning on; the conclusion was reached that they could not win with the bombing, but they could not win without it. Into South Vietnam went the paratroops and the first of the helicopter attack companies. By now there were over 30,000 American troops going into action and within the year there were a quarter of a million. The demands for men by the Pentagon appeared to be insatiable. On the on they went, pumping in men until eventually American had 600,000 of them involved. And never were they in sight of victory in South Vietnam, whatever their plans might have been for elsewhere.

That was not the impression the western would was getting as the giant build-up went on and the American boys had their first tastes of guerilla warfare. From the beginning it had to be 'victory' and what the Americans may have lacked in military success they certainly made up in the field of propaganda. For a 'good' army to stand up to the might and firepower of America was an impossiblility, and each time the Americans went into action they would have to kill the Vietcong in large numbers for minimal losses to themselves. That was the decision, regardless of what the truth might be, and that is how the military briefing officers gave the figures each day to correspondents who religiously passed them on to their newspapers. Later, when the real reverses came, some may say that witholding the true casualty figures might have been in America's interests, even if it did no more than deny the information which could have been useful to the Vietcong and Hanoi. But to begin with a policy that for every American killed or wounded ten Vietcong at least had to be claimed was not only ludicrous, it was sheer dishonesty, which soon became apparent. Monotonously the figures were read out at the briefings: 'Eighty-two VC dead, seven Americans killed and one missing,' or 'Forty VC dead, two Americans killed and two wounded.' It was not long before a few of us at the briefings, when we heard a claim of, say,

'One hundred and twenty VC killed', would murmur in unison, and without waiting for what was to follow, '. . . and twelve Americans dead and missing'.

It was amazing that newspapers, and not only those of America, blindly continued to publish the claims. If they had been true the Vietcong had been completely decimated in one year from when America openly entered the war. Yet, mysteriously, the guerillas fought on in ever-increasing numbers. Similarly, and within three years, the number of casualties claimed almost equalled the whole population and yet the war continued unabated. Early in the proceedings I got confirmation that the policy was official. Over a drink I raised the ten to one ratio with an information colonel, a tired man who was now counting the days to the end of his year's tour. 'Hell,' he said, 'don't blame me. I carry out orders, and if its ten to one then that's the way it's gotta be.'

Equally amazing was it that any and every statement issued by the Americans in Saigon was accepted and played up into headlines without question. It was still May 1965 when Lieutenant-General De Puy – 'Deepew', as he introduced himself – danced on to the platform to give us a 'special briefing'. 'Gentlemen,' he said, 'I've great news for you. On our reckoning and in view of the success we have had so far, the Vietcong will be defeated by the end of this year and South Vietnam will be at peace.' Later that day De Puy sat contentedly puffing at his cigar after dinner at the house of the British Military Attaché and repeated his forecast. Naturally, a discussion began and it went on well into the night, but I am sure the general never knew why Colonel Napier and I disagreed so violently with his views or understood the dozen reasons we gave which were to prove him wrong.

Almost as De Puy made his prediction, Saigon was in a new crisis. Its two million people were short of food for the first time. Trucks which had regularly brought rich farm produce from the lush pastures of Dalat, north of the capital and in the hills, were not arriving. Quickly the Vietcong had reacted to the setting up of American bases between Dalat and Saigon and as battles broke out they formed into battalion strength and cut and commanded the vital Highway Twenty along which the food went to the south. Prices soared as hotels and restaurants cornered dwindling supplies at black market prices, and for the masses it became a diet of rice, with an occasional relief of a little fish or, when it could be found, an even smaller amount of meat. American transport planes were taken off their military supply routes for an airlift from Dalat, but not nearly enough could be spared and the vegetable shortage continued and became worse. But that was not all. The vulnerability of Saigon, relying for every scrap of food from outside, had not been given the fullest consideration, and as the war mounted in the Delta supply roads onto the all-important Highway Four became cut off. Farmers in Vietcong areas no longer could get their supplies to the capital. And, added to this, areas around the maze of Delta canals, through which food barges had hitherto been reaching Saigon, were now battlegrounds.

It must rate as one of the oddest aspects of the Vietnamese war that Saigon, lying on the edge of one of the richest food producing areas in the world, would have starved if a massive supply operation, costing untold millions more in dollars, had not been organized as a number one priority. Soon we were to see the rice ships from America coming up the river to the capital. Much of the rice was stolen and more was hoarded by merchants with an eye to higher prices. And the Vietnamese did not like it, anyway; they protested that the quality of the rice was inferior to that from the Delta. Food ships were attacked long before they reached Saigon; the Vietcong mined the main channel; the war in the Delta had developed into the battle for food and I doubt if the military brains had seen it coming. It was certainly not in Vietcong interests to have the rice and other produce piling up in the Delta provinces; they could collect no taxes if it were not sold. But if they did not fight they would be giving up the territory.

Little has been written of the river assault group. Most of the glamour in those early days surrounded the marines, the paratroops, the pilots and then, of course, the helicopter-equipped air cavalry. But as the battle for food built up, so did a force of armoured assault boats, each no more than sixty feet long, which were shipped into Saigon from America. By May 1965 the force had grown to 130 boats and their beat was 2,500 miles of rivers and waterways in the Delta, now, after two weeks of rain, doubling and trebling as the nine mouths of the Mekong River were gradually forming into one huge lake covering over a thousand square miles. The job of the assault group was to keep the water routes to the capital open, to escort the food barges, but mostly to land troops wherever the Vietcong could be found, keep them supplied and then evacuate them. And it was a job for volunteers only; the young American lieutenants and second lieutenants who commanded the boats did not live long and locally recruited crews, despite the big rates of pay offered, were hard to come by. From the air the battle for food would hardly have given me the picture I wanted, but here, with the assault group, was the obvious way to get at it, despite the fact that my application to join the boats was greeted with raised eyebrows and the words, 'Well, if you insist. But we must warn you, it's your own responsibility.' Along the river from the centre of Saigon was the group's headquarters and I reported there – for exactly what, I was not quite sure.

It was one of my stranger journeys. It was three o'clock in the morning and I was on the armoured bridge of the leading assault boat, a gunship; four more boats trailed behind loaded with ammunition, and a sixth, which I could not see in the darkness, brought up the rear, another gunboat – and all the young lieutenant talked of was death. We were going down river, making for a rendezvous with South Vietnamese and American troops on a reasonably hard piece of ground somewhere among the maze of waterways. 'Over five hundred killed there already,' the lieutenant announced as a cheerful opening to the conversation and then went on to say at once, 'We lost Bob last night. Great man, Bob; he'd always take a chance.' Bob was a second lieutenant, I gathered, but Bob was by no means the only one in his Delta grave from the ranks of the assault group. 'Joe got it four days ago,' the lieutenant solemnly told me. 'Never thought Joe would go – he had a charmed life, been with the force since it was first formed.'

How long had this twenty-one year old, blond and baby-faced man been with the assault boats? 'Over two months,' he said. 'Lucky, you know. Not everyone lasts that long. I'm not reckoning on finishing the tour alive.' Then what was the casualty rate? 'About two-thirds so far,' came the answer, 'but it's difficult to say. We haven't been operating long enough for anyone to get through a full tour – some have left, but they got shot up.' I've seen the death wish on many people, but never quite so matter of fact as this. So why have so many volunteered? 'Well,' explained the lieutenant, 'we get a command and that would mean promotion when the tour is over.' He was peering out through the bullet proof glass and into the eerie blackness. 'Not reckoning on seeing that promotion,' he said, 'not now I know what's its all about.'

We had been going for two hours when the convoy turned into a narrow waterway off the main stream. Another ten minutes and we were in what I took to be a canal. It appeared to be narrower and dead straight. The first fingers of the pink dawn were picking out bushes and trees and our rendezvous was at five-thirty, when there would be enough light to unload the ammunition and take on any casualties which might be awaiting us. A sharp turn to starboard, but this was another river and I wondered at the superb navigation. For another ten minutes we wound our way round bend after gentle bend and suddenly the lieutenant opened the throttles wide as he called over to me, 'If we're gonna get it, it's coming soon.'

I could pick out the banks more clearly now and there must have been about twenty to thirty yards clearance on either side as the diesels strained and took the speed up to its maximum – twelve knots. All count of time was lost as we searched the bushes and trees, thicker as we went on. But when it came I did not see the first flashes of guns; they came from the opposite side of the boat from where I was. What I was really conscious of was the gun mounted above the bridge roaring into action, but by then another score of guns were answering from either bank. Fire was being poured at us and our gunners were raking the bushes. Flashes were turning the half-light into staccato daylight and the red tracers shone brilliantly as they snaked their way above, across and behind us. It was the ambush the lieutenant expected, knew was coming, and amidst the din I heard his voice. 'Bastards, bastards,' he was screaming, but he knew there was only one way out of it – straight ahead.

What seemed to be hours were, in reality, no more than two or three minutes before we were through; the firing around us suddenly ceased, but it continued as the other five boats, nose to tail to make the greatest concentration of firepower, came out of range. What our casualties were he had no way of knowing, but now was not the time to find out. For another three miles we kept up the speed along the river as our radio operator worked away, giving the position so that the planes could be called in. The sun was rising above the ever flat horizon as we drew into a hard-packed length of riverside which lined the mud of the fields beyond. The cases of ammunition were unloaded by a string of South Vietnamese troops under the direction of an American army sergeant; twenty or so wounded were taken aboard the two gunboats and one of the crew was detailed in the rear one to take the place of the original gunner who had disappeared in the fray, overboard and probably riddled with bullets, our only casualty. Within twenty minutes we were away again, in line astern and the throttles were wide open once more. 'Won't see them again this trip,' shouted the lieutenant, 'but let's get the hell out of it.' He was right. The Vietcong knew when to go and what the next move would be. We saw the Skyraiders and jets diving ahead of us but what was there for them to see, apart from the bushes, the trees and the wide open spaces?

A week or so later, two of the assault group commanders came into the hotel bar and I enquired after the lieutenant. 'Good kid, but a bit green,' came the reply from one of the naval officers. 'He bought it two nights ago. His replacement flew in today.'

It must have been a hard decision for the Vietcong, but many of those food supply routes, and the revenue which they had brought, could now be considered as permanently cut. The Delta was aflame, and no matter how many government and American troops were thrown into this preliminary battle the Vietcong matched them and usually beat them. It was another time to stop and think, but nobody did. From the numbers alone that the Vietcong could rush in from other and northern provinces, any calculation would suggest that the major part of the country's population supported them and would have to be put down eventually, if that were possible. And so far they were doing it alone, without the help of the North Vietnamese

STORY UNUSED

armies, which were to come. Everywhere the Vietcong strengthened and consolidated their position. They overran government army posts and left few alive; they kidnapped provincial chiefs who were still stupid enough to think that they were in 'pacified' areas; they ambushed and stole armoured cars and weapons by the thousand. Villages went quickly under their full control and then they proved they were powerful enough to lay siege to, and take, the provincial capital of Song Be. Helicopter trips into and out of the battle areas had to be rapid affairs; it was no use dallying for even a few hours. The Vietcong were on all sides and it was a question of using a landing pad one day and the next day finding it, from the fire coming up, well and truly in Vietcong hands. Always they moved by night and never was it known where their battalions would appear next. They attacked at night, when the American jets could not get at them. But the slower planes could, and I discovered a way of getting a grandstand view.

Nightly from Saigon I could see the flares dangling in the distant sky and when I asked to join those who were dropping them the USIS again obliged and passed me over to the air force. The big and bulbous, twin-engined C-123s, normally used only for transport, were now taking on a new role – acting as flareships and patrolling the Delta all night, ready to light up the scene of any action. Sometimes the call came, but often it did not and I was thinking that I was facing nothing but a dreary night just stooging around the sky, when the radio crackled at around one o'clock in the morning, an hour after we had taken off from Tan Son Nhut. We flew at three thousand feet and the pilot swung the plane around and onto his given course, deep into the Delta, leaving the lights of Saigon far behind. It was only the direction we really needed, for within ten minutes we saw the red glow on the skyline and in another fifteen were above it, a village, defended by government troops, was under Vietcong attack and was blazing on three sides. From the wide open, rear loading doors of the C-123 I could clearly see the explosions of grenades.

Inside the plane were stacked hundreds of canisters and at the buzzer signal from the cockpit the crew pushed two of them through the open doors; suddenly the nocturnal blackness turned into blinding whiteness behind as the magnesium in the first canister, and then the second, ignited and they hung there suspended on their parachutes, each shedding their eerie two million candle-power across the ground below. But these were just the pilot flares to gauge the wind, the attack appeared to be coming mainly from the eastern side of the village and we watched as the flares drifted more to the southeast. A quick turnaround and down went two more pilot flares on a corrected course; dead over the eastern approaches to the village they went and the scene was set.

For the next hour I lay on my stomach as we flew north to south and then south to north. Out went the canisters by the dozens, leaving long strings of brilliant pearls behind us and lighting up the ground below as though it were daylight. In came the Skyraiders and I saw their bombs straddling a road leading to the village; from a thousand feet I watched them diving and weaving below us, through the murderous fire which was being guided by thousands of red tracer shells. The Vietcong had come well prepared for an air attack and they did not forget the C–123; up snaked the red tracers, first on one side of us and then on the other but out went the canisters until the Skyraiders finished their attack and all the bombs were gone. What the final result of the action was I never knew, but there would be little of that village left by the morning. Our radio was crackling again and we turned onto a northerly course, our flares were needed elsewhere.

Saigon lay no more than sixteen miles away to the northeast and the city lights formed a giant glow in the sky as we next went into action and the flares lit up the Vam Co Dong river. Somehow the alarm had been given that another battalion of Vietcong was on the move and we could see their sampans crossing the river as the waiting Sykraiders dived to the attack. Many must have died as the boats were caught in the magnesium glare, but the fire which came up from the paddyfields on either side left no doubt who was in control for miles around in that countryside. That was the Delta; we had been only one of several flareships operating over it that night and, apart from one hour, we had been at action stations the whole time until we landed at dawn. How many more battalions of Vietcong

STORY UNUSED

had gone undetected, how big was this swarm that the Pentagon imagined it could crush in a few months? The crew chief looked up from his log back at the flight hut and announced his night's count. 'Two hundred and thirty flares tonight, sir,' he said, and grinned as he went on: 'At eighty-five dollars a flare this war's getting mighty expensive.'

So much for that understatement. If the Americans had but known, they were already paying Vietcong indirectly in hard dollars which were being spent on Chinese arms and medical equipment. A ridiculous situation had developed whereby the more men America put into Vietnam the more dollars went to the Vietcong, who equipped more men to fight them. It was the Americans conceit again: nothing was 'real' money but the greenback dollar, and they looked on the Vietnamese currency as 'this goddammed toy money'. From his monthly pay each American was allowed to draw $200 in greenbacks and the Vietcong rapidly built up an organization to collect them.

I watched it grow as I saw Saigon changing and deteriorating out of all recognition. Always there had been the money changers and the black market rates for hard currency, but these had been discrete transactions, negotiated in the privacy of an apartment or office and usually with an Indian. 'The Bank of India' it had become known as in quiet conversation and an introduction was needed before one was accepted as a customer; cheques and bills were carried out in suitcases as baggage to Singapore or Hong Kong. But now there was no need to search for a money changer; they and their touts stood on every corner of Tu Do, Le Loi and every other large thoroughfare, offering rates which gradually soared to three times that of the official rate. 'Change money?' were the words one heard twenty times in a ten-minute walk, and the most familiar sight was that of GIs disappearing into an alleyway behind a building with a dubious looking Vietnamese and then reappearing, stuffing wads of notes into their tunic pockets with grins on their faces as they contemplated how many drinks and women that was going to pay for.

But not all the dollars, by any means, were being picked up like this on the streets by the Vietcong agents; bars were the first thing the GIs made for, so enough bars had to be opened to cater for the thousands of Americans who were now filling Saigon, Da Nang and every other place where American bases were being set up. Overnight shopfronts were torn out and their counters and goods swept away to be replaced by glittering interiors and names over the entrance such as 'Hollywood Bar', 'The Manhattan' or 'Miami'. In went the girls, two or three dozen to each bar and it was open within two weeks or less, from nine in the morning until the early hours of the next. 'Buy me a drink, Johnny?'. Every girl was taught the phrase parrot fashion and they drank endless glasses of cold tea at two dollars a time, paid for by the GIs—then the young innocents were led off to be relieved of more greenbacks in a seamy bedroom. By the end of 1965 Saigon alone had 4,500 bars and 3,000 of them had been opened within that year; anyone could get a licence for the equivalent of eighty dollars and the Vietcong put up their chosen women as fronts. Thai Phung, beautiful with her raven hair, slant eyes and charming smile, was one of them I got to know quite well when she opened up as 'Olga's Bar', and she told me she had recovered the cost of equipping and stocking the bar in her first month of operating. But the profits were not going to Thai Phung, for at around one o'clock each morning two men would arrive to check and empty her cash register. She knew I had noticed it on more than one occasion and one night came over to the stool where I sat, covering me with one of her smiles and pushing a drink towards me. 'Don't ask questions,' said Thai Phung; 'it's dangerous. I am only doing my job.'

Yes, the money was rolling and Saigon was becoming a boom town. A group of GIs from the Tan Son Nhut airbase noticed it fast enough and, even if they did not know where most of the dollars were going, they saw no reason why they should not filter some of them into their own pockets. I was invited to the new 'club' which had been opened in an old building not far from the base; something special, I had been told, and it certainly lived up to that description. Within a week of opening a bar the GIs had somehow found enough women to supply the 'attractive company' it was now boasting and the accommodation to enjoy them. One room was set aside for 'blue' films and the place was packed. Within two months the business was extended to include a restaurant and a swimming pool.

For some it was a lovely war. Not every GI was a fighting soldier and many of them, with their officers, went away after their one-year tour as rich men. With the bars had come the great demand for what they sold. American stocks of drink were 'diverted' into black markets, where no questions were asked; hi-fis, transistor radios, record players, electric razors, perfume and other luxury goods by the ton were on display in a hundred city shops and American cigarettes sold by the million from kerbside dealers, complete with the 'Forces Only' labels on their packets. Corruption, wholesale stealing (with tiny children trained as thieves), prostitutes by the thousand and many of them from good families. Near the American bases up and down the country I found GIs and officers who set up women in houses and then sold them, house included, to the next man at the end of their tours. And the profits from all this?—nine-tenths of it was going to the Vietcong one way or another. The bars, the girls, the child thieves, the money touts and the black marketeers, they were all part of the operation to grab the dollars, and nearly every American serviceman, senior officers included, was playing some sort of part to make it a success.

It may have gone on much longer, offering the dollars on a plate, if, in an article, I had not pointed out that every greenback dollar going into South Vietnam was buying a bullet to kill a GI. Some days later I had a call from the USIS, 'Say, have you been writing about dollars?' I was asked. 'Hell, you've caused a stir in Washington. They're sending out a team of investigators and cancelling all our dollars for scrip.' It gave me no pride when that quickly happened; it was just another example of the amazing blindness which befogged all American thinking when they pulled the trigger in their mad desire for a war against the communists.

Among themselves the GIs started another black market, in scrip money. And it was not long before the Vietcong, and the North Vietnamese who joined them, were assured of all the arms and supplies they needed to fight the Americans, without payment.

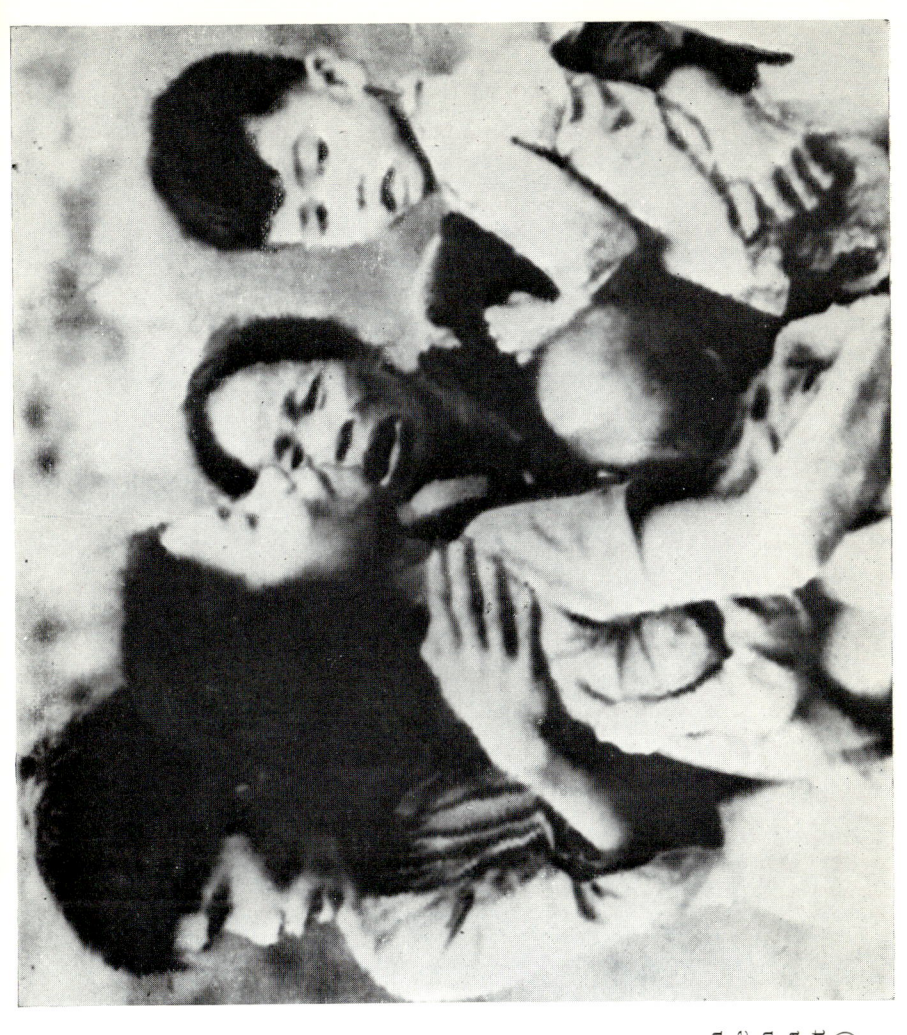

9. Some of the few civilian survivors caught in a battle between Vietcong and South Vietnamese troops in a jungle town. Photo by Horst Faas (Photo: Assoc. Press)

10. *Top:* South Vietnamese unit, hip deep in water, searching for Viet Cong guerillas in the Mekong Delta. *Bottom:* Two guerillas flushed from a flooded paddy 120 miles southwest of Saigon (Photos: Assoc. Press)

For many of the million Chinese living in the half of Saigon called Cholon it was not such a bad war until the Vietcong chose to invade the capital through that area. But that came much later. It was not considered a good security risk to have the Chinese in the South Vietnamese forces and they were left free to cash in on the American invasion in a hundred and one ways—there is nothing to match the ingenuity of the Chinese. Of course, they paid their taxes to the Vietcong, even their special position did not let them out of that. Everyone was paying Vietcong tax and the Caravelle hotel where I stayed soon learned not to get behind in its dues—a Vietcong agent booked in and left a time bomb on the third floor and the damage took months to repair. Chinese restaurants doubled and trebled in number, a large and modern dance hall in Cholon took on an extra hundred or so taxi-girls as dance partners for the GIs and the 'French' wine makers began to turn out the Beaujolais and Chateauneuf du Pape. But this was small stuff. A group of Chinese manufacturers set about the task of providing what every well-dressed GI should wear and every third shop in Saigon was soon devoting most of its space to improving the sartorial elegance of the American navy, army and airforce.

It is one of the more incredible sights I have seen around the world and I cannot imagine any other country, apart from America, allowing it. Discipline in dress is surely one of the first and basic requirements of any military man, but I cannot say that I have been particularly impressed by the type of discipline the Americans practised in any other form in their forces, where rank means little or nothing at all and GIs offer the same respect to a captain or major as they would to another GI in their own barrack room. Here was the chance to look like the Hollywood war heroes, and in their thousands the GIs discarded one article of their personal equipment after another. Government issue boots were put aside for the more attractive ones to be found in the shops; gun holsters in shining black leather became the fashion, but for the most elegant had to be worn on the Cholon made and matching bullet belts. Small wonder that the GIs became known as 'Cowboys'; it was nothing uncommon to see them, on and off their bases, dressed in cowboy style boots, complete with leather fringes and stitched designs, the bullet belt and holster, a 'battle blouse' decorated with large and painted lions, and the whole ensemble topped with a cowboy style hat, upturned at one side, Australian fashion, and in the particular colour chosen for a particular unit. The cowboy hats were in brilliant scarlets, blues, yellows and greens and shop windows were filled with a galaxy of different regimental badges and insignia, with which the GIs plastered themselves. Nobody in authority stopped them. One of the favourite shoulder flashes, Cholon made, bore the words, *Sorry about that.*

The discarded government issue equipment had to find its way somewhere and the Thieves Market, a block of narrow streets behind the flower market in Saigon, opened up with new and profitable lines. If you wished to dress as an American paratrooper, everything you needed could be found in the back rooms of the market 'shops', complete and down to the webbing, belts, boots, water bottles, knives and badges. Or a marine, an infantryman, an airforce sergeant? – it was all there at a price, with a good line in American weapons from revolvers and rifles to automatic guns. I did not attempt to prove it, but it was said that American jeeps or trucks could be obtained on 'special' order. Anything was possible in this ludicrous state of affairs and, of course, the Vietcong found great possibilities in the market. Some of the American correspondents and cameramen had great shopping sprees there and could don the uniform of any unit they were temporarily joining. Again, no questions were asked; we were not allowed to join operations out of uniform, but the American command refused to supply us with them. Most of us compromised; we found a tailor in Tu Do who made, to our own design, a reasonable copy of a battledress in jungle green, but something not too military looking, so that we could use it for almost any occasion. The two-piece suits became the hallmark of correspondents who had served in Vietnam and an immediate mark of recognition as they gradually appeared all over the Far East – in Singapore, Malaya, Indonesia and any other hot and tropical spot. They were also legitimate items on our expense accounts, although mine did raise some surprised whistles among the British troops in Borneo when I first arrived in my 'Saigon battledress'.

Correspondents can usually be relied upon to find the best eating places and, once the word was passed around, three or four of them in Saigon became our regular rendezvous when we were in town. 'Cheap Charlie's' – a great misnomer, but it could not be beaten for its giant fried crab hands – was a lunchtime favourite; service was quick and it was in the city centre. A pizzeria close by had a period when it was on our regular list. But always we had to move on; we made a place popular and the American servicemen moved in with all their invitations to Vietcong bombs and grenades.

The Restaurant Flottant, a converted boat lying on the river near the Yacht Club and away from the centre of Saigon, a group of us decided, was one of the safer places. The GIs had not discovered it and only Vietnamese ate there. It was quiet, apart from the sounds of guns which rolled over from beyond the opposite bank, and to sit with the excellent food and some of the remaining French wine on the open deck under the stars became one of our main relaxations when we had showered the grime of the day away and our last cables were safely gone.

We should have decided earlier; the nightly diners aboard the boat were gradually changing. First one and then another officer found it and even if they were in civilian clothes there was no mistaking the crewcuts for what they were. One night we did discuss giving up the Restaurant Flottant when three GIs came aboard in full uniform, but we were loth to make the decision. We regarded it as one of our own and special eating and meeting spots. For another week we continued to use it, and did no more than curse anyone resembling an American who came aboard. But for the grace of God, this holding on to a favourite rendezvous nearly cut the number of operating correspondents by eight.

The Restaurant Flottant for dinner, it was to be a few nights later, when we agreed to meet in the Caravelle bar at seven-thirty. Normally it was a drink as we foregathered, and then on to the boat where we would have been sitting on deck studying the menu by eight o'clock – if the telephone had not rung in my room at seven-fifteen. John Martin from the British

Embassy was on the line: a visitor from the Foreign Office in London was in town and John was wondering if I would be free for dinner at his house. I explained that I had agreed to join a group of colleagues and John, always the perfect host, had the answer. 'Why not bring them along,' he said, 'it's a buffet meal and there's plenty to eat'. My suggestion as we met in the bar was fine; John was one of the more popular members of the Saigon diplomatic corps and it was agreed.

That was how we were standing with our first drinks in John's garden at eight-fifteen when the first ground-shaking crash came, to be followed in three minutes by another, just as violent. Don Wise looked across at me. 'Christ,' he said, 'someone's got it. Sounded as though they came from down near the river.' We grabbed the telephone in the house and were still trying every number we could think of when John Morley rushed in to announce, 'It's the floating restaurant. Shocking mess. God knows how many dead.'

There was no dinner for us that night. As one, the eight of us forgot our drinks and the attractive dishes and made for the cars. Sirens were wailing all over town and everything was going in the same direction. Down Tu Do we raced and turned right at the bottom along the river. Crowds prevented us from driving further and we pushed through them on foot towards the spot we knew so well, forcing people aside to get at one of the most gruesome sights imaginable, and in that I include all the gory sights of the so-called 'legitimate' war.

The Vietcong had struck; too many Americans were using the Restaurant Flottant and they were the primary target. For the first time, Vietnamese civilians and others were not taken into consideration, and if they were in the way they had to die too. Against a tobacco kiosk on the riverside the Vietcong had planted a timed Claymore mine, a Chinese copy of the American original but with twice its destructive force, and aimed as a broadside against the boat. On the opposite side of the street another Claymore was fixed to a bicycle propped up against a tree and pointed towards the covered and narrow path leading to the restaurant's gangway. It was diabolical but perfect planning, and timed for the moment when the decks and the inside cabin restaurant would be crowded with nearly 200 diners. The bicycle had been standing there for fifteen minutes, but two policemen had passed it by without suspicion and the Vietcong were safely away as the infernal machines ticked their way towards the unmerciful tragedy which was to come.

At eight-fifteen the Claymore hidden by the kiosk went off with a roar, spewing its jagged pieces of metal at the boat. The glass sides of the covered restaurant shattered into thousands of pieces, which sliced through the diners as they sat; while others on the open deck, where we would have been sitting, were struck down as though under fire from a rifle-carrying platoon. In an instant there was pandemonium, as those who could still move stampeded for the gangway and the covered approach. There was a mass of struggling people as the second Claymore blasted off at eight-eighteen. The strugglers were cut to pieces, falling on top of each other into a bloody pile, and those few who had got off the boat first were cut down on the riverside pavement as the murderous mine blocked their path of escape. The road, the pavements and the covered pathway flowed with blood, and when the terrible work of removing the bodies was over fire pumps were called in to clean up the scene with high-powered hoses. On the heavily listing boat was a ghastly sight; human flesh, mixed with Chinese food, covered the floors, and unrecognizable victims, armless or legless, lay among the debris of tables, chairs, plates and bottles. Hardly a soul on board escaped that night; forty-two lay dead, and among them twelve Americans who had invited the disaster.

Eighty were terribly wounded, more Americans among them, and many were not to survive their appalling injuries.

The Restaurant Flottant was never used again; it lay in the river abandoned and half-filled with water, a grim reminder that when generals go to war they take the innocents with them.

The following afternoon I was strapped into the rear seat of a Canberra jet bomber, one of two stooging around the sky awaiting the call from a spotter plane which would give us a target onto which we could unleash our five-hundred-pounder bombs. We sat up there at 15,000 feet, first line abreast and then line astern, waiting for instructions, and Major Gerald Hamilton's voice sounded impatient as it crackled over the

STORY UNUSED

intercom from the front seat. 'Goddam,' came the word through my headphone, and a memorable conversation was opened.

'Something wrong, Captain?'

'Hell, no! But I want to get rid of this lot on someone today – fast.'

'Anything special about today?'

'Did you hear about the bastards blowing up that floating restaurant last night? One of my buddies got it; another one lost his girl friend.'

'Do you always drop your bombs in anger?'

'Can't say that, but it's kinda special today. Someone's gonna get them with a vengeance.'

'You married, Captain?'

'Sure, wife and three kids back in the States.'

'Does it ever worry you when you have to drop bombs on women and children?'

'Well, I'm an air force man and I reckon I'm a good one. I take my orders and if I'm ordered to drop my bombs I drop them.'

'But don't you ever wonder what's at the other end of them?'

'That's not my job and I wouldn't be out here flying if I had to think what every bomb was hitting.'

'Does your wife ever worry that you might be killing women and children?'

'Hell, why should she. Some of us have got good air force wives and some of them are bad. I reckon I've got a good air force wife. She never asks questions about what I'm doing.'

'Does she write about the war in her letters?'

'Nope, that's none of her business. I said she's a good air force wife. She tells me how the kids are getting on at school, you know. . . .'

The conversation was cut short. Another voice broke in on the radio. It was the spotter pilot and he had a target for us; someone was going to 'get it'.

To me it was just a village, a couple of hundred typically Vietnamese wood and rush houses, stretched either side of a muddy centre path. For miles around the flat countryside there was nothing else in sight. It made a perfect target; it was unmistakable. But did any of us know who was down there? I could see no sign of life; it could have been deserted, but from what I knew of the villagers they were in their bunkers and trenches the moment they had heard the first plane. We circled it at 3,000 feet until Major Hamilton decided on the plan. 'You go in first from the south-east,' he hold Captain Chabot in the other Canberra, and I watched as the plane manoeuvred into position and went into the dive. Dead in line with the centre path it went, a stick of seven bombs straddling the village. 'Beautiful bombing,' Major Hamilton was saying, 'beautiful'; but as he said it Captain Chabot was pulling up into the sky shouting, 'I've been hit, sure, I've been hit.'

We wheeled around to get alongside the other Canberra as the intercom buzzed between the two pilots, first one side of the number two plane we flew, then the other and finally underneath. 'Waggle her around a bit,' Hamilton called. 'Few holes on your starboard side. How are the controls?' The Canberra danced around the sky as Chabot tried the ailerons, the tail and the rudder, until his voice came back. 'Seems okay; controls feel normal.' From somewhere, perhaps hidden in the fields around the village, the fire had come, but we had not seen it. Not such a simple target this, after all, so we formated again for a minute or two as Hamilton decided on the next move. 'I'll give them a taste of cannon while you make another run as before,' he said and we went low for a run in from the north-east, spraying the village and the fields around with cannon shells for a few seconds before Chabot dived again on his second bomb run. Those were the tactics we kept up.

Next it was our turn for a bombing dive, but its shallowness surprised me. True we hit the village fair and square, all along it. But this was not dive bombing as I knew it; there was hardly a pull of 'G' as we climbed out of the dive from around a hundred feet and we were presenting a fair target for whoever had the guns on the ground. Four runs with cannon and five with the bombs we did until the village was nothing but a heap of dusty rubble. By then Chabot had reported being hit again and we collected half a dozen holes through a wing and, as we were to find when we landed, another couple through the tailplane. But it was the spotter pilot in his tiny plane who seemed to be having the roughest time: 'Say, have you finished?' he called more than once, and then I heard his plaintive voice come over the radio for the final time, 'Hell, let's get out of here,' he said. 'It's alive down there.'

With a few thousand pounds of TNT, anti-personnel and time bombs left around, to say nothing of the hundreds of cannon shells, I suppose Hamilton and Chabot felt they had done a good job. But those who had fought back certainly were not in the village, waiting for bombs, and we had seen nobody fleeing from our attacks. 'D'you reckon we got many women and kids today?' I asked Hamilton as we made our way back to Tan Son Nhut, and his voice came back sharply through the headphones, finishing off our earlier converstion. 'Hell,' said Hamilton, and there was a lot of punch in the word. 'If you're going to worry about women and kids you'd go crazy in a week. This is a bomber and you shouldn't fly it if you feel like that. I told you – I'm a good officer.'

There was time to get back to the hotel to shower and change before walking across to the USIS auditorium for the five o'clock briefing. For a while I sat there listening to the daily and dreary American claims – 83 Vietcong killed, 6 Americans killed and 2 wounded, etc., etc. I was about to leave when the briefing officer's voice stopped me, 'US Airforce planes attacked and destroyed a Vietcong headquarters twenty-four miles north-east of Saigon this afternoon,' he was saying. This was my raid, so I listened to the few details and then the claim: '138 Vietcong were killed.' From the front row came a question from a young American correspondent, new to Vietnam: 'Body count?', he asked. The briefing officer replied in his matter of fact tone, 'No, sir – pilots' estimates.'

It was all written down and flashed over the wires with the rest of the day's communique. The Americans had had another victorious day and, with those that Hamilton and Chabot were supposed to have killed, over 600 Vietcong had been eliminated for the loss of a mere 40 or so Americans, killed or mostly wounded. Or so the world was led to believe. I thought back to the conversation with Major Hamilton before we took off from Tan Son Nhut: 'Don't you put any of that cock about pilots' estimates down to us,' he had said. 'You should know. You're a pilot. MACVI thinks up the figures and makes us look bloody fools.'

A good officer. Most of them were, and I spent a lot of time in planes of one type or another. They carried out their orders and asked no questions. But if I had asked Hamilton, as I did many other pilots, the background to the Vietnam war, its history or its rights or wrongs, I would have found, as I usually did, that he did not know and was not interested. Naturally, they would say, America was right and the frightening thing I found was that many of them, in 1965, looked on it all as some sort of game. Kill as many bastard gooks as you can before it is your turn to go home, was one attitude – and you do not have to worry about enemy planes. It is true, there were no North Vietnamese in the skies then, and when there were they stayed in the north. In South Vietnam the anti-aircraft fire had not reached the degree of sophistication that was to come later but, if they were not knocking the planes out of the air in such large numbers, the Vietcong were certainly enjoying a reasonable degree of success in destroying them on the ground.

It was a Sunday morning. From Saigon I heard the explosions and the great palls of smoke rising into the air marked it as the huge base of Bien Hoa, twelve miles or so away. Near the base was the village; the bars, the girls and the night clubs were well installed and it was a hotbed of Vietcong. Blissfully unaware, as they invariably were, the Americans practically rubbed shoulders during the day with those who would be planning an attack on the base for that night. Perimeter defences, as at all bases, left a lot to be desired and, as all plane strikes went off at fairly regular times, the Vietcong who penetrated right to the flightlines during darkness had timed their explosive satchels for the first and main one at eight-thirty.

It was devastation when I arrived and time bombs carried by the planes were still exploding. Some still blasted off twenty-four hours later. Bien Hoa had been attacked only six months before and eighteen Canberras destroyed, but still security pre-

STORY UNUSED

cautions had not kept up with the prowess of the enemy. This morning five Canberras had just got into the air, three were on the runway and others taxying out from the flightlines when the neatly placed charge blew up a Canberra, still parked. The taxying planes and their crews were blown to bits and scattered over hundreds of yards, and the flames and explosions spread along the rest of the parked Canberras, all bombed up for a strike and parked wingtip to wingtip – destroying the lot. It was still an inferno when I got as near as possible nearly an hour later; a flight of helicopters parked some distance away had managed to get into the air and were diving in and out of the smoke in rescue attempts; a fire tender disappeared in a roar as the heat melted and exploded another bomb, and ground crews, air crews and rescuers died and burned in the inferno. The Vietcong raid had destroyed and crippled 41 planes; 21 Americans were dead and more were to succumb out of the 40 critically injured – but not one Vietcong had been seen. General Joseph Moore, commander of the Second Air Division, deduced that it was an 'accident' and not due to enemy action, within half an hour of the first explosion and when the flightline was still an inferno; how he did so is difficult to imagine. Perhaps he did not see the smiles on Vietnamese faces that morning; he would have had to drive no more than a hundred yards from the base main gates to realize who was claiming victory and success.

Unbelievable, incredible – there is hardly a word properly to describe the crass stupidity of the American military machine when it came to security. The Vietcong guerilla attack at the Pleiku base in February, when seven Americans had been killed and over a hundred wounded, sparked off President Johnson's order for nonstop bombing of North Vietnam. In the nearest village had been found a clay model of the whole camp, detailed by Vietnamese who had access to it, and on this the raid had been based. Yet in June, when I was next at Pleiku, four months later, Vietnamese cooks, waiters, servants, builders, electricians and carpenters were still being used, and in greatly increased numbers – all checked into and out of the base by Vietnamese guards. They wandered around at will, and then, when they left the base, disappeared into known and proven Vietcong territory, in which the base lay as a tiny island, and countryside into which any American would not dare to stray – on the ground. They coveted all the living comforts of Florida, had their personal maids and never raised the matter officially when pieces of equipment, uniform and documents were missed in case it interfered with their easy-going way of making war. Vietnamese boys sold Coca Cola on the flightlines and in the briefing rooms as helicopter raids were being planned, took off and landed again. Each boy was a potential menace; he could not withhold information from the Vietcong, who were half a mile or less away, and he could not refuse to get them information. On the day that I arrived two Vietcong, dressed as women, had been caught on the base and nobody knew how long they had been there or how often they visited. And nobody connected the shocking lack of security that night when we dived into sandbagged trenches as the Vietcong neatly picked off the main power plant, left us in darkness and went away.

I spent several days and nights at Pleiku, only leaving it in the same way as I had arrived, by air. To the north lay the provincial capital of Kontum, surrounded by hills and Vietcong land, and the North Vietnamese were moving into the war; their 101st Regiment had been in action against outposts with mortars and was forming up a few miles to the north-west of Kontum, after crossing into South Vietnam over the Laotian border. I was flying with a US Army helicopter wing and there was seldom a dull moment. A new phase in the war for Vietnam had begun and it was never certain who any new strike was against—the Vietcong or regular North Vietnamese. We were usually operating in support of the South Vietnamese army and they were taking some shocking beatings; to leave them in isolated outposts, often with families and miles from any support except from the air, appeared to me to be inviting trouble; but as every reverse for the South Vietnamese was another excuse for America to send in more troops, perhaps their insistence that the outposts should remain manned could be understood.

Le Thanh was one such outpost. It lay on the plateau about twenty miles to the north of Pleiku and east of Kontum, and for two nights now it had been attacked by mortars, a sure sign that it was on the Vietcong list for destruction. Two convoys of South Vietnamese Rangers had tried to get through to Le Thanh, but had been ambushed; on both occasions we had got into the air fast – and the Coca Cola boys were there to wave us off – but the Vietcong has melted away from the scene by the time we arrived and all we found were the dead bodies of the Rangers. By the second day something much bigger was building up; around 500 Rangers were dropped into the area, and from eighteen miles or so from Le Thanh began an advance, preceding it with heavy mortar and shellfire. At last the Vietcong were located; they were fighting back, but from the air we could seldom find anything tangible to shoot at. That evening I left a supply helicopter to join the Rangers and their American advisers on the ground. If they had stuck to the road along which the slow advance went, I would have been adequately dressed, but as dusk came on the Rangers left the road for the night and set up positions in the fields and bushes on either side of it; it had rained heavily for the past week and I was to spend a most uncomfortable night, thinking of the equipment I could have bought in the Thieves Market to protect me against the mud and soggy wetness in which I found myself lying.

Until ten o'clock all was quiet; the Rangers' advance had got them within eight miles or so of Le Thanh and, it was confidently expected, we should be relieving the outpost some time the following day. Some were allowed to sleep whilst others stayed at their guns, peering into the blackness. A quiet night was hoped for, and then back onto the road before dawn. But it was not to be; the Vietcong, perhaps with the aid of the North Vietnamese, had planned it differently, and in seconds I was out of the truck where I had been sitting with an American sergeant when the first mortar crashed down a hundred and fifty yards away. In they came from both sides and ahead of us from the gentle hills which ran up from the road and its flanking flat country; from the rate of the mortaring it could have been a main force of Vietcong we were facing, but the rifles opened up from much closer.

There was bedlam at once as the Rangers replied with their

mortars and guns; at any moment we expected the Vietcong to be among us, but instead they kept their distance and for three hours the blind shooting went on from both sides. I did not move far; most of the time was spent with my head pretty well down and I remember thinking several times that this was a strange sort of battle. The Rangers were not going out into that eerie countryside and the Vietcong were making no moves to come in after us. Then, as suddenly as it had started, the firing stopped all around. Another three hours or so were spent with everyone on the alert, fingers on the triggers, but not another move came from the Vietcong. They had disappeared completely and soon after dawn we were to discover why; the attack on the Rangers had been a feint, a diversionary attack just to keep them pinned down and unable to advance farther. There were few casualties to be counted, but elsewhere the real killing had come. Whilst a minor force of Vietcong had kept us engaged, the main force had attacked the Le Thanh outpost. And it, too, had melted into the hills; there was not one guerilla to be seen at whom a gun could be pointed.

The first helicopter landing with supplies brought the news and I hopped aboard, to get back to Pleiku. In fifteen minutes, still mudcaked, I was away from there in another helicopter with the American colonel commanding the base; he did not have the full story of the attack on Le Thanh then, but it was not long before our worst fears were realized: we could see the smoking and smouldering outpost from the distance and there could be little left alive down there. There was nothing but rubble left when we got into the outpost and now more helicopters were lifting in troops to clear it. Bodies lay everywhere in their odd postures of death; some of the fiftytwo defenders had been caught in their beds when the first mortars dropped, signalling the attack, and their charred remains still lay among the twisted iron bedframes in the burned out huts. From its tall flagpost, the only thing still standing, the national emblem of yellow with red stripes hung in strips and tatters. Le Thanh was dead, never to live again, and swarms of flies were already taking over. Not one plane had been able to take off when the radio call had come for help the night before; the Vietcong had used the low clouds to their own advantage.

STORY UNUSED

That evening I was flying on a dusk patrol. I had wanted to land at Kontum, but the weather was closing in and I was told that I could be stranded in the city for days or weeks. High hills on three sides surrounded it and Kontum could look in only one direction – along the valley running northwest to the Laotian border, the Vietcong and the North Vietnamese troops who were now on the march in their thousands. Down below we could see the signs of new digging: small holes spaced well out in lines across the lush fields where once the peasants had worked the land. Deep underground, we knew, were the Vietcong tunnels and they were creeping ever closer to Kontum. Like Pleiku base, the town was one of the few white spots remaining on military maps covering the central and northern provinces of South Vietnam. All the rest was shaded red.

For me the weeks ahead meant pre-dawn risings and flights into one battle area after another. Le Thanh quickly faded into insignificance when I saw Dong Xoai, for there every woman and child perished with their husbands and fathers who manned the village headquarters. They were piled together at the bottom of gunpits and trenches where they had taken shelter when the first attack came. Their menfolk stood on their bodies fighting until they, too, died and lifeless Vietcong were mixed among them. It was possible, as I watched the bodies being lifted out, to piece together the horror of the few hours before; possible to decide who had survived the first attack and died in the second, knowing that their families had already gone before them. Seven hundred Vietcong dead were claimed in a government and American 'victory', but no more than 200 bodies were ever counted inside the headquarters and in the rubber plantations around. One hundred and eight government troops were admitted as killed and two Americans, but no mention was made of another 126 government troops who were missing. Over 300 women and children died, either from Vietcong bullets and mortars or from American bombs which came down in the final stages of the battle – but they were never counted, or spoken of officially. A relief battalion had been landed not long before I arrived by helicopter; it was wiped out, but never accounted for in the final claims. The Vietcong were still everywhere: it was one of their great and planned victories. We were pinned down for two hours half a mile from the headquarters before we could move in, and more helicopters fell from the sky around us. The following day, as a reprisal, the eight-engined B_{52}s made a 'saturation' bombing raid over miles of the area to which it was thought the Vietcong force had gone. I went into the area soon afterwards; not one Vietcong body was found, but the stench of dead animals, old peasants, women and more children hung upon the air.

What was this madness which was mounting in a thunderous crescendo? Giant bombers, smaller bombers, cannon-carrying helicopters and every 'conventional' weapon of war America could devise only made the Vietcong grow stronger. Defoliation – the disgraceful burning of the countryside and everything which was caught in it – nerve gas, flame throwers, the murders of civilians in any village where it was decided the Vietcong had been helped or hidden: they all went to strengthen the will to fight the new aggressor.

One day I was on a 'seek and destroy' mission with American marines from Da Nang, a village had been mortared before we went through it. Few had remained for our arrival. At the door of one damaged house stood a woman and beside her lay a dead dog; she picked it up and threw it at us and spat. An old woman ran screaming from another hut and fell into a hole in the ground in terror; an American sergeant shouted at her three times to come out and then threw in a hand grenade after her. 'Why did you kill her,' I asked afterwards and the sergeant replied, 'She was Vietcong.' But how did he know, I demanded, and the terrifying reply came, 'Hell, she would have come out when I told her if she hadn't been Vietcong.'

The smell of death was heavy on my nostrils when the cable came from London, suggesting that I take a rest from Vietnam and return to Singapore. I thought of June and my daughter Anna, safely at school in Switzerland. It had been so long since I had seen them. Was this possible now? Somehow the thought frightened me; they did not seem to be real people any more; they had become something vague, a dream. I was not real, nothing was real any more. Nothing could be.

But for a newspaper to pull its correspondent out of Vietnam at this crucial moment – I was still more than a little mystified as I boarded the plane. Later I heard from my foreign desk in London that the editor had recently been in Washington and had decided that, in future, reporting on the Vietnam war would come from our correspondent there.

Chapter 7

JUNGLE WAR

The other undeclared war, Sukarno's 'confrontation' against Malaysia, must not be forgotten. The troubled pot of the Far East was brewing dangerously and, although there was no direct connection between Indonesia and Vietnam, one situation had to be watched just as closely as the other. Sukarno's favourite expression 'Go to hell' had been applied to America. He had used Russia to re-equip his forces, and now, by the end of 1964, he was having a wonderful courtship with Peking. The large Chinese population of North Borneo had a section orientated towards its mother country and, after secret training in Indonesian Borneo, were stirring up the cauldron quite effectively. Prime Minister Tunku Abdul Rahman just threw up his hands in despair and called for United Nations help, to be slapped down smartly by the British, who certainly did not want that sort of interference. But the situation had to be faced; more troops, ships and planes were needed to stop the audacious Sukarno, and Britain had to find them. In went more Marines, paratroops, the Guards and a few more regiments, Hunter and Javelin jetfighters, Canberras and even a few V Bombers when Indonesian planes appeared over Singapore and Malaya. The navy got every available minesweeper out of mothballs at the Singapore base and the admiral lost his personal barge – now needed for something more serious.

Between my quick dashes to Vietnam I was flying over to North Borneo to join the Marines or the Gurkhas for a few days, or rushing into Malaya whenever Indonesian troops landed. First, and the reports were hard to believe when they came in, the Indonesians dropped by parachute and there was much scuffling around Malayan villages, jungles and rubber plantations before that lot were eliminated. There was no more fool-

STORY UNUSED

hardiness in that particular method of 'confronting' again, but somehow Indonesian boats were evading the naval night patrols and getting ashore in the mangrove swamps of western Malaya, crossing from Sumatra. The British navy was by no means asleep, however; their patrols did some good work and supplied some excellent despatches for me – as was noted by a World War II acquaintance, commander of the Far East air force and now Air Marshal Peter Whickham. He was mildly complaining that the army and the navy were getting all the publicity and asked if I could not arrange a little for my old service, the Royal Air Force. What we fixed between us caused a stir among the rest of the senior air force officers and brought near apoplexy to the public relations staff, all of whom had been by-passed and found themselves powerless to countermand the C-in-C's orders. I joined Twenty Squadron, whose pilots were longing to take a crack at those Indonesian invaders with their rocket-equipped jet Hunters.

I shed twenty years when I settled down in the crewroom at Tengah air base among the young pilots I was to fly with. The language and the talk had hardly changed in all those years since I had worn the same uniform, except that now, with jets replacing the Hurricanes and Spitfires I had known, it was, perforce, somewhat more technical. Of course, it was hardly to be expected that I would be offered my own single-seater Hunter; not only did I know that I would undoubtedly bend it, but Twenty Squadron had a twin-seater which was just as potent and Flight Lieutenant Dick Smith gave me a meticulous cockpit briefing. I had never used a pressure suit – automatically inflated from the legs upwards to keep blood circulating in the head when the force of gravity tried to drain it and effect a well remembered blackout – and I was given one and briefed on that, too. Helmet and headphones, parachute straps and the rest of my equipment, they were all checked, some left in the cockpit and we were ready to go; we discussed tactics for when a call might come and I found that I was talking as much as these youngsters so many years my junior. There was so much I was remembering; it was only the speed and not so much the tactics which had changed since 1945, and the squadron pilots, without realizing it, were accepting me as one of them. But the call did not come that day, nor for another three, as we waited at readiness, and if more Indonesians had landed they had not been spotted. On Christmas evening the telephone rang as June and I were leaving the house for a dinner party: Squadron Leader Max Bacon, co of Twenty Squadron, was on the line and he was speaking in the code we had prearranged – 'Happy Christmas,' said Max. 'Do you have time to join us for a drink tomorrow – usual drinks time, around six?'

Six o'clock did not mean the following evening. Max did not have to explain, but the call caused me to spend one of the most abstemious Christmas nights I could remember. By six o'clock in the morning I was at the flightline, flying suit on, maps in my pocket and trooping into the briefing room with four others. There was Max, for the last minute briefing, and he was to lead the flight of four: Dick Smith, with whom I was flying, Flight Lieutenant 'Black' Ferguson, who got his name from the most persistent stubble which made him shave three times a day, and Flying Officer Tony Harper. During the night a force of Indonesians had got ashore in Johore on the Malayan mainland, troops could not get near them in the dense and swampy jungle and, for the first time, the Hunters had been ordered to winkle them out.

With the seven and a half hours time difference, the last hour of Christmas Day was fading in London as we nosed the Hunters on to the rainswept Tengah runway. Dawn was just up and the 'party' was on. We streaked into the sky, formated and made for the target, leaving the sleepy island of Singapore below and behind us. A strange sort of Christmas; but then, it was no festive season for the Indonesians we were after. They were Moslems.

We pinpointed the area, less than two miles long and a mile wide, where the Indonesians were known to be. The briefing had been precise and we each had a quarter of it on which to concentrate. Down we went in line astern for a dummy run and then climbed to 3,000 feet again. Max was first in and he dipped his Hunter almost vertical as he went into the dive. Two or three seconds later Dick Smith swung our plane into a vicious turn and I could feel the G-suit working, stabbing at my legs; then down we went, aiming the nose at our small piece of jungle at over 450 m.p.h. At 800 feet the first two rockets shot out ahead of us and we were still going down; Dick pulled back on the stick and suddenly I realized what the G-suit was all about. With only a few hundred feet to spare we were coming out of the dive and into a climb at force six gravity. The pressure suit inflated with a jerk, holding my legs, my stomach and then my chest in a vice-like grip, forcing the blood back into my head as my mouth, my cheeks and my eyelids were torn downwards and the veins in my eyes became red hot needles as they were all but drained – but only to a state of greyness. On, off, then on again; the pressure suit compensated for every sharp manoeuvre of the Hunter. If only we had had them twenty-five years earlier.

Now we were back at 3,000 feet. 'Black' and Tony were coming out of their dives, Max was going in again and our nose was down for the second time. Away went two more rockets; we were tearing into another climb and this time the jungle was no more than a hundred feet away. But the G-suit was in control, the grey-out was less, I was getting used to it.

Four more times we went in until all forty-eight rockets from the Hunters had done their job. The gap of twenty years had completely closed; I was the scientific killer once again, and strangely, I was enjoying it. At a hundred feet we raked the ground with thirty millimetre cannon fire until every round had gone, what havoc we wrought beneath those thick trees we did not know, but at least we were trying to kill men who would themselves have killed – if they escaped; no innocent women and children were down there. Was it this subconscious thought which gave me no compunction when I pressed the firing trigger as I had pressed them so many times before? Killing to prevent killing – war, but between fighting men alone? I do not remember dissecting what innermost thoughts there may have been in the early hours of that Boxing Day morning; within forty-five minutes of take-off we were landing back at Tengah, the job done, being debriefed. And the next thoughts in our minds were of the mess, bacon and eggs and hot strong coffee.

It was a merry lunch-time, half the Twenty Squadron pilots brought their wives to the house for one of those air force parties which only air force pilots can understand, and which their chosen women witness a thousand times without appearing to be thoroughly bored. The talk was of planes, naturally, fighter tactics, dive bombing, technicalities and performances; and when the news came that only thirteen Indonesians out of a possible force of a hundred well-armed men had survived our attack to give themselves up, champagne glasses were raised to wish them a Happy Christmas. But it was a Singapore Christmas, hot as it was always hot, and the sun blazed down between the monsoon downpours. The only snow around was artificial.

By now we had found a permanent home, a vast colonial mansion with its tall palms and taller, spindly betel nut trees closing us into a private compound; twenty or more species of orchids I had carefully planted, while bougainvillaea, morning glory and a host of other exotic blooms covered the house and lined the lawns to remind us that there was still so much beauty left in the world. And short, dumpy Ah Keow, the housekeeper, stood smiling on one of the terraces, with her Chinese family which now, and devotedly, belonged to us – enjoying every moment of a celebration, the reason for which she would never know.

Our little victory by no means stopped Sukarno's plans, but with others like it, it did temporarily slant his approach to confrontation in the hope that Malaysia could somehow be turned against the British. 'I'm for a peaceful solution of the issue,' said Sukarno. 'We love the Malaysian people. We are not against Malaysia itself – only against the British imperialists.' At the same time he infiltrated the large and fanatical Pan Malay Islamic Society in Malaya, which declared it would not fight against Indonesian Moslem brothers. By some means Sukarno got ultra left-wing Malayan politicians into his clandestine payroll, and added to this there was the danger of the untrustworthy Chinese, in Singapore and Malaya, as well as in Borneo. Tunku Abdul Rahman was forced to drop his pretence that Britain's part in Malaysia's defence was 'negligible.' and that only the United Nations could control the gathering conflagration.

The Tunku was glad for a while to sit back and watch as British army forces built up to well over 50,000 men. The air force increased its strength once more and the navy had seventy ships in the area including guided missile destroyers, the commando ship *Bulwark* and two aircraft carriers – *Victorious* and *Eagle* – always on station. But Sukarno was building up too, especially with his guerilla raids in North Borneo and across the Sarawak borders. British and Gurkha casualties mounted. For some time I had wanted to get into those Sarawak jungles, to live and patrol with the troops, but never had I been able to find enough time. Things were moving too fast and, like the proverbial fly, I was buzzing from one place to another, keeping up with them.

Then, in January 1965, the opportunity came, but tragically. Winston Churchill died, and for at least a week and until after his funeral there would be practically no space in British newspapers for Vietnam, Borneo or anything else, apart from the last honours to that great man. I flew to Kuching and, by helicopter, on to join a platoon of Irish Guards attached to a battalion of Scots Guards – Micks among the Jocks, and right on the Sarawak border with Sukarno's Indonesia.

'This is the border and all the best of British luck,' said the voice over the helicopter intercom and we plonked onto a fifteen yard square of hillcrest. With my kit I was clear in ten seconds and in another five or so the helicopter was rising above me, churning up the stones, the earth, and sending bits of foliage flying in all direction as though I were in a hurricane. But where was I? I had no idea until ten pieces of thick jungle nearby came to life in the shape of Irish Guardsmen with guns a-bristling; there was no mistaking the fact that I was among friends.

Who could mistake the Killarney voice which was calling, 'Don't stand there, sir, unless you want to get your f— head blown off.' It was an extended four-letter word to which I was to become accustomed, it was included once in every three other spoken words and fifty times in a two-minute conversation: as much a part of the army as a pair of boots, and just as well worn. During the next week I often wondered if anything I said was understood in the slightest. I did not appear to be putting the same accent on every verb and noun. But what grand and dedicated soldiers, even as I heard the same same phrase over and over again – 'when I f— get out of this f— army!' – a finer bunch of youngsters I could hardly wish to be among.

It had been raining, as it can rain only in Borneo – all-soaking blankets of pounding water for weeks. Through the jungle path I slid and slithered until, thankfully, we came to bits of bamboo stuck across the trail to form rough steps through the slimy, ankle-deep mud, up among forty yards of tangled, barbed wire defences. I followed up some more professionally made steps and along a bamboo catwalk to the 'office' of twenty-one year old platoon commander, Lieutenant Tim Eugster. The tall blond boy rose to greet me and it was then that I noticed the roughly painted sign which hung on the wall beneath the palm leaves – 'The Pentagon'. I was in time for a rationed can of beer and then tiffin – an iron hard lamb chop, a wad of mashed potato, tinned fruit and a messtin full of steaming, sweet tea. Tim's language was pure and devoid of the usual epithet, but there was little room for passengers here – better get myself sorted out and decide which bunker I was to sleep in. There were seven of them, sandbagged and pointing in all directions. It looked like a 1914 war position, with mud-filled trenches communicating one to the other. But I discovered this position had not been built for Tommies when I cracked my head the moment I tried to get into my newly appointed home. 'The Pentagon' had been built by Gurkhas and had been taken over from them. And Gurkhas are very tiny people.

A twenty-year lack of shooting practice was going to need some attention so, in the late afternoon, I tried my hand with an automatic rifle, a stengun and a pistol. Not at all bad! I rather suprised myself. Those days at the Royal Air Force college at Cranwell, when I could rely on friendly competitions on the range to augment my meagre pittance, had not been completely forgotten. The guards showed me how to set landmines and explode them electrically from the gunpit; if the Indonesians chose to get near us in darkness – and our rattling tin cans told us they were there – we could turn night into day a hundred yards away among the spiked defences. But, just to make it a little hot for them, I spent an interesting half hour with a corporal, lobbing mortars onto the six or seven jungle path approaches we knew of.

We could see no farther than five yards – just the weather for an attack, but not until just before dusk. That is when the

Indonesians preferred it. The high spot of the day: rum ration and two cans of beer all round and then the sergeant shouting, 'Stand to.' Into the bunkers and cracking my head on the beams, every man to a gun and peering through the narrow slit as the monsoon-soaked greyness faded into black.

Corporal Michael O'Donaghue ordered stand down and told three of us to get some sleep. Groping around for the camp bed and bashing my head for the umpteenth time. Boots on – everything on – for nobody ever undressed here. Gun beside me and feeling the hard but welcome pillow. The place was alive with rats – one of them was running across my chest. That four letter word was being used with a vengeance until the hissing came from one of the guns: 'Quiet, d'you expect me to f— hear anything outside when you f— lot make all this f— noise?'

He considered himself an old man at twenty-eight and, beside the rest of the youngsters manning the Pentagon, I suppose he was. Nine years in the Irish Guards and only another eleven months to go. Mike O'Donaghue told me softly as we stood together on the guns between the hours of four o'clock and dawn. 'Beginning to count the days,' said Mike, 'and this time I mean it. Lost my girl friend last time I signed on again. Time I settled down, back in Tipperary.'

A strange situation in which to strike up a friendship, but some sort of bond formed between us, and if I met Mike again it would have to be as a brother. There was something different in the way he thought and the way he spoke; something deep, honest and sincere, which emanates from few, as we talked among a mad cacophony of screeching owls, madly screaming monkeys and the high-pitched buzz of a million cicadas.

Eerie shapes appeared in the early morning mist and Mike saw that my finger was tightening on the trigger, calmly he said, 'Take it easy – everything moves if you look at it long enough.' The quiet voices at the other guns were now becoming faces and I found myself comparing them for age with Mike's – Frank Harris, a fresh-faced kid from Liverpool and eighteen, as I found later, Jimmy Lightbody, no older and 7,000 miles from his home in Bangor, County Down. Bill Donley, and his voice unmistakably linked with Belfast; but Bill was slightly superior – he was 'nearly nineteen', he insisted.

Now it was time for breakfast; fried eggs done to a dozen turns by the 'cook', who had never touched a frying pan until he arrived at The Pentagon, sausages and tea. The brogues were rich and to the point as each man gave his verdict on the meal; the chaffing never stopped during the whole week I was among them – but never once was it in anger.

From intelligence reports it was estimated that around 2,000 Indonesians were massing about five miles to our north-west and another 8,000 to 9,000 were building up to the east, now that the rains were easing off. They were busy days, with patrols going off and patrols returning, with special steaks awaiting those coming in with reports of ambushes, jungle fights or just 'nothing seen'. I wanted to get on to one of those patrols, but Tim Eugster was reticent in putting my name down for a detail; he was most apologetic about it, and about my age, but pointed out that no personnel over thirty were allowed on patrols except those with special medical clearance. However, when Tim's commanding officer, Major John Morrogh-Bernard, flew in to discuss new tactics and brought a Pakistani barber to smarten up his bunch of guardsmen, the issue was settled. There were no orders against me going on patrol, the major agreed, so therefore the decision was mine; he warned me not to expect a picnic and, looking back, I might have saved a lot of trouble if I had heeded Tim's words.

There was plenty happening around The Pentagon for the next three days to satisfy most correspondents. Constant alerts and a couple of half-hearted Indonesian attacks, the big guns firing over us from behind and the Hunters diving in with their rockets to break up an assault before it could get under way. When one flight had finished its work the leader came on the radio to The Pentagon and, having recognized the markings on the Hunters, I took over the conversation. It made the day for the guardsmen when an amazed voice came back from the leading Hunter, 'Hey, this is "Black" Ferguson – what the bloody hell are you doing down there?' A detachment from Twenty Squadron was operating from Kuching and 'Black' and his friends gave The Pentagon the best low level display of flying it had ever seen as a greeting.

Stand to, stand down, dry and clean clothes, now that the

sun was occasionally shining. Repairing the outer defences, letter writing and the long talks as we sat on the bunker sandbags. I had become one of them and my accent had been accepted. They were my close friends and I was theirs. Mike O'Donaghue told me of his plans for 'civvy street', of his family and his beloved Tipperary. We were our own tiny world and sharing it together – so much that, one afternoon as I stood naked under a punctured beer-can shower on a raised bamboo platform, Bill Donley shouted up to me: 'Don't be too long with your f— pants off, those f— so and sos can see you and you'll look f— funny if they attack now.' Bill was not joking; he meant every word, including those which were superfluous. He was giving me some very sound advice.

An Iban, one of the head-hunting tribe which had dealt with a few Indonesian guerillas in their own particular way, took the lead as we filed out of The Pentagon at eight o'clock on what was to be my last day with the Guards. The sun was shining and the weather was promised fine as the heat – already around ninety – drew the dampness out of the ground in gently rising clouds of steam. Lieutenant Tim Eugster went next, a trooper with a weighty radio set strapped to his back was number three, I was fourth and behind me was Mike O'Donaghue and five others – ten of us altogether and spaced out at six to seven yard intervals. For the first half-hour any climbing we did was gentle, but by the end of it sweat had soaked my jungle kit and a towel wound around my neck was catching more as it ran in rivulets down my face. Despite the greasy pole act, I successfully negotiated bridge after bridge as we came across them – two lengths of bamboo, each five to six inches wide and thrown across streams or gullies – and I was considering myself an expert. I was breathing rather heavily – something I would overcome, I thought, as I got more accustomed to the pace. Was it the twentieth or twenty-fifth 'bridge', we had crossed so many on this winding and rough trail where all sense of direction had long disappeared? The Iban, small and thin, was across it, hardly noticing that it was there and Tim Eugster, tall but slim, had reached the other side as I eased myself on to the bamboos. Mudcaked boots on wet and slimy poles which gently bounced up and down with every step – that was presenting no difficulty for me now and I criss-crossed my feet as I went. Half-way across the bridge I glanced down, but even as I spotted the rottenness of the bamboo on the right and before my subconscious thought warned me of the danger, it collapsed on me and I was crashing down the rocks ten to twelve feet below and sinking, up to my waist, in oozy and foul-smelling, slimy mud. I felt no pain then; perhaps because all my limbs had begun to ache, and Mike O'Donaghue was climbing down over the slippery rocks to get me. I grasped one of his hands and his lion strength drew me up from the mud and steadied me as we climbed back onto the trail. Stupid thing to happen but not due to my inexperience, as all agreed. Tim was worried that we should go on, but I assured him I was not hurt. We were only one hour out on a scheduled eight-hour patrol and I was determined that it would not be cancelled through any fault of mine. The 'bridge' was repaired with another bamboo and we went on to the next stream, into which I waded to get rid of the mud.

Again I was to realize that I should have taken Tim's advice; if the trail so far had been rough, it resembled a country walk compared with what was to come. Ahead was the mountain, three thousand feet high, and our patrol was to take us over the summit. If I had known it was there, surely I would have realized that age and lack of training, plus a knee which was now stabbing every step with pain, were not on my side. Up we went, grabbing at any foothold and grabbing at ferns, bamboos and thorn-spiked branches, anything to stop the slip back which could have sent another six men crashing below. On and on for another hour or so and my heart was thumping as the soft bird whistle came from Mike O'Donaghue which stopped the patrol; I sank beside the path as the troopers stood listening and at the ready, and Mike beckoned to Corporal Archie Byrne, the medical orderly. This was the second time I had held up the patrol; for ten minutes I had to rest as pep pills and a dozen salt tablets were forced into me. Then it was on and up, forever up and stumbling and sliding – no battle school could ever have devised training for this, and the guardsmen never appeared to tire. At last the ground flattened and we were on top of the mountain; the going would have been easy, but for the pumping heart and the knee which I now knew was badly injured. It was one o'clock and now we were behind schedule by nearly two hours. I lay beside a hut for fully another as tiffin of biscuits, tinned meat, jam, chocolate and water was passed around and Archie Byrne went off to do what he could for a pregnant Dayak woman who was crying out in pain nearby.

Sure, I was ready to go when Tim Eugster called the patrol to its feet. My heart was back to normal and, apart from the knee which I could feel was swelling ominously, most of my other aches had gone. Into file we got and made across the ridge looking down into Indonesian Borneo on our left and across the mountain range which hid the massing enemy. Gently the descent began, but quickly became steeper; within half an hour I was sliding again, but this time forward, crashing into huge and gnarled tree roots to stop the fall to certain death a thousand or more feet beneath. Mike was close behind me now and slithering down to keep up with my crazy and headlong plunging. Then I was out of control and nothing could stop me going over the edge this time. Mike was shouting, 'Hold this,' and from three yards behind snaked down the line with a wooden toggle at this end; the line was attached to Mike and his amazing strength stopped me at the brink. On and down, my right leg now almost useless, and but for the lifeline to Mike I would not have survived a hundred perils against which I had not been trained.

Again I was completely out of control and pulling Mike faster and faster. Why should I take him with me? My wretchedly tortured mind was asking. So I let go of the toggle – again to be saved by Mike O'Donaghue who threw himself down this near vertical trail and on top of me to stop me once again and no more than two yards from a fall into oblivion. What could I say. Words would not come, but Mike was forcing the toggle back into my hand. Twenty times or more his voice came from behind when he was sure I was about to give up: 'Hold it, hold it,' and the command was a military one. I thanked God that once I had been drilled into accepting orders and remembered.

The ground was flattening again and on either side of us rose the tall bamboo when the next bird whistle came; the Iban guide had stopped dead on the trail and looked around with his hands raised as the whole patrol stood crouched, fingers on triggers and straining for any telltale noise which spelt danger. For ten minutes we stood like statues. A twig cracked somewhere in that dense bamboo and a monkey screeched as we heard it rushing away with a noise which sounded like thunder in this deadly silence. The Iban was pointing and I saw the nods come from Tim, Mike and the troopers stretched along the trail behind. Now it was certain; it was attack or be ambushed, and at the wave from Tim they went into the bamboo, guns blazing.

I might have gone too, but now I was little use to anybody. I stood on the trail in the unbearable heat; a huge and black cobra slid in panic from the bamboo and passed my feet, three feet away, it disappeared again on the other side as the firing moved farther from the trail. Then Mike was back beside me, his sweat-soaked face breaking into a grin. 'They're not stopping to fight,' he said. 'Running like hell, but I'd better cover things here.' The 'things' were me, I knew, but there was nothing in Mike's look to suggest that I was a bloody nuisance. His grin was pointing in all directions for the next three minutes until the guards were back on the trail and we continued in silence, a silence stark with tension and every nerve working overtime against the next possible attack.

We reached a small clearing, well away from where the guerillas had been, and I was confident that they could not have followed these magnificent jungle fighters when Mike's bird whistle brought us to a halt. He had watched me, every step, and now I almost fell to the ground. Corporal Byrne was ready with more pep pills, salt and a shot of something to ease the pain as the rest stood to alert, sometimes asking me with upturned thumbs and smiles if I was fit enough to carry on. That is how we continued for several more hours, walking a mile and resting, then half a mile before I had to stop and finally a halt every two hundred yards or so – all for me. Once I felt I could go no farther and told them to go on without me, and it was Mike's voice which spoke first in a reply so definite that I found a renewed energy to drag myself along. 'If you stay, we all stay,' said Mike, 'even if we're out here all night and carry you in tomorrow.'

The last two or three miles were almost like that, first one and then another guardsman would prop me up, one of my arms around his shoulder. Somehow they got me across all the bamboo bridges and I felt like crying when The Pentagon finally came into view. We had been out for thirteen hours and the steaks awaiting the returning patrol were five hours overdue. I had not heard one mention of them, not one grouse against a damn fool correspondent who had kept them hungry. We reached the bamboo steps up to the catwalk, but that was as far as my legs would get me for another half hour; Mike brought me down some food, a stiff rum and a can of beer and ate his meal sitting there beside me.

The camp bed was heaven that night. I did not notice the rats; but for me it was evacuation early next morning and all the inhabitants of The Pentagon were shaved and looking spruce to give me a cheerful send off to the helicopter. They helped me to the pad and carried my kit. Corporal Mike O'Donaghue was the last one to grip my hand as I climbed aboard. It was difficult to say all I wanted to say to such a man and I confined it to the one word 'thanks'. Mike grinned. 'Sorry you're leaving us,' he said. To which I replied, 'We'll meet again.'

June was at the airport in Singapore to meet me that afternoon. The knee was in pretty bad shape: this torn and that torn. There was no sense in operating on it, but it was going to take a long time to mend. 'Two to three months,' was the doctor's verdict, 'and you must rest it all the time'. What a dismal prospect. Enforced inactivity and so much going on in my parish. I agreed that I must rest for the moment, but for just how long I would have to decide later.

There was plenty to do, of course: mail which had piled up could now be answered, especially a letter from London, complaining that, for such a small island like Singapore, I was spending too much on taxis. I offered to send a map, pointing out that it was not usual to walk miles in temperatures that were always in the nineties, or through the monsoon rains. I also had to suggest that I might be needing quite a few more taxis, now that I could hardly walk at all. I have no idea what was thought of my suggestions; no reply ever came, so I presume attention now turned to some little home reporter who could not produce a bill for the beer he bought an informant who had produced a front page scoop.

It was a busy time, no doubt about that; my office was in one wing of the house, the telephone hardly stopped ringing and the visitors came and went in a constant stream, particularly when my article appeared in London. I had caused an international incident; at least that is how the Foreign Office in London regarded it and how a hot and puffing member of the C-in-C's diplomatic staff put it to me. I had written that for eighteen months Sukarno had refused me a visa into Indonesia, but there I was, sliding down Sukarno's side of a mountain. I had suggested that British troops violated Sukarno's territory by crossing his borders; I had played into Sukarno's hands and the whole world would now look on Britain as the aggressor. The furore raged for several days, between the diplomats in Whitehall and their opposite numbers in Singapore; oddly, Sukarno did not appear in the uproar. Nothing was heard from him. I can imagine the answer Whitehall would have got from the boys at The Pentagon: 'Don't be f— idiots, it's the only f— way down that f— mountain.'

Two weeks were enough. With my knee tightly bandaged, I could get around after a fashion and the cables were coming from London office suggesting I had had long enough 'holiday' and things were looking black in Saigon. The Buddhists were making it known that they did not agree with the way things were going and they were having their turn at rioting in the streets. I hopped on a plane and hopped around Saigon for a while till things quietened down. Much to my annoyance, and to a few stern words from the doctor, I was hopping even worse when I got back to Singapore. That damned knee was to cause me trouble for the next two years and it never did get back to normal. For a long time it interfered with my water ski-ing, in the early morning when I was in Singapore and the lights were going out back in London. An hour on skis normally pepped me up for the day ahead, but now my boat was out of the water and on the racks, and it was to stay there for a long time.

Five weeks after shaking his hand at The Pentagon I was to see Mike O'Donaghue again. I had predicted it, but what a tragedy that the meeting had to come like this. Mike was unconcious when I first visited him at the British Military Hospital in Singapore; he had been in the operating theatre and the doctors told me that his condition was 'serious, very serious'. A high wire cage protected his legs, from which the flesh had been burned away up to his thighs, and in a smaller cradle lay his right hand, swathed in the dressings and bandages which hid the fingers, raw to the bone. During an attack on The Pentagon, three grenades which had been fired at the Indonesians had failed to explode and Mike had volunteered to be lifted into the area by helicopter to render them harmless. The first two he had dealt with, but the third, a phosphorous grenade, had exploded in Mike's hand and before he could hurl it away. For nearly twenty-four hours he had been in the agony which nearly killed him, as they got him out of the jungle to Singapore; and now he faced months of skin grafting if he survived the terrible burns. For a long time after he came round from the anaesthetic, Mike lay there but there was no sign of recognition. For several days more, when I went into the ward, it was the same until one evening I was met by the smiling nursing sister who told me, 'He's recovering, today he has been talking.' I crept into the ward and stood there for a full two minutes before Mike's eyes cleared; the pain seemed to drain from his face and he smiled faintly: 'Hello, sir,' he said, but that was all he could manage. It was two nights later when he could talk coherently and then the first thing he asked me was, 'How is your leg?'

Soon it was Vietnam again for me and it was several months before I saw Mike again; he was due to convalesce in the hills of Malaya but, the sister told me, he had no clothes apart from army kit which could be supplied. It was so little that I could do in return, but I am glad I was back in time to leave a small case filled with all that Mike would need. We shook hands again as he left the hospital and I saw him for the last time. 'Still thinking about that demob, Mike?' I asked. Mike did not answer for a moment and then the reply came: 'I don't know sir,' he said: 'I've had plenty of time to think over the past few months. I want to get back to the boys in Borneo, if they'll have me.'

11. *Top:* A long line of U.S. helicopters setting out on a large search and destroy mission. *Bottom:* A U.S. supply helicopter unloading ammunition in the jungle north of Saigon (Photos: Assoc. Press)

12. Mrs. Sirimavo Bandaranaika, Prime Minister of Ceylon (Photo: U.P.I.)

Chapter 8

MEETINGS IN CEYLON

Each place one visits in the world leaves certain and indelible marks on one's mind and, whether they be of people, events, scenes or particular objects, they come to the fore as the memory is stirred by the mere mention of its name. Momentous, at times, were the happenings which sent me there on the first available plane, but now, as I think of Ceylon, and ludicrously perhaps, I remember two things above all else – miniskirts and that most delightful of all tropical fruits, the papaya.

Miniskirts in Ceylon! – unbelievable, and in the country once known as the Paradise Isle where, for centuries, custom and religion have dictated that a women's legs shall be covered down to the ankle, with that most attractive garment, the sari. But that is where I first saw the miniskirt, not one but a couple of dozen, and all at the same time – and, I must admit, I was shocked. Of course, I had read about them and seen the photographs in western newspapers and magazines, but to come face to face for the first time with the real thing, I suppose, was bound to bring forth some sort of violent reaction, and mine was of horror. I wanted to flee, to banish the first glimpses of this new 'culture' forever, but there was no way out. I was surrounded by them at the tiny shack which served as the country's air terminal, twenty miles or so from Colombo, and the customs and immigration officials were not assisting me with their long drawn-out formalities.

Maybe I had been away from 'civilization' for too long, had grown too accustomed to my eastern surroundings; but no one can deny the attractiveness of the colourful *sarong kebaya* which the women of all Malay races drew around themselves, knotted at the waist, the high-necked *cheong sam* which hugged the slim figures of the Chinese down to the slitted and calf-length skirt,

STORY UNUSED

the *ao dai* of the Vietnamese or the *kimono* of Japan. Nor the grace of the silk and patterned saris, among which these miniskirts were now, deliberately and devoid of all inhibition, mixing to create, with all their garishness, the never-to-be forgotten scene. I am not easily embarrassed, but the miniskirts had just landed from a British plane; daughters were *en route* for Singapore, Kuala Lumpur or Hong Kong to join their British parents for holidays, and the British girls were out to show the world the new and sophisticated trends of fashion.

Miniskirts soon became a familiar sight, adorning the figures of British visitors, and more than once they were banned from places where they were worn with such complete blatancy that they caused unwelcome troubles among less sophisticated males, who never before had been able to gaze on a woman's limbs until married.

The papaya – or paw-paw as it became known to the British Raj in India and Ceylon – is part melon, part pumpkin, but really nothing of either; its delicate flavour, enhanced by a sprinking of fresh lime juice, becomes an acquired taste. I consider myself something of a connoisseur when it comes to papaya, and there was just that particular hint of something, a mixture of sweetness and a tang which was to be found in the Ceylon papaya exclusively; a something I could distinguish the first time I ate one and a distinction among all my papaya-eating in a score or so of tropical countries. Breakfast, to me, was never complete without a slice or a half of a papaya, according to its size. They grew in my garden in Singapore, but these papaya of Ceylon were shorter and rounder, and the trees had the intriguing habit of growing to the height of a few feet and from there branching into two separate trunks, each forming its own tree and bearing twice the normal amount of fruit.

Papaya trees grew in great profusion for almost the whole length of the airport road into Colombo; narrow and winding, it had thick walls of tropical greenery and flowers on either side and passed through ten or more villages before reaching the city outskirts – and it acted as a barometer. For me, that is, for local change is seldom noticed by locals themselves when it approaches and devours them gradually. Over five years Ceylon had seen changes which had reduced it to complete economic collapse. It was in the grip of sinister people and the road showed it all.

On my first visits the road had been a happy one; the small houses were well painted, trucks piled with local produce caused traffic blocks, but nobody appeared to mind and there were smiling faces; gay advertisement posters showed a certain amount of prosperity, and the international oil companies vied with each other in the service, slickness and smartness of their roadside filling stations. Those were but a few of the signs to gauge the changes, and for the worse, through which Ceylon was passing. Once, and when I had not been to Ceylon for many months, I saw the results of oil company nationalization. Every petrol station on the road had its former name crudely painted out; some were open and some were not; stocks of accessories were non-existent; service was bad and the places, mostly, were filthy. Advertisement posters were not renewed and many hung in tatters; the firms which imported or manufactured the goods advertised were no longer in business; trucks and cars were dumped and propped up on stones for want of spares, houses were looking dowdy from lack of paint and people with smiles on their faces were scarce. New signs, scrawled in whitewash, covered the walls of previously well-kept buildings, and nine out of ten of them were communist slogans.

But all this took time; nothing as dramatic as the tragedy which had overtaken Ceylon happens overnight. Three-quarters of a million workers do not lose their jobs in the same week, and the country which had been the favourite call for the cruise ships plying the eastern routes does not suddenly find that no more than one ship a month is using its huge harbour at Colombo – and that one unloading second and third rate rice from communist China or taking the palm oil in return for the rice, to sell it elsewhere at a profit.

The female of the species is more deadly than the male, and nowhere for many years had that oft-repeated saying proved more true than in Ceylon. Madame Nhu of Vietnam might have qualified, had not her brother and husband restricted the deadly power she wanted; but here, in the shape of Mrs Sirimavo Bandaranaike, had arisen a potential female

STORY UNUSED

Castro, a female tyrant – Ceylon's own Bloody Mary. No one in the world would have predicted it in 1960, when she had been elected a Premier on the tears being shed for her late husband, the assassinated Prime Minister. Great numbers of Ceylon's people poured out their sympathy and love to her, a sedate and seemingly gentle woman, a mother of two young children.

She changed; she dreamed of being a dictator and, as her parliamentary colleagues deserted Mrs Bandaranaike in her bid for total power, she had remained in office by drawing opposition and left-wingers into a coalition until in March 1965 her only political bedfellows were communists and Ceylon's sole economic and trade connections were with Peking. The country was facing an election, Mrs Bandaranaike was fuming and threatening to deal out retribution to the parliamentary Speaker who had dared to defy her on a point of procedure and had forced the downfall of her coalition. But the Speaker was but one on the list: police chiefs and high army officers were already in jail, many were those who faced the next few hours in fear. The only people still defying her were the press men.

Shelton Fernando, my stringer for a long time in Ceylon and an astute and fearless political journalist, had never before failed to meet me at the airport, but this day, despite the cable I had sent him, I drove into Colombo alone. Hours of telephoning did not locate him and in most places I contacted, including his newspaper office, frightened and evasive voices either disclaimed all knowledge of Shelton or said that they had no idea of his whereabouts. But a forceful anti-Bandaranaike article under his name had appeared only that day. The two newspaper groups which had previously been in opposition were still publishing with small four-page newspapers when they could; they had pooled their diminished stocks of newsprint, which Mrs Bandaranaike had denied them for weeks, and were continuing their fight for constitutional freedom to the last, whatever the consequences. The weaker members of the profession had forsaken them for 'safe' jobs with a new communist newspaper. Shelton and many others had not; they were being hunted and hounded by Mrs Bandaranaike's strong-arm thugs, as I was to realize at ten o'clock that night when Shelton's voice came on the telephone for a few moments to fix a rendezvous – two miles from the hotel and in a Tamil cafe I knew from a year or so before. We ate the hot and spiced food together as we had done on the previous occasion but no longer was I with the smiling and witty Shelton Fernando I had known. There was much to talk about but now the Tamil café owner had locked his doors. Shelton's once neat and well-pressed suit was now crumpled, his shirt was dirty and his beard showed days of growth. His wife and child had been hidden with relatives miles away in Kandy for three months and Shelton had not dared to go near his own home for a week.

There was one day of electioneering left before the fate of Shelton and many others would be decided and, early next morning, I took the road out of Colombo towards the huge oil-palm estate, twenty-five miles to the north, where Mrs Bandaranaike had her family mansion. Several times I had met her, in the days when she had been a quiet and grief-stricken wife, and later, as she gradually took the political reins. But what had caused the complete transformation into the megalomaniacal figure which the last few months or year had seen, what mystic power had she acquired with which, apparently and purposefully, she could reduce a rich and hitherto, happy country into one of ruin, with police and thugs acting to her command and striking fear into the hearts of everyone whenever and wherever they appeared. Mrs Bandaranaike was a great believer in astrology, that I knew, and Shelton had recently told me that her astrologers seldom left her side. Was this ogress really under the impression that the heavens were guiding her? I was more interested in who those astrologers were – and who was paying them. I had many questions for Mrs Bandaranaike, if she would answer them.

All tropical countries are startling in their greenness, but there has always been a certain touch of emerald which makes Ceylon just that slight shade more enchanting, and I noticed these again as I drove through the gently rolling countryside that morning. Beautiful, yes, it was still beautiful, but a practised eye could have seen the neglect in even greater abundance than was obvious to me; nowhere did I see workers in the fields, bushes were overhung and the bamboo grew out of control; the broad-bladed grass was long and wild, untended like the rest.

Few cars were on the roads; there was a shortage of petrol and it was expensive. But as I drove nearer to the Bandaranaike country the blue and nationalized buses were appearing from all directions and heading north onto the main road; they were packed with people and adorned with posters, which that day were undoubtedly political. It was at a filling station that I learned the destination of all the buses, they had been commandeered by Mrs Bandaranaike to take 'supporters' to her election-eve meetings in her constituency. If anyone for miles around wanted a free ride the buses would take him; but if he preferred to hear the speeches of the opposition United National Party candidates, he walked, for every bus that day in southern Ceylon was taken off its normal routes and was working for the communists. It was just a matter of following any bus in the area in which I was and it would take me to the Prime Minister.

At the first meeting I visited I saw from the back of the crowd that she had her sixteen-year-old son with her on the platform – and she was introducing him as Ceylon's leader of the future – 'When, one day, I am too old to lead my people in their glorious march forward.'

I trailed around another five meeting but did not see much enthusiasm from the crowds; there was precious little else they got free from the government except the bus ride and they were taking advantage of it. What they might vote was impossible to judge and police were out in force with guns and clubs to see that every meeting was orderly. Mrs Bandaranaike did not appear to worry whether she was cheered or not as she confidently rambled on from one gaudily adorned platform to the next, and it was late evening when her heavily escorted car turned for home, with me taking up the rear.

There was much studying of my credentials before I was shown into the large and expensively furnished drawing room, but although the chairs were deep and comfortable I was not invited to sit and there was no handshake. She stood on the white Indian carpet, more plump than I remembered her in the years before, but still a fine-looking woman, her hair well oiled and drawn tightly back across her head and into a coil at the nape of her neck, her short-sleeved silk blouse in the party colour of green and the flowing sari matching, with only a slight pattern to detract from the 'national' colour I had seen so much of all day. One might have said that for her forty-nine years Mrs Bandaranaike still retained some of the beauty of her younger days, but the face was now hard and set, and the dark eyes glared rigidly at me with not a flicker of recognition. 'Why do you wish to see me?' she asked, flatly, 'I am a very busy woman.'

'Mrs Bandaranaike, do you think you will win tomorrow?'

'There is no question about it – the country needs me to lead it.'

'With the help of police and troops, all opposition suppressed and people you do not like thrown into jail?'

'How dare you speak to me like that! I decide what is good for Ceylon, the British are not our masters now.'

'Why have you tried to suppress the newspapers? Are you afraid that they tell the truth about what has happened to Ceylon whilst you have been in power?'

'The press is rotten, reactionary. It will not exist after tomorrow.'

'And the journalists who have told the truth will go to jail?'

'Just retribution will come to all those who have opposed me.'

'Will the newspaper for which the Chinese Embassy has supplied the presses cease to exist?'

'You print lies – all the British press prints lies.'

'Mrs Bandaranaike, there are three-quarters of a million unemployed since you became Prime Minister and the only trade you have is bartering with China; this was once a thriving country – do you consider your policies are what the people want?'

'I do not want advice from the British. I know what is good for this country.'

'You have visited Peking?'

'You know perfectly well where I have been.'

'Mrs Bandaranaike, who are your masters?'

'You will leave this house immediately.'

'Thank you, Mrs Bandaranaike. You have been most helpful.'

Her last words had been final, and if I had been a local journalist I may not have had the opportunity to accede to her request. I saw no necessity for offering my hand in the normal courtesy and there was the long drive back to Colombo ahead of me. And a long drink – I needed refreshing.

Polling day I spent among the desperately poor of Colombo, drinking tea with them in poverty-stricken back rooms of families who now had forgotten the days when a man of the house came home once a week with money in his pocket. An occasional few hours' work could be found, but only for the lucky, the few; and the rupees it produced were shared among brothers, sisters, cousins and grandparents. Transport workers and dockers were practically all the wage earners left and they were in communist-controlled unions. They could be relied upon to vote for Mrs Bandaranaike's party, but long before polling finished that day I could have forecast that, at least in Colombo, she was due for a shock.

I sat in Shelton Fernando's office that night as the results came in, and cheers went up each time the hated woman suffered a reverse. By the morning she had been defeated, unless she could gather around her another coalition; but now she found that friends were hard to find. In one last desperate, maniacial fit of fury she set the mobs to work and for twenty-four hours they clashed with police and troops who, fortunately for Ceylon, had realized that they had long been misled. Things had reached the brink of anarchy when the Governor-General, William Gopallawa, finally stepped in and dismissed Mrs Bandaranaike, which must have been yet another shock for her, for he was her uncle and she had appointed him.

However, she did not forget me. In those last few hours when she was trying vainly to cling to power, a group of journalists and photographers was standing outside Temple Trees – Colombo's Number 10 Downing Street – awaiting the next moves. I was standing alone when the bunch of strong-arm men suddenly rushed from the house and there was no doubt about who was to be their first target. They made straight for me. Unfortunately for the first one to reach me, my left fist barred his path and the five others were not so eager after that. A fine old melée broke out. One photographer needed new equipment after it and bruises were plentiful, but I'm sure the press won on points. We came off much better than a Japanese television cameraman who had been filming in another part of Colombo at the time; he was unlucky enough to be mistaken for a Chinese and received a severe beating at the hands of an anti-Bandaranaike crowd.

Nearly three years later a letter from my daughter, then at a university in France, told me of a new and charming friend she had made. 'You would remember her,' wrote Anna, 'she is the daughter of the ex-Prime Minister of Ceylon, Mrs Bandaranaike. I have not explained in detail who you are. I seem to remember that you and her mother are not on very friendly terms.'

Dudley Senanayake, who took over from her, certainly needed co-operation; Ceylon was in a shocking state and to right its ills would take many years of superhuman effort – and an awareness among backward-minded workers and peasants that the wiles of a power-crazy woman could still send them sliding backwards from any possible gains.

I spent hours with Dudley; so much assistance was needed, and the first problem was to woo back the western nations who had been dealt with so rudely, and whose assets had been ruthlessly expropriated. I promised to do what I could, in my writings and privately, and just over a year after, Dudley was able to tell me of the aid which had come, principally for a new agricultural plan we had talked of. I had borrowed the idea from Prince Sihanouk of Cambodia, who, cleverly, had turned farm work into fun and got youth onto the land, more as a holiday than the toil as it had been, hitherto, regarded. Proudly, Dudley took me to see the schoolchildren as they worked in the rice fields; half a million of them, from high classes as well as low, had learned that they could enjoy feeding themselves. 'Holiday' camps had sprung up and charitable organizations fed them and the children sang as they bent over the rich paddies. Senior students were to be presented with plots of land and enough money to work them; a new élite of farmers was being created. In sixteen months Ceylon was being transformed from a country of ten million people which had imported 45 per cent of its staple diet from China into one which now, and so quickly, needed no more than fifteen per cent. Within another year, it was planned, imports would drop to zero and Ceylon would be able to export some of her rice.

But it was not to be, the utter rot which had been created by Mrs Bandaranaike proved too much to overcome. Dudley Senanayake was no magician and could not transform the scene overnight; too many remained jobless and living in a state of near starvation. And never for one moment did Mrs Bandaranaike give up her dream of returning to power.

It took her just five years and one election; May 1970 saw her party returned with a majority in its own right. I felt a real and personal sadness when the result was declared, a sadness for a people who had never had a real chance to think for themselves. And now, perhaps, never would.

I could only hope that Mrs Bandaranaike had learned from her previous and dangerous errors. That she would, in future, choose her bedfellows in a way more befitting a woman of her original class. And that she was no longer planning 'just retribution' against Shelton Fernando and all those others who wanted no more than a free life in a free country.

I doubt if I shall see Ceylon again. I cannot imagine that I shall be welcome; but for a while, at least, it was a happier place to visit during Mrs Bandaranaike's absence. They spruced up the main buildings, a new hotel in Colombo and even the old Gall Face Hotel got a few licks of paint here and there to brighten up its Victorian and dusty drabness. In fact, at times it was quite gay; good food was to be found in a newly opened grillroom, foreign businessmen were entertaining and being entertained.

The women were seen again in all their finery; and for sheer beauty, tall stateliness and poise a younger Ceylonese woman of the higher class families can take her place at the fore in any international and feminine gathering.

It was a delight to be among them at the gatherings and equally delightful to sit in the Gall Face lounge at any time of the day and watch the graceful and sari sheathed figures float past towards the stairs and lifts. Although I did wonder why I never saw these lone females again, sitting at meals in the dining room or anywhere else in the hotel, for that matter.

It just shows how the ways of the world can pass unnoticed under one's very eyes. They were callgirls, a planter from up country explained to me, but only from the very best families, the wives and the daughters. For a small fee the head waiter in the grillroom would supply a telephone number. The planter told of the wealthy man who took a room in the hotel and called a number he had been given; I cannot vouch for the accuracy of the tale, but it was said that fifteen minutes later his own wife appeared at his bedroom door.

My last visit to Ceylon was an unusual one, to say the least. A foreign correspondent's life is not entirely occupied with politics, wars, revolutions and the like; excitement can come in other ways, and when the cable from London reached me in Jakarta, asking me to go to Colombo as quickly as possible, I was mystified. Ceylon was quiet enough at that time, July 1966, as far as I knew, and the cable asked me to await further instructions. I might have anticipated them when I arrived at the Gall Face Hotel to meet a reporter from a London Sunday newspaper renowned for its 'exposures'. A gentleman well known for his lavish living had disappeared from London, following the failure of the insurance company of which he was the founder. With this gentleman had also disappeared a sum of around £600,000. He had been traced by the press to a nursing home in Switzerland, where it was said he was suffering from 'a heart complaint', and from there, evading the press, he had returned to his native land. Emil Savundra he was known as in the best European circles, but now he was reclining in bed at his sister's Colombo home under his fuller name of Savundranayagam. A reporter in London had unearthed dates and amounts of money transfers and now all that was needed was confirmation from Savundra. A simple matter, especially as Scotland Yard's fraud squad was enquiring into just those vital transactions – at least our London 'investigator' imagined it might be, as, excitedly, he read out the exact details over the telephone and down to the last penny. But I doubted that Mr Savundra would be anxious to discuss his affairs at such lengths, and to other newspapermen he had shown the gun he kept constantly in a drawer beside his bed because, as he said, 'my life is in danger'.

The house, modern and obviously expensive, lay back from the road in one of the more desirable districts of Colombo and I left the taxi outside the drive. Yes, the matter I had to discuss with Mr Savundranayagam was 'most important', I explained, but I must admit that I was somewhat surprised when, three minutes later, I was shown up to his bedroom.

He lay in the bed, propped up with pillows, and I noted the bedside cabinet and the drawer. I noted, too, the dozen small bottles on top of the cabinet as Savundra moaned, took tablets from one of them and murmured, 'My heart.' One did not need pharmacological knowledge to recognize them all as vitamin tablets of one sort or another.

Savundra switched on a small tape recorder, asking me to proceed, and I safely got through the first three, reasonably innocuous questions – not that the replies impressed me – before coming to the main question of the huge money transfer. I gave the bank, the date and read out the amount, '£384,534 15s 6d – yes, even to that last sixpence. But my 'interview' was over – the 'sick' man was coming out of the bed, bellowing and charging like a bull. He grabbed at the paper in my hand but I moved it out of his reach, the tape recorder crashed to the floor, and as Savundra tugged at the cabinet drawer it, too, fell to the floor with all the bottles and the bedside lamp.

I really thought it was time to be leaving and backed out of the room as Savundra raged and fumbled among the unholy mess. It would have been stupid to invite a possible bullet in my back, and under Ceylonese law right was on the side of the householder – not the visitor.

For a short time I stopped on the stairs as Savundra came to the landing rails to give a recitation in the foulest English – quite unrepeatable, even among the troops in Borneo. But now his sister appeared beside him and suddenly Savundra realized that he was not acting in the way expected of someone 'dying' of a heart disease. He clutched at his heart and groaned, half fell, but made sure the rail was there to grasp. 'My heart, my heart,' he cried; 'you have killed me.'

Savundra's doctor friend was coming up the stairs. 'What's going on here?' he demanded, but I imagined he knew as much about the 'sickness' as I did. I passed him by. 'I think he has been having too many vitamin pills,' I said, and went on down, out and to the taxi.

If Savundra had but known, I had not heard of that sum of money until I had taken it down on the telephone an hour before. To him, no doubt, I was the clever investigator who had hounded him across the world and confronted him with the evidence he had imagined was safely hidden for all time. Even so, I did not expect him to pursue the matter as far as he did.

Three hours later I was called from my dinner table to find the hotel filled with reporters and photographers and a police inspector, who with his burly sergeant, was waiting to question me. First, Savundra had called the press and then, nicely timed, had summoned the police. To both he had given his carefully prepared charges and the police inspector began to read them out: 'Calling him a black bastard; attempting murder by holding him down in his bed by the throat; stealing vital evidence, namely, a cassette from Mr Savundranayagam's tape recorder; falsely accusing him of illegally transferring the sum of £384,534 15s 6d. . . .'

How interesting! I checked the sum with my notes and not one figure was wrong. When had Savundra worded the charges, I asked the inspector? Just half an hour before, I was told. Now, I asked the inspector, please repeat the sum without looking at the book in your hand, and he began. 'Three hundred – er, three hundred and . . . I'm sorry, sir, I can't remember it.'

What an amazing man was Mr Savundranayagam, to be able to repeat that sum two and a half hours after I had read it out and you, inspector, cannot remember it thirty seconds after reading it. Much scratching of heads followed and I asked, 'Do you wish to arrest me, inspector?' But that worthy man was studying his notes again, apologized for intruding on my dinner and said he would have to refer it all to his superintendent.

Next morning I was famous – or infamous, according to where one's sympathies lay. At last I had made it, headlines and pictures on the front page of every Colombo newspaper – and all about me. For a change I was being written about, and tucked away somewhere at the bottom of each long report was the time-honoured, journalistic phrase opening a paragraph: 'Interviewed at his hotel last night Mr Arthur Cook said . . .'.

The danger of serious charges was by no means past, however, as I gathered next day when the superintendent called to see me. 'Of course, we are not proceeding with the charges, sir,' he told me. 'We know you well and we don't believe them.'

Very comforting to know, but the superintendent continued; 'But I should warn you, sir, that Mr Savundranayagam has instructed his lawyer to go to court tomorrow morning to file a private prosecution against you; and under Ceylonese law you cannot leave the country until the case is finalized.'

Sometimes that great and British nationalized airline flies the Far East routes on schedule and the VC-10 rose into the air ten minutes before Savundra's lawyer stepped into court the following morning. And eventually the uncontrollable conceit of Savundra – the man who had boasted that he could drive his Rolls-Royce through the loopholes in the British insurance laws – persuaded him that he was untouchable and he returned to England.

Twenty months after our one and only meeting he still remembered me. Savundra was standing in the dock, facing trial at the Old Bailey in London when prosecuting counsel came to the main charge: '. . . fraudulently converting the sum of £384,534 15s 6d . . .'. It was too much for Savundra. Across the court he shouted. 'It's all lies. I've been persecuted by the press. That man Cook tried to strangle me in my bed in Colombo. . . '.

Chapter 9

THE BREAKUP

The sudden transition from months of Vietnam to the normal life of Singapore was no simple matter. One's mind cannot suddenly be switched from death and destruction when they have been part of it for so long. People had become vague but animated objects which one saw only briefly before they took their place among the rest of the dead; they were things unreal, ephemeral, from which voices floated but were not attached. The flight of less than two hours had been all too short to prepare me for the change and for seconds I stared at Ah Keow, greeting me from the terrace, before the bounding and barking dogs shook me into the realization that this world had no connections with the one I had so recently left. The garden was in fine shape and Ali was there to show me new and flourishing plants; orchids were in great profusion and soon large bunches had been cut to fill the house which opened up and became home again as if by magic. Ah Keow and her family busied around, chattering excitedly, 'Where Mem?' and I told them that June would be returning in two days. 'Where Missy, Missy come?' and they were satisfied with the news that, 'Missy come tomorrow.'

Before I left Saigon the cables had gone off to June and Anna. I needed to see them, but at the same time I was glad they were not at home awaiting me now. As much as I needed them, I needed some time to adjust myself, to take the first steps back to normality before we were together again. More than anything I needed to dispel the ghosts which persistently refused to disappear completely, to send them back to that other world where they belonged.

Alone I sat on the terrace after dinner, listening to the familiar tropical noises, but this night they were not disturbed by the sound of a plane, a scream or a gun. The cicadas buzzed away in their thousands, forming the permanent backdrop of sound to which one became accustomed and which usually went unnoticed. In the distance monkeys squabbled in high-pitched screams, arousing the wrath of a host of dogs who always failed to reach them, and a nightjar began its nocturnal game from a nearby tree, defying any mere human to join in. 'Tok-tok-tok', went the bird and, after a short pause, 'Tok-tok-tok-tok'. Irresistibly, one found oneself predicting the numbers of toks and counting them, up to a usual maximum of about eight, and cursing the nightjar for being so damned unpredictable. The Chinese swore that the game gradually sends humans insane, but this night I was willing to take the chance – I found the tok-tok bird strangely comforting.

In another two days of homecomings the family was assembled and seldom could any of its size have had so much to tell each other. Plans to be made for the long summer break from studies, water ski-ing, a horse at the polo club, and the date for Anna's usual teenage party: the whirl of entertaining and being entertained starting all over again, with invitations to dinner parties with admirals, air-marshals and generals, all anxious for firsthand briefings on Vietnam. Everyone, except myself, wanted to talk of Vietnam, but nobody appeared to notice the cloud which was creeping over Singapore itself; as the days went on it was everywhere, and among the Chinese, from whom the ready smiles had vanished, inescapable. Tension between them and the Malays, between Singapore and Malaya, had built up over my long absence until now, and suddenly, it had reached alarming proportions, and one felt that the tiniest spark invited an explosion.

Fifteen months earlier, in April 1964, Singapore's premier Lee Kuan Yew had caused a fright among the Tunku and his Alliance party by putting up candidates in the general election. The rules of the Malaysian Federation might be democratic but the Tunku drew the line at this; it was no more nor less than a Chinese attempt at domination, said the Tunku, and he did everything in a vain attempt to prove Lee's action illegal. So few months after the formation of the federation, it could be said that Lee had moved with undue haste, perhaps impetuously, but he had gone into Malaysia wholeheartedly and he saw no reason for any delay in spreading what he thought was best for everyone. Lee would have to admit now that he went too fast; the Tunku and his Malays were by no means ready for change and certainly they were not ready to regard the Chinese as anything but second-class citizens, despite the constitution. Patience on Lee's part might have paid off eventually, said many at the time, but I am inclined to think that his patience would have had to last a good fifty years and then the answer from the Malays to any of his suggestions would still have been a determined 'No'. However, if Lee showed his hand too soon, it was quite obvious that the Tunku and his cronies were going to slap him down without delay; they caused a riot between Malays and Chinese, sending Malay troublemakers over from Malaya, so that they could tighten their grip on the Singapore police. Deputy Premier Abdul Razak was most to blame for this, for I am sure not even the Tunku would have done such a thing. But the Tunku was with the others, falling in with most of the suggestions to grind Lee and Singapore down until the planned day when Lee and most of his ministers were in jail.

In fact, Lee's arrest had been openly demanded in the federal parliament and by the fanatical Malay politicians. But when the speeches on both sides were reported by a British freelance journalist, Alex Josey, the Youth Association of the United Malay National Organization demanded his expulsion and the Tunku and his inner government quickly bowed to the request and Josey was given one week to leave. Josey was not the only target; more, it was a deliberate attack on Lee Kuan Yew, who for a long time had used Josey as a part-time press adviser. Nothing could have been a more calculated personal blow and many expected Lee to react violently. In fact, at a farewell dinner he gave for Josey, I was shattered to hear Lee mouthing facetious phrases which never at any time approached the issue at hand. He appeared to be a scared man, beaten into utter defeat by the Malay bosses in Kuala Lumpur, and now lamely awaiting their next move. The same feeling had spread throughout the whole of Singapore's one and a half million Chinese, and not one of them could see a way out, apart from a ghastly racial war which they did not want.

Naturally I wrote about Josey's explusion and the bitter

racial and political disputes which formed the background; they were threatening to divide the Malaysian Federation, I said, when it was not yet two years old. Nine days later I had cause to write another warning; the Federal Government was closing down the Bank of China in Singapore, which extended credit to hundreds of Chinese shops and businesses. Internal trade was about to collapse in what was probably the final and most vicious blow yet at the Chinese by the Malays in Kuala Lumpur.

As I have said before, I cannot blame the Tunku for everything, but then I cannot excuse him for his gross lack of knowledge or the crass stupidity with which he approached situations, especially those he felt were aimed against him. All his years in England had left him with only a thin veneer of western sophistication, and his passable, but by no means perfect, English did little to hide the fact that underneath it all worked the mind of one of the more backward Asian nations.

The Tunku was in London for the Commonwealth Prime Ministers conference at the time my articles appeared and in a vast fury the man who considered himself to be a world figure and statesman unleashed an attack on me, the like of which, in all its ferocity, has seldom been experienced by any foreign correspondent before or since. It began as the main item on the evening radio news bulletin and was repeated on the hour throughout the length and breadth of Malaysia; the next morning every newspaper, including the English language *Straits Times*, headlined the Tunku's attack in the largest possible print. The Tunku alleged that I had created mistrust between Chinese and Malays and if trouble was coming, then the cause could be laid squarely at my door. I was Public Enemy No. 1 and the newspapers vied with each other to produce more 'disclosures' day after day. *Utusan Melayu*, a fanatical pro-government Malay daily which held the greatest sway, created the line on which the main attack on me was formulated. I was not a journalist, it said, but was using that title as a disguise; my real job was to break up the Malaysian Federation and hand it back, piece by piece, to the British government.

It was now only a matter of waiting for the next move; the demands for my explusion came from all sides and the Tunku said he would 'deal with' me on his return. There were three weeks to wait and seldom during that time did the press or radio leave me alone. Even Leslie Hoffman, an Eurasian who loved to be regarded as completely westernized and edited the *Straits Times*, went overboard in an attempt to show the Kuala Lumpur government how far he would back them. Leslie had been considered a friend until then, but he was soon to be crossed off my list. 'I'll write exactly what I wish about you,' he told me openly. 'I'll tear you to pieces in any way I please.'

If nothing else, I was in good company, but if anything I was ahead of Lee Kuan Yew when it came to vilification at the hands of the Malaysian press. The pendulum swung over us both, but Lee's betting was that I would be 'dealt with' first on the Tunku's return and any other voice like mine would be silenced before the axe really fell on himself. Good reasoning, I had to agree, and in all probability, that is the way the Tunku had planned it. In the event we were to witness a classic example of how momentous decisions can be taken without any consideration of the views which may be taken by the head of state. Tunku Abdul Rahman returned to Malaysia on Saturday, August 7, 1965, and walked straight into a *fait accompli*; during his two months of absence the fanatical elements of his United Malay party had drawn up an order expelling Singapore from the federation and all that was awaited was the Tunku to give the order. Deputy Premier Abdul Razak, who had been left in charge of the country, had shown his 'strength' once again; he had been scared to stand up to the fanatical elements and the dismissal order had been written on his own notepaper.

I certainly had no intention of meeting the Tunku at the airport that Saturday afternoon; expulsion for me meant little more than a move to Hong Kong and that was not an unpleasant prospect, and the Tunku could send for me when he was good and ready. It was a slight surprise when the Tunku did not leave Singapore airport, but flew on the first plane to Kuala Lumpur. The same evening it had become apparent that something far more serious than my expulsion was afoot, when Lee Kuan Yew and most of his ministers were summoned immediately to Kuala Lumpur. There they were told to resign or face the possibility of racial war between the Malays and the Chinese. They held together during two days of threats and wrangling

STORY UNUSED

and the Tunku was forced into the only alternative left him by his colleagues: he dismissed Singapore from Malaysia. All the plans for a multi-racial society, for which Lee and Singapore had earnestly hoped and had been prepared to work, were thrown to the winds. In so many ways, apart from the simple geographical ones, Singapore and Malaya should have been part of each other. Now a long period of bitterness was to come, mostly initiated by the Malays, whose overall desire to dominate the Chinese left little room for co-operation.

On Monday, August 9th, a stunned Singapore heard the radio news that the island was now an independent country and no longer part of the Malaysian Federation. That was all it said and everyone, in fact most of the world, was given to understand that Singapore had walked out of the federation of her own accord. A further shock was to come the following day, when Lee called a press conference to explain just exactly what had happened. There really was no excuse for the international press sitting there; they had jumped to conclusions when the radio broadcasts came and for a full twenty-four hours had misled the world. I sat through the conference to hear my own version of the events reiterated, but my real object was to take things further with Lee Kuan Yew himself. I had asked his secretary to call me from the conference room when he was ready, but before he left Lee made it obvious that conversation was not going to be easy. He broke down and tears came to his eyes in front of the television cameras as he said: 'All my life I have believed in this union of races.' It was a strange contrast to all those in the streets outside. They did not know how the split with Malaysia had come and they did not really care. All the Chinese knew was that a great, persecuting sword no longer threatened them, and there were smiles all round.

Few people, I feel, knew Lee Kuan Yew in quite the same way as I did. The friendship was mutual and was not to be presumed upon. Built under circumstances of difficulty and adversity, it was an understanding, and forged out of a deep respect, one for the other. In public – on Singapore Television – we fought and I never had the feeling that I should pull my punches. But Lee liked it that way and gave as good as he took. He had a habit of hogging the screen and effectively holding off any interruptions, until I insisted on breaking into his monologue and saying that, as I had been invited to the studio, I expected to be able to speak; otherwise I considered I was wasting my time. Lee took it, on the chin, and the cameras continued turning. Surprised, perhaps, but here was a degree of magnanimity which showed itself at the end of the programme with the question, 'Well, how did we do?' Our televisions bouts became the talk of Singapore, but I trust we were both completely constructive, and to his minister colleague who wondered why he continued to appear with me when I 'attacked' him so much, Lee used one of the English colloquialisms he had stored away in such profusion – 'Aw, shut up,' he said. 'Arthur and I understand each other.' Strong and capable, of that there was no doubt, and so far as I was concerned, he could be excused for his impetuosity in wanting to get things done for the people he had been chosen to represent.

Lee sat in his office nervously playing with a paper knife, as I walked in and closed the door that morning he had faced the press, and my opening words brought the tears to his eyes. 'Pull yourself together, man,' I said sharply, but the events of the past forty-eight hours were still too heavy on his mind to allow any new horizons. Compulsively, Lee went through the shattered dreams and the events in Kuala Lumpur. I tried to head him off, but it was useless, everything had to be poured out and Lee felt he could do that with me. But this man could not be allowed to dwell on what was past; the future was now too important. 'Stop crying,' I ordered. 'That was yesterday and now we have to think of tomorrow.' For a full five minutes the talk became reasonably rational, but then the tears came again. Something drastic had to be done and I have wondered since if anyone else would have used the words to the Prime Minister which now came so naturally. 'Shut up,' I shouted. 'Will you stop crying. Big things have to be done and the whole of Singapore is relying on you to do them. Are you prepared to talk about tomorrow, or do you insist in living in the past?'

Lee sat bolt upright and stared me straight in the eyes. He wiped his eyes and that well-known look of determination took over in an instant. We talked of the future for a long time, and enough of the future to acquaint the world that, as small as she was, Singapore was ready to fight for the future as she had planned it. Tears became a thing of the past and if they were ever seen again, they were tears of sweat.

Later, I did have to speak sternly again to Lee Kuan Yew; he introduced me to a group of foreign guests at a large reception in the grounds of Government House with the words, 'The Tunku was going to expel him.' I pulled myself up in mock dignity to reply, 'Mr Prime Minister, to keep the record straight, it was a question of whether you were to be expelled or I was to be expelled – and you were.'

Now, of course, living in Singapore, I was no longer under the Tunku's jurisdiction, but I saw no reason why we should not have the meeting he had promised me on his return to Malaysia. When I left Lee in his office, I telephoned to the Tunku in Kuala Lumpur and left a message that I would be presenting myself the next morning. Just three and a half weeks after my warnings that trouble was in store for Malaysia the Tunku, with all pomposity, sat in his palace and told me that, a month earlier, he had decided to expel Singapore. He was in the London Clinic receiving treatment for shingles, the Tunku said, when the idea came to him. 'It was an act of God that I was ill. It gave me time to think, to work out the whole problem,' he explained. But weren't the terms of the expulsion worked out in Kuala Lumpur during his absence, I asked; after all, I had seen the letter on the notepaper of Abdul Razak? The Tunku became vague about detail, but suddenly his hatred for the Chinese came to the fore as he pointed out that they owned all shops and businesses whilst the poor Malays owned none. It was evident that nothing constructive would emerge from this conversation, and the Tunku was not at all pleased when I suggested that the reason was, perhaps, that the Chinese were willing to work whereas the Malays were not. But what of his allegations that it had been me who had created mistrust between the Chinese and Malays, I demanded; strange man that he was, the Tunku did not remember – or he chose to forget – that the subject had ever arisen.

Inexplicable would be a more suitable word to explain the workings of the Malay mind. On each visit to Malaya, even in transit or on my way home to Singapore from other countries, the mere sight of my passport set customs and immigration officials into action to make everything as unpleasant as possible for me. It got progressively worse until, one day at Kuala Lumpur airport, an immigration man rudely pushed me, but cried out in terror as I held him in a grip until the arrival of the Chief of Immigration. Then, one evening, a large Jaguar car swept up the drive to my house and four Malays descended on the quiet household, unannounced, to talk and drink me out of brandy. Not that they all talked; the short and bespectacled one, who commanded all the respect and introduced himself as Dato Jamal bin Abdul Latiff, the new Malaysian High Commissioner to Singapore, did most of it whilst a press officer took second place in the conversation and the other two, the driver and the bodyguard, sat quietly saying nothing. The following morning the driver arrived with a beautiful bracelet for Anna and which bore a note, 'From Uncle Jamal.' June and I became guests of honour at most of the Malaysian receptions and Jamal was on the telephone from morning to night, asking my advice or for introductions among the diplomatic corps. Without being positively rude, it was difficult not to help, and I must say that Jamal was one of the more charming Malays I have ever met.

After a week or too, however, my curiosity could wait no longer and I asked Jamal, who had sent him to me. Amazed, he replied, 'But you do not know? The day I left Kuala Lumpur to take up my post, the Tunku ordered me to contact you immediately. The Tunku regards you as his greatest friend and said that you would be able to help me in everything.' I could not lay claim to such wide powers, but at least I was able to impress reason here and there which narrowly avoided serious clashes between Malaysia and the newly formed Republic of Singapore in those early days. It was becoming most interesting, but I had no wish to continue indefinitely as an unpaid diplomat, particularly as it would have been in nobody's interests if one tiny part of what was going on behind the scenes had appeared in a newspaper.

August was drawing to a close. So far it had been a busy year, but it was by no means over. And the sinister sounds of war were rumbling across from Kashmir and the Indo-Pakistan borders.

Chapter 10

END OF A DREAM

The last day in September, 1965, and the plane was hurrying me to Beirut. Behind lay the short-lived and abortive war which was to set both India and Pakistan back financially for a long time to come, behind lay the wasted lives and behind lay the clinic in Rawalpindi. It was a journey I have no wish to repeat; for so long had my mind been unconsciously winding itself up to a pitch at which rest and a slow unwinding was the only antidote; but now, on the plane, events were crowding in on each other and the scenes were changing with such swiftness that little made sense – except the overriding revulsion against war, wherever it may be and in all its futility. Ahead, and I thanked God that only a matter of hours separated me from my many friends, lay the tranquility of Beirut. Surely this was the complete change and relaxation I craved for. Now it was Thursday and I could rest for a long weekend, I told myself, before thinking of flying east again and home to Singapore.

It was all that I could have expected. Mansour Braidi, the concierge at the Hotel St Georges, lined up the staff and greeted me as though I were a king; Ali, the barman, remembered my favourite drink and was already shaking it as I entered the terrace bar. One of the best suites overlooking the bay was at my disposal, and within half an hour telephones had announced my arrival and I was sitting among a group of my friends and colleagues on the most famous terrace in the world.

Five days. Yes, that was my plan, and arrangements were being made for lunch parties, dinner parties, drives into the mountains and cocktail parties in the lazy atmosphere of the beaches and their palm-covered huts. Could anything have been more superb: to live the life of a millionaire once again, if only for a matter of days. The prospect was warming as we lunched in the sunshine, overlooked by the mountains which swept round the bay towards Byblos and then northwards to Tripoli. All that might have been mine if I had not gone to my room after lunch in the hope of having a few hours refreshing sleep to prepare me for the evening. But sleep, that was a thing of the past and refused to come. In half an hour my mind was working in leaps and bounds again: I must get back to Singapore, something was telling me, and no excuses could budge what had now become a compulsion. By six o'clock I had booked myself on the VC-10 flying eastwards that night and by eight oclock I was on the way to the airport after hurried excuses to my surprised friends.

What was the compulsion? I had no way of knowing as the plane flew into the dawn over the Arabian Sea, put down at Colombo and then set off again for the long hop to Bangkok and the final, but shorter leg, south to Singapore. A warm greeting from the immigration man at the airport and one of my more friendly taxi drivers, to tell me of the weather they had been having as he drove me home in the setting sun of Friday evening. The dogs, yes, they were leaping around as usual and dear Ah Keow was on the main terrace.

'Mem?' I asked and Ah Keow pointed upstairs. I hurried up. Was this the unknown reason for my headlong flight home? But no. June's fever could not have been; the doctor had assured her it was nothing serious; even so I was glad to be at home with her, and perhaps now, at last, my mind would relax. Slightly, perhaps, it did and sheer fatigue allowed me to sleep that night; then, on the Saturday morning, came the first news of the events which had been tugging at me, telling me that Beirut was the wrong place to be. Even as I had decided to leave there on the Thursday, communist troops in Indonesia, under the command of a Lieutenant-Colonel Untung, had attempted to take over the country. Leading generals had been put to death and President Sukarno had been kidnapped, or so it was said, by the communists. Battles had raged in and around Jakarta until Untung and his troops had fled. The crack, which had been so long awaited in the Sukarno myth, had come – and it was a crack through which I must try to slip, to penetrate the barricades against such people as myself which Sukarno had now been keeping well manned for over two years.

For no more than two hours did I see Jakarta and I had to wait until the following day, Sunday, before it was decided that a plane would be able to fly in. The Dutch airline manager was a friend who listened to my argument that, as I was not a permanent citizen of Singapore, the rules made by Sukarno did not prevent the issue of a ticket. But a visa? That was something we both conveniently forgot to discuss. All hell was to break loose from the Indonesian authorities eventually, which rebounded all the way back to Amsterdam. But no harm came to my airline friend; somehow he kept out of the line of fire. Being the only passenger aboard the plane, I walked into the airport building with the crew and promptly disappeared, well away from the airport, before my arrival was realized. An Italian diplomat and his Dutch wife, a friend of several years before, played their part, and without their help I would, no doubt, have been picked up sooner. By that time I had been able to acquire a fairly full picture of the situation, and its confusion at that time, no doubt, was all that saved me from a rather uncomfortable jail when I was finally arrested, back near the airport, and escorted by a most irate major and a platoon of troops to the aircraft, which had not been allowed to leave. So it was back to Singapore, but with a bottle of champagne as a mild celebration; from what I had seen and heard in Jakarta I felt sure Sukarno's days were now numbered. It was a question of watching and waiting through his twilight hours; no regime with foundations as rotten as these could hope to defy all the rules and survive all the time.

As true as that proved to be, the most incredible aspect of the fall of Sukarno was the length of time it took finally to get him out of his palace and banished from Jakarta. Seventeen years as dictator, Bung (brother), and the only voice recognized by a hundred million people were not going to be wiped out overnight, and for five months Sukarno defied the generals who thought they were in control. He brought back pro-communist ministers and when the generals remonstrated Sukarno sacked their Chief of Staff, General Nasution. By February, 1966, he appeared to be firmly back in the saddle and not one general was there with the guts to pit his strength against a President who sat back, openly laughing at them. The generals, or the army, never did overthrow Sukarno; that was left to thousands of students, who finally decided that the rot had gone far enough and, if nobody else was prepared to act, they would go it alone.

I was a regular passenger on the planes between Singapore and Bangkok at the time, as Bangkok housed the nearest Indonesian embassy from where a visa might be obtained. But how or who decided which correspondents should be allowed into Jakarta, and when, was one of the greater mysteries; each visit to Bangkok cost something in excess of $200 in air fares and hotels, but it became fairly normal and expected to be met by a smiling ambassador with the excuse: 'Sorry, your name is not on the list this week – come back next week. I assure you, your visa will be ready.' Oh, yes, my name came up eventually, but by then the visa had cost over $1,000, quite the most expensive visa I ever acquired and, no doubt, duly noted by the accounts department in London, who never would have understood the importance of that stamp in a passport. After all, they never required such things for their annual package tours to France, Italy or the Republic of Ireland.

There were some rather 'old' students in the movement against Sukarno and when I eventually, and legitimately, flew into Jakarta, I could have sworn that several among the organizers would not be seeing their fortieth birthdays again. But they had had success after success. For weeks they demonstrated and then rioted for the banning of the communist party. They demanded the sacking and final arrest of such people as Foreign Minister Subandrio, and got it. They had sacked and burned the Chinese embassy and Peking's New China News Agency offices and then ransacked the Foreign Ministry and found all the damning evidence that was necessary to prove that Sukarno and his clique were about the pass over their country completely to the Communist Party. When troops were set against the students, the youngsters threw themselves against guns and bayonets, until eventually the lily-livered generals decided that, if they were not to embark on a wholesale killing of the students, they had better join them.

STORY UNUSED

The usual meeting point for any new demonstration was in the big square below the towering Hotel Indonesia, Jakarta's only hotel, built with Japanese war reparations and run by an American hotel chain, and my first few days were kept more than busy keeping up with what the students were taking over next. They feared nobody and they had nothing to lose; the schools and the university had been closed for months anyway. After one of their bigger victories, they commandeered every workable piece of transport they could find for miles and brought Jakarta to a standstill, a hilarious one, by parading in their thousands past Sukarno's palace – with a miniature 'President', dressed down to the inevitable sunglasses and pitji, aping Sukarno with his known gestures from the front of each truck.

Never, perhaps, have I seen a country so completely run down and dilapidated as was Indonesia at the end of the Sukarno rule in 1966. The immediate effect was that someone had produced the greatest vaudeville show on earth and the stage props still jutted skywards here and there among a sprawling and single-storeyed Jakarta, where shops displayed empty cartons in their windows but had absolutely nothing to sell inside and three million people went from one hungry day to the next. Sukarno's ghastly and grotesque monuments to 'freedom' rose three and four hundred feet into the air and millions had been spent on an unfinished skyscraper which, Sukarno had planned, would house world conferences of 'newly emerging nations'. Jakarta alone had had a fleet of nearly 700 modern buses, but in three years no more than 150 were in working order and the rest lay on waste ground everywhere, cannibalized of all spare parts and rusting. Apart from a misguided gift from America of Jakarta's main highway, not one other road in the capital, or, in fact, thoroughout the country, had been repaired in the least degree since the Dutch had left. They were broken, pock-marked and dusty, or they had vast flooded holes and broke the vehicles which used them. No more than twenty taxis could be relied upon for any journey of more than a few miles and a hundred mile trip or more, to any part of Java – and all of it was as broken down as Jakarta or worse – was a highly planned affair with no guarantee that the vehicle would ever survive the battering it was to get.

END OF A DREAM

The decline of the country which, less than thirty years before, had been the world's greatest producer of raw materials, was a depressing reminder of what happens in this world when freedom and independence gets into the wrong hands. Textile factories and other small industries had run to a standstill and gone to rot; the people had become too lazy to work their crops, and rice and wheat had been eaten by rats long before they attempted to gather it in. The Dutch had been accused of beating the Indonesians to make them work, but, God knows! it had been for their own good. Indonesians left to their own ends can best be explained by describing the picture of the drive from the centre of Jakarta to the airport. For two miles the road runs alongside the main canal, and, especially in the early morning, the banks are crowded with men, women and children, squatting side by side defecating into the filthy, brown water. This operation over, the Indonesians then lower themselves into the canal to complete their ablutions and finish off by washing their clothes in the water as they stand there. With this sort of hygiene there can be little wonder that diseases had spread alarmingly throughout Java, Sumatra and practically every tiny island, and if their had been medicines available, which there were not, there was no means of getting any sort of aid to those who needed it.

A giant world rescue operation was needed even to arrest the rot and decay of Indonesia. Her income and production was nil and her foreign debts ran into thousands of millions of dollars. But confrontation to Malaysia still went on. British troops were still fighting in the Borneo jungles – and getting killed – so it can be imagined with what surprise I heard the news that Britain, of all countries, would be the first to offer a monetary gift, with no strings attached. What nonsense this was! For months British diplomats had been working hard to stop other countries from giving aid to Indonesia until she dropped her confrontation, and now, at the end of April 1966, Britain was breaking all the rules which she herself had tried to lay down. I was back in Singapore when I heard of it: the British Government – and that could only mean Harold Wilson, assisted by his Foreign Minister, Michael Stewart, had offered one million pounds sterling, naturally accepted with alacrity in

STORY UNUSED

Jakarta. Wilson and Stewart had no doubt hoped that their little game would go unnoticed in Britain, but when my article appeared, telling of the free gift, the situation exploded. Orders were issued that my informant should be discovered and sacked immediately.

Several days went by before I realized what a stir had been caused in the dark and dusty corridors of Whitehall, and by then three most senior British diplomats in Singapore – all friends of mine – were under the gravest suspicion and their original reports to Whitehall had been turned down as unacceptable. It was obvious that someone was determined to find a scapegoat for the leak to the press, and if one of the three diplomats would not admit that he had been my source of information, then all three heads must be chopped – three distinguished careers ruined. They never knew why the searching enquiry was dropped but, luckily for my diplomatic friends, an under-secretary from the Foreign Office came to the Far East at that time and we were able to discuss the situation quietly. Most certainly, he admitted, Mr Stewart was livid about the leak. How interesting, I was able to reply, but I would like a message sent to Mr Michael Stewart immediately – if he had chosen to inform the governments of Singapore, Malaysia, Australia and New Zealand of his intention to offer money to Indonesia, he should not be surprised that the information would eventually reach me. I had no intention of disclosing who had been my informant, my message continued, but I would be watching with interest the careers of three senior diplomats in Singapore and would be only too willing to reveal more if any one of them was victimized.

It was to be almost four months after the million-pound gift that any sort of peace was signed between Indonesia and Malaysia, but long before this I decided to get up to Indonesian Borneo. Not that the army authorities in Jakarta appeared to be in any sort of mood to crown my plan with a blessing and even now I wonder why they did not ban it altogether and make sure that I was not allowed on any plane flying in that direction. First I had to find the colonel who had been appointed as press 'liaison' officer, a lengthy procedure which occupied all of three days until I discovered that the colonel, like most

Indonesians officials, regarded an office as a place to visit perhaps once a week and any 'liaison' could be effected only if he could be tracked to his own or one of his friend's homes. Mine was an unusual request and would need the highest clearance, the colonel informed me, but when another four days had passed and no official passes were forthcoming, I presented him with the *fait accompli* that I would be arriving at the garrison headquarters at Pontianak the following morning and if any harm befell me I would hold the colonel fully responsible. To my astonishment there was no curt order forbidding me to do any such thing and I found that it was me giving the orders – telling the colonel that I expected him to signal Pontianak immediately, warning them of my arrival. It was sheer bluff, of course, but how else was one to get any satisfaction in obtaining official permission which otherwise could have taken another six months?

If this was security, it was no small wonder that the communists had been so close to taking over Sukarno's empire. With a ticket I bought openly at the Garuda airline office at the hotel I presented myself at the 'internal' section of the flight departures early next morning and not a soul queried the reason for my flight. All other passengers on the plane to Pontianak were military – going back to 'the front' – and they nodded or smiled at me with all the friendliness in the world. A captain who sat in the seat next to mine offered me a sandwich once we got airborne, was pleased to find that he was talking to an Englishman and even more pleased to tell me that he had learned English at a Dutch school many years before. Going to Pontianak to see the general, that meant quite obviously that I was a most important person. And when we landed at the garrison town on the west coast of Borneo – named Kalimantan by the Indonesians – through which the equator ran exactly, the captain made sure that there was a place in the small Russian transport for this V.I.P. who, if the truth had been known, was even then not quite sure if he would ever see the outside world again.

There are no words to describe the devastation at Pontianak air field: plane fuselages lay stripped of wings, engines and wheels. Of six Russian helicopters only one still had rotor blades, or tyres on its wheels to give it any semblance of being airworthy; and the road to the main airport building, doorless, paintless, windowless and housing an incredible stack of useless military rubbish, was a dusty and broken track. But this, as I was soon to find out, was reasonably smooth and comfortable compared with the twelve miles of 'built up' road into Pontianak which had yet to be negotiated; never have I had such a terrifying and back-breaking ride and the trucks, jeeps, troop carriers and even tanks which lay in hundreds by the side of thirty years of neglect bore witness to the fact that nothing mechanical on earth could be expected to stand up to such battering for more than a limited number of times. I let myself go limp as we bounded into the first craters, but was thrown in so many directions that a rigid posture seemed preferable, until the spine nearly cracked in two. Off the seat and trying to take the bucking and rearing with the knee-joints, every other known position to combat a sudden death from a broken neck, which could have come at any second, but on we had to go at a speed which averaged no more than six miles an hour. It was a drive I remembered every hour of my stay in Kalimantan, and remembered with horror that it had to be negotiated once more if ever I was to see that airfield again.

After such a conditioning the sight of the army headquarters was, to say the least, bizarre. All around it was the devastation of broken roads, dilapidated and tumbledown houses, shops with nothing whatsoever to sell and cafés – I was surprised to see that most were Chinese run – that were nothing more than dirty and ill-kept holes in walls, while among it all rose the great modern façade with fifty or so white steps leading up to great halls and offices through which stiff and starched uniformed troops marched briskly, with every outward show of intense efficiency. I had been expected, much to my amazement; a signal had, in fact, arrived that morning from Jakarta. A Lieutenant Moechsin had been assigned to me to facilitate any request; but to visit the forward troops, that was impossible. The headquarters had only two jeeps in service, the general needed one and the other was in constant use.

How it ever reached Pontianak I shall never know and how it had not fallen into military hands yet was a larger mystery,

13. *Top:* Tunku Abdul Rahman, Malaysian Prime Minister in 1965. *Bottom:* Lee Kuan Yew, Prime Minister of Singapore in 1965 (Photos: U.P.I.)

14. Corporal Michael O'Donaghue in Borneo, 1965

but that evening I discovered a British Land Rover which actually worked. It was in pretty good shape too and was owned by a Chinese café proprietor, whose eyes glistened at my suggestion of fifty American dollars for its hire for a few days. If he had contact with a black market, and I had no doubt that he had, he could be the local millionaire for a while; but word gets around fast in such a place as Pontianak, and when I presented myself and the Land Rover to Lieutenant Moechsin, demanding an escort, he quickly worked out what it would cost for himself to accompany me, our rations (nothing but rice) and the petrol 'which would have to be bought from the army' – in American dollars.

However, I was mobile and early next morning we set off with Moechsin driving at his own insistence; to my eternal gratification there were very few miles of 'main' roads which could be used, and by nightfall we had driven more than 100 miles northwards, mostly over tracks, and drew into a jungle camp from where Indonesian guerillas made their way into Malaysian North Borneo. It was too dark to see how close we were to the border; in fact, that night I saw nothing but the mud which squelched above my ankles and the inside of a rough and ready wood-and-rush hut I shared with Moechsin and two other Indonesian officers. But next morning there they were and no more than six or seven miles away – the hills over which I had clambered with Tim Eugster, Mike O'Donaghue and the other Irish Guards. Naturally I could not make out where The Pentagon might be hidden, or any of the other forward posts which had been holding this border for so long, and I must admit that I was hoping their heavy guns and mortars would not be concentrating on the particular area where I was to spend the next twenty-four hours. There was something uncanny in the feeling that I was looking at the wrong end of the British artillery – and without the wherewithal of letting them know that they were aiming at a 'friend'.

Again it was amazing that, as a Britisher, I was accepted by these Indonesians, who did not appear to raise an eyebrow when they were told who I was. Captain Margono and Lieutenant Rozak, whose hut I was sharing, both spoke enough words of English for us to have, albeit laborious, conversations and it was more than interesting to learn their opinions of the British and the Gurkhas they were facing. When I had been on the other side the perpetual complaint from the British had been that they were desparately short of helicopters, but here was Rozak praising the speed with which the British moved their troops around by air. He and Margono had every respect for the heavy artillery too; all the British equipment was superior to theirs, they admitted, and on this it was easy to agree when one had seen so much lying around derelict and coming from all corners of the globe. Margono and Rozak themselves were perfect specimens of how Sukarno had begged his way through the years, and at the same time they were damning evidence of the disgusting practices of developed nations in supplying arms and other war equipment to those who never could manufacture them for themselves. Margono and Rozak wore American made, camouflaged jungle uniforms, with American webbing and helmets, but their soft peaked caps had been made in Japan. Their rifles and machine guns were a mixture of American and Russian, their pistols Belgian and their long leather jungle boots Czech.

Activity along the border was on the wane now, as nobody appeared to know who should be giving the orders from Jakarta, but two patrols did come in whilst I was at the forward camp and, although they had no action to report, it was obvious that they had been out a long time. There was no real action that I could report myself, but I had never had any intention of joining these Indonesian troops on a jungle patrol; that would have been tempting fate just a bit too far. I was, however, able to clear up the mystery, until then, of the fate of the pilot and crew of a British helicopter which had been missing for several months. Rozak told me the story in his halting, schoolboy English, but I understood it accurately enough for all the details to be checked eventually and the relatives of the missing men informed of their end. The helicopter had strayed over the border in bad weather and had been shot down two miles from the camp; the crew were killed and given a military funeral but the pilot, who died later, was cremated and his ashes sent to Jakarta. There they were finally located by the British Embassy and flown back to England.

END OF A DREAM

I might have stayed with the forward troops much longer, but Moechsin was impatient to get back to Pontianak; he was more of a headquarters wallah than a fighting soldier, like Rozak or Margono, and did not appreciate the hard boards we had for beds and the squelching mud through which we plodded every time we moved from the bare and uncomfortable hut. Secretly, I agreed with Moechsin, but the trip had been my own idea and I was prepared to put up with it for a while longer; but if there had been just some little thing, a piece of dried fish or a papaya, to augment our rations our diet could have been much more pleasant. Our rice just went in with the general handout – and that is all we got, for breakfast, lunch and dinner.

We left after the second night, with Moechsin more cheerful than I had seen him since we started out from Pontianak, and again we made the journey by nightfall. There a message awaited me that the local commander wished to see me the following morning and Moechsin, taking this as a great honour, said that he would take me to a café for dinner. It was a meal I would gladly have missed; nothing was eatable except for the rice and I was not in need of that. And when it was over Moechsin asked for money to pay the bill – in dollars and at some calculated rate of exchange that only he could understand.

Brigadier General Ryacudu was charm personified, with his thin moustache he could have doubled for Ronald Colman in any film, and his uniform, sporting more medal ribbons than ever Eisenhower or Montgomery could have claimed, seemed as though bound to break into pieces each time he moved, so great was the weight of starch which held it – and him – upright. Of course, he had won the war so far, Ryacudu told me and if the Central Government ordered another full-scale offensive he would go into Sarawak and beat the British again. I am sure the general was not boasting for boasting's sake; his mind was no different from Sukarno's or any other Indonesian, for that matter, and the more I nodded my head as though in agreement the more he liked me and the more he expanded to my apparently innocuous but loaded questions. He first claimed, for this had always been the official Indonesian line, that none of his 10,000 regular troops had crossed into Sarawak, but as I

STORY UNUSED

worked him into a greater enthusiasm on his 'victories', Ryacudu gave me graphic details of battles, including locations, where his regulars had trounced the British and Gurkhas, 'despite their superiority in equipment and mobility'. But it was the Sarawak 'freedom fighters' which interested me most, and Ryacudu was eventually telling me how he had trained them by the hundreds as they came across, equipped them 'idealogically and mentally as well as with weapons and equipment' and then sent them back to train others. Even with the end of confrontation in sight, Ryacudu's efforts did not augur well for the future of Malaysia and a dangerous force which had always existed in Sarawak was going to need an even closer watch in the future.

If Ryacudu was proud of his achievements, who was I to argue with him? I was in his territory and that was a point which it might have been dangerous to forget. The general regarded me as a good fellow, and, to prove it he produced a green and sickly drink over which we clinked glasses a dozen times. If I left him with any doubts I can only imagine that Ryacudu might have wondered if Sukarno had been right in ordering him to fight such friendly people as these British. And I say that with absolutely no conceit. I had a job to do and the way it was done had to suit the circumstances. Just as an added possibility that I may have been right I have never disposed, as one does of so much junk collected around the world, of a silver and mounted plaque bearing the crest of General Ryacudu's division. With all due ceremony he presented it to the first Englishman with whom he had come face to face in three years of war, and my profuse thanks left him in no doubt that I considered myself duly honoured. I have kept the plaque, as I have said, not so much as a momento of General Ryacudu or his West Kalimantan Division, but to remind me eternally of the worst road on earth along which I was obliged to run the gauntlet, and almost lost the battle, an hour or so after the presentation.

It could be wondered how anything I might have written after such an expedition, for in no way could it have been complimentary to the Indonesians, ever passed the rigid censorship imposed on all press cables from Jakarta to the outside world. The answer is that the censors never saw it, any more than they saw ninety-nine per cent of the articles which were written in Indonesia and filled the newspapers of the outside world. Difficulties placed in our path were difficulties to be circumnavigated and Indonesia had nothing which was insurmountable or anything which a bunch of foreign correspondents had not encountered somewhere before. Six days a week – and it would have been seven if there had been a plane that day – a bulky packet of despatches and films found its way past the ever watchful airport customs officials, who invariably emptied suitcases in their vast suspicion that everyone should be treated as a spy and an enemy of the country. One day it might have been a diplomat who acted as our courier and the next a correspondent who was moving out or, if we were stuck for known collaborators, we never failed to find a helpful passenger, pilot or stewardess. It was never necessary for the courier to take the risk of carrying the package through customs, for we had our own ways of getting the precious cargo delivered to them on the plane and after that it was simple. At Singapore airport messengers from news agencies met every plane in from Jakarta and our despatches were in London, New York or elsewhere within hours, via the Singapore cable office. Perhaps the Indonesian censors themselves were happy about the whole arrangement; it meant that they were never seen at their office, not even once a week, and were rather displeased at being disturbed occasionally at home.

I doubt if history will ever record its immensity, but the largest massacre, perhaps of all time, took place in Indonesia in the days following the abortive communist attempt to take over the country on September 30, 1965. With practically no communications, however, it was weeks and months before the reports filtered through to Jakarta and other main centres, and by that time nobody was interested apart from diplomatic circles. That is not to say that I was not interested. Naturally I was; but it is one thing to write a report of a massacre at the time it happens, with all the gory details to horrify the world, and quite another proposition to interest an editor weeks after the event, when all he needs is to be able to label a story 'old' and 'stale' to make sure that it does not clutter up the columns when such monstrosities as the Beatles are making 'big' news or the editor himself is running a campaign against a racket in babies' nappies.

The earlier reports of the massacre, from Java, were gruesome enough and it soon became obvious that thousands of communists had been put to death when the majority of the people turned on them as the cause of all their deprivations, starvation and oppression. Then came reports from Sumatra, and the numbers said to have been killed rocketed to tens of thousands, half a million and eventually – with all reports painstakingly added together – to well over a million. Whether or not that was the true figure, of course, will never be known; it could have been half or just as easily it could have been double. Who was going to miss a mere million or two in a population of a hundred million? But we did get many first hand reports which, although they were not exactly pretty reading, were surely within the duties of newspapers to inform their respective readers.

On the road from Jakarta to Surabaya, which one young diplomat had driven in search of some of the truth, human heads were stuck on posts for miles along roads and others decorated bridges crossing streams and rivers. Children played a game of kicking more human heads around the open padangs of their villages, whilst adults had full time jobs pushing the bodies along the river past their villages to the next one, as the sheer weight of human flesh blocked the rivers and flooded the surrounding land.

From Sumatra – and this was first hand – I heard of the tiny and elderly woman who for years had stayed on in a small town looking after the dwindling interests of a Dutch trading firm. One of the senior members of the firm had at last been able to visit her from Jakarta, to find that the meek and quiet woman clerk was now the town leader, wearing pistols at her hips alongside vicious-looking knives. She had organized the rounding up of several thousand communists in her area alone and each morning took a number of them from their makeshift prison to have them tortured and finally put to death before large crowds of her followers. To be branded as communist anywhere throughout Indonesia meant certain death when the tide turned, and when it is considered that ten million at least

END OF A DREAM

were open communist party supporters it can only be a matter of conjecture that the eventual massacre must certainly take its place among the greater, or greatest, horrors of history.

For one man to attempt to project such a ghastly picture as an on-the-spot report was a sheer impossibility, but an opportunity did come to make a partial effort when news filtered through that there had been another shocking massacre, this time on the paradise island of Bali and only a few weeks before. Again it was a matter of asking no permission, but booking a seat on the internal flight which went to Bali three times a week. No particular department ever knew what the next was doing and it was a fairly safe bet that I would not be stopped. The only real query on an expedition such as that was whether or not the plane would be serviceable to take off and, once in the air, if it would stay there. However, the wing and the prayer were both working for me and I had one of the most intriguing flights in years, once I got used to the occasional cough from the starboard engine. There was the long string of volcanoes to see all the way eastwards and beyond Surabaya. Some of the volcanoes were smoking and rumbling as we flew within a few miles of them, and one of the crew came back into the cabin especially to point out the volcano which had erupted only a year or so before, killing hundreds in the valley below. Then, leaving the easternmost tip of Java, we swept low over the calm sea for two miles to the most lush and green island it is possible to imagine.

Bali had been the favourite retreat of President Sukarno. He had built a palace there, and more Japanese wartime reparations were being spent on modernizing the airfield and on the building of a huge hotel which were eventually to put Bali firmly on the map for any eastern tourist. Sukarno had not worked it out that way, it was just that he liked Bali more than any place in Java; perhaps he preferred the people to his lazy Moslem brothers of Java or Sumatra for, alone among the thousand islands of Indonesia, the Balinese were not Moslem – they were attached to an exclusive Hindu sect, similar in their worship and customs to the Hindus of India, but by no means the same.

Just two and a half million in all, the Balinese were a separate race from the rest of the Indonesia peoples; Indonesians from the mainland were not welcome and there was absolutely no intermarriage. Small and beautifully formed, the Balinese had always been known as courteous, easy-going and lovers of their music, poetry and intriguing, if sometimes frightening, national dancing. They worked hard and had had no inhibitions; it was only when I arrived in Bali in early 1966 that the younger women had taken to covering their breasts – a great pity, for women of forty or even fifty, who still adhered to the old tradition, shamelessly showed their perfectly shaped breasts, which would be the envy of many sixteen-year-olds in other parts of the world. But if they had been able to stay as a race apart, the Balinese had not been able to fight off the spread of communism, which gradually overran them from mainland Java and changed their whole communal existence. The communist teaching was that everything belonged only to its believers and would come to them naturally on the appointed day when the disbelievers would be overthrown; as September 30th drew near, large graves had already been dug by the communists around most of the Balinese villages and long lists had been drawn up of those who were to fill them. The day came and with it the news that the communist coup had failed all over Indonesia. Now it was the turn of the Balinese communists to wait in fear, but not a soul moved against them – not for the two months during which the massacres swept through nearby Java, and not until, so I was told, the Hindu gods could point out all those who must pay for their sins and gave the order to act against the transgressors.

Considering that it was little more than two months since the Balinese massacre ended in January 1966, there was little for a casual visitor to see which could give a picture of the ferocity which had swept the island for about eight weeks. Nature, with all its tropical swiftness, had done its work and the mass graves which now contained the communists were already overgrown. Not that there was any attempt to hide them. I told an official at the government tourist office in the capital of Denpasar exactly why I had come to Bali and he immediately supplied me with two of his senior guides to take me anywhere I wished. They were not warriors said twenty-three-year-old Oka, the senior and most intelligent guide, but had acted as the gods had told them and until every communist had been put to death. Now it was over and they must get back to the life their religion ordered.

I went to the remains of countless villages where only charred timbers poked into the sky like blackened fingers as a reminder that once had it been a workers' commune but had strayed away from its true gods to the communists. Ubud was one of the silent and overgrown remains that I saw: six hundred bodies were in the communal grave, Oka told me, and he went on to describe his part in this particular killing. 'Sometimes I helped hold them and sometimes I killed them with the sword,' said Oka, and he demonstrated how the victims had been hacked to pieces. No, Oka had never used a sword before, he admitted, 'But it was all very quick,' he said. 'The communists had to be finished.'

From others I heard the tales of those who had been hacked and left as dead, only to crawl away and to be put out of their misery when they were found again. Each night the village elders would have their conferences and decide was who to be killed next, whether people in their own village or everyone in a village nearby. But it was always the gods who pointed out the communists before any action was taken. It was insisted time and time again that the only rule that the Balinese made themselves was that every boy over the age of fifteen whose father had been a communist must be put to death too in order to avoid future hatred.

Were the Balinese happy now that the gods had been obeyed and their fear of the communists was in the past? No, the evil spirits of the communists were still inhabiting Bali and would continue to do so until the remains of every one of them, according to the Hindu religion, had been cremated and that was a task which, they sadly admitted, could take years and might never be completed. Many bodies had been washed down rivers into the sea and it was everywhere believed that pieces of human bodies had been found in fish. No longer did the fishing boats go to sea and no longer was fish eaten. Those who were still alive were surrounded by evil spirits from which they saw no escape. Again, how many those spirits may have been was impossible to estimate accurately; 'official' records, kept as a list by the military who moved in from Java, put the number of dead as around 150,000, but others insisted that more than twice that number had been named by the gods and put to death, whilst the lowest figure I was given was 75,000.

When my story arrived in London, it was queried from start to finish, because I had not quoted a witness by name and address for every incident I had mentioned or for every statement made. It was not history the office had been expecting or looking for; here was but another article to be weighed up among the rest for available space, but every word in it was not qualified by the magic words 'Mr Albert Smith, a postal worker of Bali, who was there at the time, said last night...'. Mr Albert Smith, however fictitious he might have been, would have meant that the reader could be expected to read the truth. As it appeared, my readers learned only a part of the truth for my article was hacked to pieces just as surely as the communists themselves had been.

There was much else to be seen in Bali, apart from graves, and it was one of those few occasions when I took time off to be a sort of tourist. I would say that some of the finest wood carving in the world is created on the island and, still with Oka as my guide, I was able to find a few pieces of the most exquisite workmanship when we toured the mountain villages. In Denpasar the carvings filled the street-side stalls in their thousands; Hindu gods and goddesses mounted on fantastically ornate eagles, traditional Balinese women with headdresses which alone could have taken one man three or four months to carve, fishes and birds carved by young beginners and all being sold in the same currency, the only currency Bali had known for years, now devalued a hundred or more times. This was not the type of workmanship I was seeking; the figures I acquired had been fashioned by Bali's master carver and I watched him squatting in his workshop, holding the wood with his toes as he chipped away at it. They had kept much of the tradition, but were embodied in modern grace. Each one had taken six months or more to make and the only reason that any of the specimens were still available is that tourists and art seekers had not been seen on Bali for two years or more. In rupiahs the prices were astronomical compared with those for the higher class carvings, but the outside world had not yet caught up with Bali and, at the rate of exchange I was enjoying, none of the carvings cost me more than a few dollars each. I regard them as being among the few bargains which ever came my way. It was not long before the master carver was discovered by an American art expert, who sponsored him and arranged exhibitions of work in New York. Carvings such as mine now sell for thousands of dollars and they are still rare but, more important than the price I paid, I have the satisfaction that I went to Bali, to the carver, to find my treasures.

In some villages every man one met was an artist – of sorts – and they were all anxious to show their work to this rarest of all creatures, a visitor. A dozen, or two dozen times, I was stopped in village streets and, as they were opened up, it gradually became apparent that every other house or building had its large studio where two, three or more artists painted and exhibited their work. Unusual, I had to admit, and every canvas had its stamp peculiar to Bali and a style which could be found nowhere else. Mostly they were of traditional Bali scenes, depicting the Balinese at their communal and agricultural tasks, and tiny figures in every imaginable pose and attitude decorated the paintings by the dozens and sometimes hundreds. But it was clear to see that, although some of the paintings had been done by the few competent and stylish artists of whom Bali could be proud, their copies abounded in every studio, 99 per cent of which had been set up by mostly mediocre 'pupils'.

Of all the Balinese dancing I saw, the Monkey Dance left an impression which, even now, can send a slight shudder through my bones as I remember that evening, the blackness broken only by an occasional and tiny oil flare, when at any moment I imagined I would be disappearing among the Hindu gods or devils, never to return. Perhaps twice a week, if one could discover where, a village would present one of the many ritual dances, and on this particular evening I was driven twenty miles or so into the hills north of Denpasar. The village was far from any main road and approached by narrow lanes, and I could vaguely make out the wood and palmleaf huts as I was led to a group of villagers with whom I squatted on a long and rough bench. Gentle people, that was their history, but as the

STORY UNUSED

night wore on I was plainly watching the ever heightening frenzy, and of that I was certain, which had turned these Balinese into maniacal killers and made them use the swords and krisses on human flesh when, until that time, they had known no other use but ceremonial. The krisses appeared this night and I saw their glint as the pale flames from the flares sometimes penetrated the forbidding darkness. About a hundred village men, each wearing a hideous mask, formed a circling mass in the dusty village centre and their prostrate figures swayed in frightening and intricate rhythms as they half rose or sank back again to the exultations of two others, equally hideously masked, bangled and painted, who vied with each other in their attempts to control the minds of the mass. The writhing mass were the monkeys, one of the two fighting over them was an evil spirit, whilst the other was a Hindu god, determined that his charges would not be taken from him. For two hours the performance was fantastic and at times petrifying, as the monkeys howled, screeched and moaned to the hoarse screaming of the evil spirit or the Hindu God. I wanted to move, to get as far away as possible, for I felt that the frenzy was getting completely out of hand; but so transfixed had I become that to flee, I was sure, would only be into the arms of equally or more terrifying creatures.

The early sunshine and the waves lapping the nearby beach were welcome sights and sounds, although I rather wished that my last evening in Bali had been, if not gay, for that would have been impossible, somewhat brighter. A taxi had called to take me to the Denpasar airport for the mid-day plane to Jakarta. As things worked out, I would have had ample time for another tour of the island; with two other passengers I fumed the hours away until the plane eventually appeared at five that afternoon. The pilot had been on one of his usual shopping expeditions, it was explained, and the fact that six hours had already been completely wasted was completely beside the point. The plane had been dropping in on all the islands within a radius of a hundred miles – collecting eggs. The pilot – and I presume the rest of the crew got its cut – bought the eggs for the local price of one rupiah each and sold them in Jakarta at fifty rupiahs each. Good business, and it was never explained who paid for the high octane fuel which had been such a necessary part of the operation. But that was Indonesia.

Summer 1966 and still the shadow of Sukarno hung over Indonesia, damning any effort to patch up quarrels with the outside world or to entice rich foreigners into making investments. The students continued to demonstrate, but the generals were still scared to back their demands to the hilt and Sukarno's voice boomed out, declaring that he was still the boss, every time anyone made a move which could have made it appear that he was not. Only one man appeared to have no fear of the President, Adam Malik, the newly appointed Foreign Minister; but even he could not keep Sukarno completely under control unless he had the backing of the generals. Malik was a most amiable and friendly man and we became firm friends. His audacity when it came to dealing with Sukarno knew no bounds; and if Sukarno fumed, Malik just turned on one of his bland smiles. One day Malik told me that he was going ahead with arrangements for peace talks with Malaysia, and when I asked what the President's views might be on that, Malik just grinned and said, 'He won't know anything about them until they are concluded – and I won't allow Sukarno and the Tunku to meet. That would ruin everything before we started.'

Malik said much more that day, and if it was going to cause a furore here and there he was the last one to care. British bases were no problem, he said, provided there were guarantees that they would not be used against Indonesia, and then the Foreign Minister had a few pointed words to say about America. From talks with the American Ambassador I knew that Washington was well pleased with the turn of events, but I had no idea that America was already acting in her usual blatant and naive ways until Malik told me: 'The United States is being stupid; she's pressing too hard with promises to solve all Indonesia's financial difficulties, but she is thinking only of her own world strategy and sees us as part of it in Southeast Asia.'

To begin with, it was going to cost $200,000,000 to pay off the most pressing creditors; was America still under the impression that she could buy anything with money? Said Malik: 'Of course we want a united Asia, but not the American pattern, just because we accept American aid. We would like to keep some sort of independance and would rather deal with several countries, such as European ones, than make the mistakes of the past when we relied completely on America, Russia and then communist China.'

Strong words, to be sure, and they were the cause of many red American faces around Jakarta when they came back, requoted from my article by the news agencies. And there was an explosion, of course, from Sukarno, who sent me a message that he wanted to see me at his palace; but Adam Malik made sure that, this time, Sukarno was not going to put a spanner into the works. Sukarno was able to say little more than, 'I am still the President and I rule this country,' when Malik and General Suharto arrived to announce that the Government had decided, as from that day, that the President would be allowed to make no further statements to the press. I still wonder if Malik had timed it for my benefit; certainly in no other way would I have had the opportunity of witnessing such a scene.

Sukarno went beserk; he shouted and raged and waved his fists as though, at any moment, he were about to attack the men who had virtually told him that he was now under their orders. The General must have anticipated the blows, for he quickly backed behind the tiny Malik. Sukarno's fist swept within inches of the Foreign Minister's face, but Malik did not budge an inch and continued smiling until the President swept from the room and slammed the door. It is in moments such as these that I have deplored my lack of knowledge of so many languages, although to have learned the tongues of every country I was obliged to visit would have been a life's work in itself.

'What was all that about?', I asked Malik, and he told me: 'He was rather annoyed to discover that he is no longer the boss, but someone had to tell him.' I was probably the last journalist to be received by Sukarno, but this restriction by no means meant that he was finished. A peace treaty with Malaysia was signed by Malik three months later in August 1966, and Sukarno had no part in it; but it was still another six months before he agreed to hand over complete presidential powers and capitulated to General Suharto – and even then there were grave fears that there would be a second massacre throughout the country, so many were Sukarno's supporters still.

END OF A DREAM

If little else can be said in Sukarno's favour, he had a certain way with women, and his two favourite wives, although they never met, agreed to share him and comfort him right through those last days when he was being cut down to nothing. I never met Wife No. 2; Sukarno kept her and their grown up family forty miles from Jakarta at his Bogor palace, and it was to her, and a house provided for him in the palace grounds, that the ex-president eventually went to settle in enforced exile. Sari Dewi, the Japanese fourth wife, whom Sukarno had married in Tokyo, where he found her as a nineteen-year-old geisha girl in the Ginza bar district, I did meet and it was a most interesting and enlightening few hours. Saturday, but not before eleven o'clock, she had told me on the telephone and then, quite openly, that from that hour each Saturday she was competely free to receive friends, as her husband left to spend the weekend until Monday morning at Bogor with his Wife No. 2.

It was July 1966; the President was not having an easy time by any means, and Sari Dewi was the target in a campaign which had gathered a lot of strength among the higher-class Indonesian wives. It was another of those inexplicable things that the demonstrations had not already forced her out of Indonesia; for her house was not more than a couple of miles along the American-built highway and another mile of quiet country road, and I did not see one soldier or guard who might have stopped an unwelcome visitor. A high wall surrounded the sprawling pink bungalow and its grounds, and a servant admitted me through a heavy steel gate. But I am sure these would not have deterred a mob of students if they had decided to act. Maybe it was because she was expecting a baby that the Japanese woman was surrounded with an automatic safety barrier. But I could not be sure, nobody could ever be sure of anything in Indonesia.

The long drive was lined with young fir trees and the well-kept lawns, stretching around a fishpond and on to the further and palm-lined fringes, were ablaze with the inevitable hibiscus and bougainvillaea. From the terrace a servant girl invited me inside and then for fifteen minutes whilst I awaited the appearance of Sari Dewi I was able to wander discreetly on a little study tour of how a world-renowned President lived domestically with his five-days-a-week wife. Every floor was of the best marble and the heavy doors were the most ornately carved to be found anywhere in Indonesia. Furniture was in abundance and enough to accommodate large numbers of guests in individual comfort, and much of it – I cannot imagine that they were originals – was made up of copies of European period pieces. But any sense of arrangement was completely lacking, and in true oriental and middle-class style the chairs and sofas were pushed back against walls in long and uniform lines. The treasures in the house most probably amounted to untold wealth, but a cursory glance around would hardly have revealed them among the Japanese and other eastern bric-a-brac. Priceless pieces of jade and porcelain lay side by side with worthless and rubbishy souvenirs, heaped together in great glass-fronted cabinets when just three or four of them, tastefully arranged, would have graced the finest museums in the world.

Exquisite pieces of Ming china I discovered, too, but only after a search of cabinets where it lay, roughly stacked with modern Noritake which, perhaps, had come as wedding presents from Sari Dewi's Japanese family and friends. Beautifully worked silver and gold *objets d'art*, and heavier statues and caskets which, from their inscriptions, had been presented by a dozen or more foreign governments or potentates; it was all there, but hidden in a setting which was manifestly dull, uninteresting and devoid of flair. In the sitting room a photo portrait of Sukarno, suitable addressed to his bride, stood on the grand piano and beside it, in a gaudy frame, was the wedding-day picture of Sukarno and Sari Dewi, sitting with her proud parents. The two men wore lounge suits and Sari Dewi and her mother looked neat and ordinary in western dresses; there had been no flags, bunting, carriages and horses or cheering crowds that Tokyo day in 1959; but then I presume that would have begun to pall, even for a President, when he was but adding one more to his array of spouses, and that particular one a foreigner and a third of his age.

Near the photographs stood a round and gilded, empty birdcage, its tiny door flapping open. I was studying it and wondering at what might be its significance, when she arrived and ended my inquisitive meandering. I was with Sari Dewi, but a woman, I was quickly to discover, who bore not the slightest resemblance to the columnists' accounts. They had all, without exception, been mesmerized by a single factor: that she had once been a geisha girl.

Although it appears to escape many a western writer, the word can imply a host of desirable attributes and, if she had not acquired them all, Sari Dewi possessed several of the best. She was as delightful a hostess as she was beautiful, as natural and unaffected as her conversation was gay but, when necessary, perfectly serious; and her occasional excuse for imperfect English in no way veiled the fact that here was an outstanding and intelligent woman. Petite and slim, her pregnancy hardly noticeable, she lounged easily on her favourite sofa and assured me that the rest of the day, if need be, she could devote to me.

'My husband,' she said and never did she refer to Sukarno in any other way, 'left two hours ago and will not return until Monday. It is always like that, but it does give me time to relax and see my friends.' Many had been among the diplomatic staff of the Japanese Embassy and their wives, but did Madame Dewi not see less of them since her husband's position had changed and with it had come the end of possible contracts, in some of which she had taken personal interest? 'It is true,' said Sari Dewi; 'I do not see my friends so much now, but these are difficult times'. Behind the delicately painted face and undisturbed poise lay hard reasoning. 'This change had to come sometime,' she said; 'the people of Indonesia are tired.'

She still preserved an intense loyalty to Sukarno, but as we wandered through the gardens Sari Dewi told me of the weeks and months of daily discussions she had had with her husband. 'It has been politics, politics all the time and we have discussed everything together,' she told me. 'My job is to comfort and calm my husband, but we have had many arguments. There have been several things on which I could not agree.'

What sort of life had they had together and what ranting and shouting had gone on behind these pink and stuccoed walls, for it appeared that Sari Dewi had opposed practically all that Sukarno had done to bring his country to ruin?

'I disagreed over confrontation with Malaysia,' she said; 'it was such a waste of money and manpower when there was so much to be done inside the country. It is so rich, but we import rice, eat it and still have to pay the credits; we import steel, but there is so much here. How much better if we had imported the machinery and produced what we need ourselves?' This was sound reasoning, but the practical brain of Sari Dewi had overlooked the most important factor in the equation: someone had to make the Indonesian work to make it all possible. What a Madame Pompadour she might have been if she had been dealing with a lesser man than Sukarno.

'I didn't agree with his economic policies and I didn't agree with Indonesia leaving the United Nations,' she said. 'We had many arguments on all these things.' Until a few days before Sukarno had been fighting everyone in sight to keep what was left of his flagging power. 'But now,' said Sari Dewi, 'he has taken my advice and decided to accept the decisions of the people and remain quiet.' But for how long could she persuade her husband to follow this advice? We were back in the sitting room and Sari Dewi looked up at me from the sofa. 'I think this time he will listen,' she said, 'it is better if he does. But the politicians and the generals should show some commonsense too.'

I will never know if it was entirely because of her influence, but we heard little from Sukarno after that day. It was said that Sari Dewi could talk to the generals when Sukarno could not, and that she arranged the deal which saved Sukarno's life. An astute woman, well endowed with feminine charm and no less endowed with the financial wherewithal which enabled her to live most comfortably when her reign as fourth wife of a President was over. She noticed that I was looking at the empty birdcage and she smiled as she said, 'I think I know what is on your mind, but it means nothing really – I shall stay here for a long time.' If several months was her interpretation of a lengthy period, then Sari Dewi must be excused for that remark. She agreed with my suggestion that perhaps the cage would lose much of its significance if the tiny door was closed and there was something pointed, if not particularly inscrutable, in her reply as she said, 'I like it that way, so I leave it that way.'

Ratno Sari Dewi – Sukarno's name for her that meant Goddess of the Essence of Jewels – left Indonesia, never to return, three months before her daughter Kartika was born.

Chapter 11

HONG KONG

The cigarette and cigar smoke hung in heavy layers, and from the other side of the haze electric guitars crashed out the latest pop music. Our negotiations did not go far enough for me to discover her name, but I had just been mistaken for a 'businessman' and one of Suzie Wong's head girls was anxious to talk business if I were interested in making a fortune. Naturally, I was; but money in the sums being discussed had always and somehow eluded me; she had $150,000, the Chinese woman told me, and if I would put up a like sum she would turn our $300,000 into $900,000 in six months. In Hong Kong dollars, for that is where the discussion was taking place, this was no confidence trick in early 1966. Suzie's girl had been in the night club business long enough to have fifty or so girls who were willing to follow her, she had the club premises and the 'house' arranged and all that was needed was the hard cash to get the operation going.

I was sitting in Suzie Wong's own night club in the neon-bedecked and closely packed Wan Chai district and it was simple to see, around me, that the financial promises were more than a distinct possibility. Eighty or more American servicemen were sharing the company of Suzies' fifty girls, with drinks which had trebled in price in as many months, and another $100 went to the house later in the evening when, inevitably, the girls were 'taken out'. And in every nearby street premises were changing hands at vastly inflated prices as the bars and clubs opened up at the rate of another three or four a week.

Like Bangkok, the British colony of Hong Kong was cashing in on the boom which, the previous year, had sent it 160,000 GIs on a few days 'rest and recuperation' from the war in Vietnam, and this was but the beginning. Each American spent an average of 180 of his own particular brand of dollars – the greenback being six times or more the value of the Hong Kong dollar – and if the overnight tailors took some of this for a couple of lightweight suits per man and some went on a comfortable hotel room, there was still plenty to assure Suzie Wong and her friends that they would not be having a bleak old age.

Not that this worried Mao Tse Tung either way, and, of course, out of Hong Kong's teeming four millions the masses were not making a cent from the dollar-loaded Yanks. Mao just saw their presence as an excuse to launch a propoganda offensive against Hong Kong, alleging that she was allowing America to use the colony as a springboard for a future attack against mainland China. He was wrong, and most probably knew it, but with such weapons of war lying around the harbour as the 85,000-ton nuclear aircraft carrier *Enterprise*, plus half a dozen other warships, including guided missile frigates, the rumblings and threats from Peking all played their part, however small or large, in the communist led and mounting criticism against the Hong Kong government which finally exploded in dangerous and bloody rioting, shaking the colony to its roots a year later.

Until then Hong Kong had been the haven of so many correspondents who, like the GIs could get a break from Saigon and the battlefields. With my home in Singapore I did not look on it in quite the same way, and I flew westwards from insanity when the others flew in the opposite direction for their sojourns in peace and comparative quietness. But Hong Kong I always regarded with pleasant anticipation if my plane was heading that way. There was something spectacular about it all which began with the plane coming down between towering peaks and skimming skyscrapers to land on the runway, man made and jutting out across the harbour crammed with craft of every shape and size. Then came the rush of traffic through Kowloon, where every visit found at least one huge new block of workers' flats and perhaps a new school to go with it. The crush on the ferry which ran at clockwork intervals to Hong Kong island – a rise of one penny in the first class fare finally triggered off the rioting – and the lushness and plushness of the Mandarin Hotel, which offered the best in western service but considerably polished up with an oriental veneer. It was always the Mandarin, and an hour in the bar for drinks before lunch or dinner was a guarantee that one knew practically everyone who was in town and who was not from the fast moving international set which peddled business, politics, steel or guns from Cairo to Sydney. We did take over the top floor of the Hilton as the Hong Kong Press Club, but that was for our own specialized gossip, where any but journalists would have found themselves distinctly on the fringe.

Apart from Japan, nowhere in the Far East did life move so fast and with such bustle as in Hong Kong, and nowhere else did it appear that so many people could live, exist and work in such a cramped space. It was bursting at the seams and its industries overflowed into the new territories on the mainland, which surely will cause one of the larger problems if and when that portion of the colony is handed back to China when its lease expires at the end of the century. But Hong Kong goes on, as though that day will never come. On one of my earlier visits the colony was suffering from its worst water shortage ever, but by the following year it had sailed into one of the most ambitious conservation schemes imaginable – on the land which reverts to China. From a distance, and when I first saw it, ants could have been swarming over their own hill; but actually the hill was a small mountain and the ants were hundreds of trucks climbing it, filling themselves with part of it, rushing off and rushing back to repeat the process all over again. By the thousands of tons the earth and rock were dumped in the sea to form a permanent wall around a large and natural harbour. The harbour was then drained of its seawater and Hong Kong had a giant reservoir, but had lost a mountain. On each visit I made my pilgrimage to see how much of the mountain was left, until it finally disappeared completely. For some reason modern progress was proving more fascinating than the centuries-old, walled Chinese villages in the new territories, or the mountains still standing along the eighteen miles of frontier which separated Hong Kong from a revolution where all the rules are written down in a little red book.

Hong Kong was a shopper's dream, whether one was seeking eastern treasures or modern fashion, but strangely for a British colony, the most difficult thing to find was a British label on the goods which filled the showrooms and shops – the Japanese, the Germans, the Italians, the French and every other manufacturing nation had grabbed the lion's share of the trade. So much so that someone at the Board of Trade in London decided early in 1966 that these nasty foreigners had gone too far and Hong Kong's four million should be told that Britain, too, could make shoes, clothes, machinery and cars, and a few other things as well. So it came to pass that a British Week was arranged and an office was set up to prepare the colony for all the British goodies which would be on display. Fashion was to be one of the main lines in the drive, the French and Italians were having it all their own way and Miss Hong Kong was spending a lot on western clothes.

I do not know quite how I got involved or why I recount the tale, unless it is to illustrate how Whitehall can win friends and influence people – the main object if the British Week were to be a success. Things started off well at a press conference and the local Chinese reporters made copious notes when it was revealed that the Queen's sister, Princess Margaret, would be flying all the way from London with her husband to open the big event. They listened carefully and accepted all the photographic handouts on electrical equipment, office chairs, machine tools, cutlery and cricket bats which were to be among the exhibits, but a special interest was aroused when the pictures of fashions, and the British girls who would be modelling them, were passed around for all to admire.

The great moment had come; if photographs of printing machinery could not be got into the Hong Kong press, no editor would be able to resist awarding the space to a gorgeous blonde in slinky culottes. Headlines, of course, were a little too much to expect, but we got them, in every newspaper next day. 'Why,' came the simple question, 'why do you bring models from Britain to show clothes which you hope will be worn by Hong Kong women when there are so many beautiful Chinese models already here?' Always ready with an answer, it came as quick as a flash; 'Good God,' were the words used, 'We can't use Chinese girls – they're all bow-legged.'

Whatever the love-hate relationship may be between Hong Kong and the Chinese mainland, and whatever the threats which emanate from Big Brother from time to time, Peking has always found it rather rewarding that the colonial state has continued to exist and Hong Kong has provided her with her chief source of foreign exchange. An admirable arrangement for both sides, it has always appeared, but I did query the fact that Hong Kong was allowing itself to become a shop window for the mainland and, what was infinitely more dangerous, for her politics. It was something which crept up on the colony, insidiously and apparently unnoticed from the inside. One had to be an irregular visitor to see that now there were six cinemas showing communist Chinese films, whereas there had been only one eighteen months before, or that one could now buy a dozen China-produced magazines when once they had been impossible to find. In the city centre where sites were invaluable communist bookshops opened up, and premises were acquired large enough to house the communist Chinese emporiums, huge departmental stores which undercut the prices of any and every Hong Kong store. It is little wonder that the Hong Kong Chinese flocked to the emporiums; shirts, shoes, blankets, tinned food delicacies that came only from their homeland, and practically everything else they needed for their normal daily living, could be had for half the normal price or less – all subsidized by Peking and served by assistants carefully chosen by the communist party. First it was one emporium which opened quietly, then a second and a third and each one was beseiged by grateful shoppers.

Who could blame them if they imagined that life on the mainland could not be so bad if there were such goods in such abundance and at such prices? It was clever propaganda, for the emporiums in Hong Kong – and later Singapore – were getting every priority from the mainland. They were so much more subtle than the films being shown in the communist-owned cinemas or the communist newspapers which were now being printed in Hong Kong on communist presses. And not only were they selling everyday needs; exquisite jade ornaments, jewellery, sewing machines and perfectly made musical instruments from trumpets and accordions to grand pianos were on display to ensnare the higher class shopper.

I wrote of the growing infiltration and of the danger it could become; I wrote of the ever increasing strength of the communists in Hong Kong, and although the inevitable explosion which came was eventually brought under control, I cannot help but feel that it all might have been avoided if the Hong Kong government had taken more notice of the dangers which grew around it. I do not remember that much of what I wrote found its way into print, but then, that is the way with most newspapers: Hong Kong is a long way from London, too far to be of any interest unless there is real trouble, preferably with a few deaths to brighten up the headlines.

It was all so different when America blacklisted three British ships for trading with North Vietnam and it was found that they were owned by companies registered in Hong Kong. Now here was a dangerous state of affairs, an international incident in the making, suggested the cables from London. The owners must be traced and exposed. Urgent, urgently, urgentest – London took the word to its limit in impressing on me the speed with which I should get from Singapore to Hong Kong. One would have thought that I, and I alone, could avert an imminent declaration of war by Washington on Britain, something it had not seen fit to make clear when it came to dealing with North Vietnam. I trust the British Government was duly appreciative of my efforts, for my editor very nearly was not, and if the circumstances had not been quite so ludicrous they could easily have led to a rapid severance of all connections between us.

The first of the three ships, the 7,000-ton *Wakasa Bay*, I traced easily enough to its agents and they professed to have no control over its movements. That was a matter for the owners, they said. Now that might have been straightforward enough, but for my unbelieving journalist's mind, and my suspicion that I was not being told all was confirmed when I checked the company registers to find that two of the Chinese directors of the agents were also directors of the owners of the *Wakasa Bay*. That was significant enough, to be sure, but my diggings went deeper, until I had confirmed that the same two men were on the board of other comapnies which owned another fifty ships, fifteen of them tankers, some of which were on charter to American oil companies. It was all a bit too much for the directors when I placed my discoveries firmly on their office table; although the *Wakasa Bay* was chartered to Japan, they would order it immediately not to go to North Vietnam and, moreover, would make sure that all future charters had clauses in the contracts forbidding the ship for this use.

The agents of the second ship assured me they would follow suit when the present charter contract soon expired, but I met with stony looks and even stonier replies when I approached the agents of the third ship, the *Shienfoon*. They were communist Chinese, operating from Hong Kong, and the *Shienfoon* was chartered direct to the Chinese Government. With her British master and British first and second engineers, she was plying regularly between Chinese ports. North Korea and North Vietnam and it was really none of my business anyway, I was told. However, success there had been, although I had not been looking for it in that particular way, and especially with the *Wakasa Bay*. Off went my cabled despatch to London with all the details of how the *Wakasa Bay* had been suddenly turned round at sea as she had left Whonpoa, the Chinese port thirty miles west of Hong Kong, when she had been bound for Campha in North Vietnam. Captain Thomas Brown, the *Wakasa Bay's* master, would have been on the bridge when the signal came and I could almost hear him bellowing the order, 'Hundred and eight degrees to port, we're heading back to Japan.' In the star-covered South China Sea that one manoeuvre would prove to America that little brother England was with her all the way. It had drama, it had excitement, it had everything an editor could wish for; all I had to do now was to buy myself the most expensive meal in Hong Kong, on the expense account, whilst I confidently awaited the cabled congratulations on my world shattering story.

The cable was there when I got back to the Mandarin Hotel and the concierge looked up startled when I opened it and laughed out loud. '*Decided unuse your story unless you can supply immediately full details of Captain Thomas Brown comma his age comma his home address etcetera proving he exists,*' the cable read.

It was all too simple. Thomas Brown could not possibly be a living person; the name was too ordinary; he had been nothing more than a figment of my imagination, the first name to enter my head. The London office, hardened to all these tricks of the trade, did not believe me or my story for one moment. It was one of those moments to send a reply in terms from which one could never retreat, or enjoy immensely, as had been my spontaneous reaction. I cabled Captain Thomas Brown's family address in Glasgow, the date on which he was born in 1921, his height, details of his service on the *Wakasa Bay*, when he was promoted to master, and the colour of his eyes. I did a similar rundown on the chief officer, the chief engineer and second engineer, all British, on information taken from the files I had been shown at the agents' office. And the message went at the most urgent and expensive cable rates, just to remind London I was always at their service.

Grudgingly, the story was given space in the newspaper, but oddly it was no longer regarded in the news category which warranted the bold and eye-catching headlines it might have automatically commanded if Thomas Brown had been blessed with any other name. That worthy seaman will remain fond in my memory for many a long day, for whilst making enquiries about the *Wakasa Bay* I was introduced to the merchant navy officers' club on Hong Kong waterfront and from there learned more of the boats and ships and those who sail them into and out of Hong Kong than I might have gathered in weeks of wandering alone. The big ships, the medium sized ships, and the junks which plied between mainland China and the colony, filled with vegetables, rice, canned Chinese foods or meat, still alive and standing on four legs–perhaps the most fascinating of all.

Side by side, and with hardly an inch between them, they lined the quaysides. Whole families lived aboard the junks, for these were their homes from the day they were born until the day they die. Their dogs and their cats were just as much a part of the scene as the washing fluttering in the breeze on lines across the decks, or the entrancing smells of cooking which blended, one junk to another, as they wafted ashore. This was Hong Kong, the same as it has always been since the days when the British first went there, and the same as it will be until they leave.

Chapter 12

THE LAST PLEA

The beach shelter was roughly made: just a roof of palm leaves supported by bamboos, but sufficient to keep off the scorching rays of the sun which, for some reason, always appeared to be more unbearable in southern Thailand than anywhere else. Cold beer in cans was on the wooden table. The American Air Force officer seemed to be reasonably well pleased. 'Reckon we can make quite a place of this,' he said. 'Clubhouse over there, some boats, beach chairs, parasols – yeah.' The three other officers nodded in approval and one of them voiced what, inevitably, would have been under discussion sooner or later: 'A few little Siamese girls running around in bikinis and we'll have a home from home,' said he.

Behind us was growing a vast new airbase with the longest runways in the Far East and in front of us, as we looked out to sea, was the Gulf of Siam. This was Sattahip in the early summer of 1966, and a couple of miles away another 'biggest' was under construction, a deep water harbour at Utapo, through which would pour the supplies of bombs, materials and oil for seven fighter-bomber bases, almost all of them now in operation. Thailand had become America's main airbase for the war against North Vietnam, but officially no raids were made from Thai soil and the American bases did not exist. It was all a secret, particularly from Ho Chi Min and Mao Tse Tung.

Ridiculous, of course. No trained spies were needed to inform Hanoi and Peking what was going on and I am perfectly certain they did not have to wait for the publication of my revealing articles before deciding to increase the activities of the communist guerillas in the already fomenting areas of north-east Thailand near the Laotian borders. Thailand had been sucked into the conflict and the fact that she had signed no agreement with America did not hide the fact that she had made her virtual entry into the Vietnam war. Not even the protests by Foreign Minister Thanat Khoman, when I talked to him in Bangkok, had sounded very convincing. Neither country considered it had violated international law, said Khoman, as no war had been declared on North Vietnam.

For a week I had been on a tour of Thailand and the picture had pieced together without much difficulty. Eleven squadrons of US 13th Air Force Thunderchief and Phantom jets – or some 200 aircraft – formed the main force to pound North Vietnam, and hundreds more transport, reconnaissance, radar, communications and every other type of warplane had taken over what were still being referred to as 'Thai Air Force' bases. From Sattahip Boeing 720 airtankers staggered into the air at thirty-minute intervals for twenty-four-hour stints on stations over and around North Vietnam, acting as mothers to the fighter-bombers and suckling them whenever they were thirsty for fuel. And when the second runway at Sattahip was completed the giant B52 bombers were to move over from Guam, so that they could drop three or four times the weight of bombs than had been possible so far.

If nothing else, the Americans had moved fast once it had all been decided, but the Thais were not too far behind when it came to providing the 'comforts' for the 30,000 air force men who moved in with the planes within a matter of weeks. Sleepy towns in central and east Thailand saw their first changes in centuries as the garish bars and clubs sprouted overnight and an entirely new style of woman appeared, clothed in skirts and dresses and hair arranged as it had never been seen before. Outside Sattahip a whole new town was in the process of being built, but from the typical signs and names above the teak structures I saw at every turn, I could only decide that nine-tenths of it was designed solely for pleasure. At the restaurant where I lunched a large notice clearly suggested the shape of things to come: 'Dollars only accepted here.' Thailand, a country which had prided itself that it had never been occupied by a foreign power, was about to discover what occupation meant.

Escalation, and in American language that meant in only one direction – upwards. America was still not fully aware of what she had been led into and it was around this time that the findings of the statisticians working for the Pentagon were telling her young just how lucky there were. 'The war in Vietnam is building a new type of youth,' the experts had decided. 'They are becoming filled with a sense of duty and patriotism and there is little doubt the war will do much to reduce juvenile delinquency in America.' Just to instil that extra bit of pride in the hearts of the draftees, a letter from a Milwaukee mother to President Johnson was issued to the newspapers: 'I pray that when my little boys grow up they will be able to fight for the American cause in Vietnam,' she wrote.

Noble sentiments for Milwaukee, but I doubt if they would have been received with much enthusiasm in the streets of Saigon, filled with tear-gas, to which I returned that May morning. Apart from one brief visit, I had been absent from the Vietnam scene for ten months, as Washington reports took precedence over all others. But now, as the headlines would put it, the country was aflame; two million Buddhists had risen in a rebellion which was to prove the last cry for peace. In Da Nang government troops, who backed the Buddhists, had revolted, and farther north in the Buddhist stronghold of Hue another 400 troops had followed suit and put aside their arms. Of all the riots and revolts of the past, none had reached the dimensions of this. I sensed it as I drove into the city from Tan Son Nhut. But then, and even before I reached the hotel, I was involved and the first nauseating wafts of tear-gas had set my eyes streaming.

It filled the centre of Saigon and drifted with the breeze, emptying shops, offices and houses. Everywhere people in their thousands rushed this way or that, trying to escape it, but as soon as one area became clear masked paratroops were lobbing more gas canisters along the broad boulevards at the Buddhists —monks and nuns – who formed in chanting columns. As the troops swept into action, clubs flailing, the Buddhists stood their ground, but only until the tear-gas forced them to flee. In twenty minutes they had somehow formed again in another and gas-free area; sirens wailed, the troops came, the gas came and the clubbing began all over again. It was still going on as dusk approached and the tropical rains came, mercifully, to wash the hate-polluted air clean. By then the barbed wire barricades were up, cordoning off government offices, the President's palace, the American Embassy and every American headquarters – until the morning when the Buddhists swept them away and Saigon was filled with gas once again.

Back and forth across the capital for another three days the battles went, but battles in which only one side carried arms. Some time the weight of guns, clubs, barbed wire and gas had to defeat the chanted peace slogans. On the fourth night the Buddhists were bottled up in their main pagoda, but only when every surrounding street resembled a battlefield.

A mile and a half from the centre of Saigon the Vien Hoa Dao pagoda lay on the city limits, its temple, administrative offices and quarters for the high priests surrounded by rough but extensive ground leading up to the big gated entrance. On that side of the wide road it stood practically alone, as though plans to develop a new suburb had come to a sudden halt, and barbed wire topped the fences which formed its perimeter. On the other side of the road the thickly clustered houses marked the edge of the populated area, and it was in the cafés of the narrow streets which forked inwards from here that we made our headquarters for the siege now begun. From somewhere two photographers had acquired gasmasks and by now most of the press corps were equipped with eye-protecting shields at least. In front of the pagoda gates the troops had erected the deep wired barricades and at every few yards they waited in their trucks ready to force back any monk or nun who tried to enter or leave; to cut off the Buddhists from all outside contact was the main objective, and especially to sever their links with Tri Quang, the Buddhist leader who was directing the whole rebellion from Hue.

For a day and a night all was quiet and only food was allowed to be passed through the pagoda gates. On the open ground the monks squatted in meditation and prayer, but if there was a calm it was but a prelude to an even bigger storm to come. Two Buddhist nuns burned themselves to death in a Hue pagoda and, as if by magic, the signal reached the high priests in the Vien Hoa Dao, 400 miles away in Saigon. As though a giant bugle had sounded, the Buddhist forces rose in every corner of the capital and 10,000 of them were on the march. We saw the rescuing column as it suddenly turned into the road beside the pagoda and we saw the monks from inside rush the barricades. Then there were bodies in all directions, splashes of saffron and crimson splashes of blood; batons and rifle butts, single shots and the frightening rattle of a machine gun – until the tear-gas cleared the streets, monks were dragged or brutally forced back through the pagoda gates and their would-be liberators had either fled or were on the way to jail by the truckload.

Why is it that one flaming suicide can electrify the world, but the slaughter of hundreds and thousands of troops and innocent civilians in war should be regarded as commonplace? But here were two Buddhists who had offered themselves up in the supreme sacrifice, and they were women. The shock was tenfold and their superiors lost no time in issuing the texts of letters placed by one of them beside her self-chosen pyre. She called on the Government to stop persecuting Buddhists, 'before the country goes up in flames'. The second letter was addressed to United Nations Secretary-General, U Thant, demanding that America withdraw from Vietnam. The letter to President Johnson was in similar terms, but Tri Quang quickly added to the tension with an outright condemnation of Johnson by blaming him for the death of the nun. Furthermore, Tri Quang threatened, two more monks or nuns would burn themselves on the morrow, and three on the following day if Johnson's support for the Saigon Government was not withdrawn by the coming dawn. Nobody except, perhaps, some of the Buddhist hierarchy, expected Johnson to oblige and so the dawn was awaited with trepidation. To contemplate two more holy bodies enveloped in flames was frightening, and in Saigon streets that night I saw the people kneeling in prayer for the souls which had not yet left for eternal peace.

Who the martyrs would be or where the self-sacrifices were to take place, nobody could foresee and this, I am sure, was the impact on which the Buddhist leaders were relying. The drama could suddenly and personally hit any town or village still under Government control. Any action or reaction in Saigon was most likely to come from inside or around the pagoda, again beseiged, and from early morning the pressmen were there in their dozens. The Government, too, had reacted with the same anticipation, but this time they were not to be caught unawares, as they had been the previous day. Every approach had been barricaded and troops stood behind the barbed wire, gasmasks on and ready for any move. Inside the pagoda grounds the monks moved quietly about their business and made no attempt to approach the gates, and outside, apart from the military, the only ones allowed on the road were those who lived there.

Hour after hour passed by, the sun beat down and the troops became restless. On the hour we switched on our radios, but the Buddhists were determined to prolong the suspense. It was four o'clock in the afternoon before the announcement came: a monk had died by fire, but 140 miles away in the highland town of Dalat. The Buddhists had carried out half their threat, and now the vigil was to begin all over again. Inside the pagoda we could see the monks praying; they too had heard the news. Troops were ordered to a renewed alert – and nothing happened.

There is no real explanation why I returned to the pagoda that night. Most of us had left the dreary scene two or three hours before to type our cables, reasonably sure that the military were in such control that we could expect no repeat of the battle to free the boxed-up Buddhists. I had showered and changed from the sweat-dampened garb of the long day. I could have relaxed, gone to a restaurant or bar and checked later on anything which may have happened in the meantime – if this had not been Saigon. Nowhere else have I been so conscious of that nervousness, that edgy uncertainty, and yet certainty, of impending action of some kind; and particularly that night. Automatically I turned the car into Le Loi and headed out past the roof-top-high mountains of uncollected rubbish which served as my landmarks for the quickest route to Vien Hoa Dao.

Even as I drove along the road beside the pagoda, I wondered why I had come, and at that hour. If it had been drab and uninteresting before I left at dusk, now and in the darkness the scene of the siege appeared unbelievably dull. The dim street lamps cast watery rays upon trucks where – those who were not still patrolling streets or manning barricades – soldiers dozed. The pagoda gates and their particular barricades stood in the deep shadows, unmanned and forgotten, and from the pagoda

15. Arthur Cook with British troops in Borneo

16. *Top:* Militant Buddhist leader Thich Tri Quang in Hue, 1966. *Bottom:* The Vice-President of South Vietnam, Nguyan Cao Ky, and his wife.
(Photos: U.P.I.)

itself no more than two tiny lights winked to remind one that any of the hundreds there might be awake, or even alive.

I might have turned and driven away immediately if I had not seen an American agency colleague and his photographer. For twenty minutes we talked and smoked, drank coffee at our café headquarters of the earlier hours, until we decided that in fifteen minutes it would be ten o'clock, and we would leave. Why ten o'clock, why any time at all, why did we stay another minute? Radios were crackling, telling troop commanders that Saigon was quiet and recalling half the troops back to barracks. I looked at my watch and it was three minutes to ten, but as I did so the photographer saw the movement of the pagoda gates as they opened slightly. Through them came the figure and moved around the barricades. Two soldiers walked from a truck, began to move across the road and we hurried after them – but none of us could have reached the figure in time. It knelt in the road, in that instant came the flicker and then the sheet of flame. In a split second of illumination I saw the long black hair reaching to the ground, but then all was lost in the inferno. The flames picked out the saffron robes of the monks and nuns kneeling in the pagoda compound and all at once I became aware of the people, dozens of them, who had left their houses already and were bent in prayer. The Buddhists had kept to their promise, two more had died and now the count was four – the flaming body before the barricades was that of a girl of seventeen. It was she who brought forth before morning the appeal from President Johnson in Washington: 'End these acts of desperation, these tragic suicides are an unnecessary loss of life.'

In all the troubles Saigon had seen since it first began to resemble an American provincial town, never before had there been cause to fear for the lives of the GIs themselves, except from the direct action of the Vietcong. On several occasions, and prudently, GIs had been told to stay clear of demonstration areas, but now the order went out from headquarters, 'Get off the streets'. For a day and a half there had been no more suicides, as a severely shaken Government called Buddhist leaders into negotiations with promises that civilians would join the administration immediately. And then, even as the talks

STORY UNUSED

were going on at the Presidential Palace, someone threw a grenande at a car carrying the Buddhist youth leader Thien Minh and sent him to hospital bleeding, unconscious and near to death. I heard the explosion, no more than a quarter of a mile from the hotel, and when I found the wrecked car Buddhist youths were draping it with a huge poster proclaiming, 'We accuse America of trying to murder Thien Minh.' Nowhere, except in Saigon, could this have happened so quickly, and nowhere else could word travel with such incredible speed.

I made straight for the Vien Hoa Dao pagoda, but the troops had been in action long before I arrived; hundreds of young Buddhists had been forced back behind the barricades in the streets around and an American jeep lay battered and on its side. The message from headquarters to get to a place of safety had not reached them and two GIs, badly bruised, with uniforms torn, stood surrounded by Government troops who had saved them from an uncomfortable end. Opposite, in the pagoda compound, young monks paraded with a coffin topped with a picture of Johnson – 'The assassin', they chanted, 'the bloodthirsty assassin'.

I cannot think it would have happened so quickly and suddenly if Tri Quang had been in Saigon and not cut off in Hue, but later that day a group of more moderate Buddhist leaders agreed to the compromise of a part-civilian government. Misguidedly, it appeared, they imagined it as the first step towards their original demand of a fully civilian administration –and they were now as frightened of the violence they had stirred up as they were of the expanding war which they believed a civilian government could end. In Hue, when the news reached there of the grenade attack on Thien Minh, orders came from Tri Quang which sent hundreds of Buddhist students, led by robed and girdled monks, racing through the streets to the American Consulate. They sacked it and burned it; they sacked and burned the adjoining Consul's house and they burned every picture they could find of President Johnson. No troops attempted to disturb them; they completely agreed with the Buddhist cause to put an end to bombing, death, dollars, black market and war profiteering. For a short while Hue was to remain as the last stronghold in the last bid for peace that

South Vietnam was to see, in whatever form it came. It had been a long war within a war, doomed from the start just as surely as Hue was doomed now.

That same night I was witness to the most bizarre scene I shall ever, I am sure, be able to record. Four thousand Buddhists stood in the Vien Hoa Dao pagoda compound to hear the decisions of the leaders; the gates had been opened to all for the first time in days and the high priest's amplified voice rose higher as the murmurings increased, telling us that not all agreed with the call for an end to active resistance. Suddenly they broke from the crowd and made for a corner of the compound, twenty monks and nuns, and the air was filled with hysterical screams as we saw them holding jerrycans high, frantically pouring petrol over themselves and over each other. Immediately, a fight started as other monks threw themselves on the would-be martyrs. Petrol flowed as they rolled on the ground and, miraculously, a nun was pounced upon as she tried to strike a match which would have sent all sixty or more of them to their fiery deaths. Above the din the high priest's frenzied voice called for calm, but this did not come until every one of the petrol-soaked twenty had been dragged away, sobbing or crying out in protest. They had been on the planned list for self-sacrifice and all of them had been due to die within the next few days. Now the holiest of holy acts had been denied them; it would never be known if the deaths of these few may have saved the lives of the many.

Four o'clock in the morning in the military departure hut at Tan Son Nhut airport, where the negro air force sergeant rudely interrupted one's bleary-eyed attempts to doze in an uncomfortable chair until the order came to get-the-hell-out-of-here to the next attempt at sleep in the more uncomfortable metal bucket-seat of the C123. Cowboy boots and cowboy hats, glistening, black bullet belts and gun holsters – all reluctantly on their way back to land-locked and Vietcong-surrounded island bases, leaving the fleshpots of Saigon behind. My plane was well off schedule that morning; ammunition was the priority for where I was hoping to go, and the extra that was being stowed aboard was playing havoc with the passenger list. Only three could travel out of the twenty listed and I hoped my USIS passes, giving me the priority of an officer, would receive their due recognition. Then we were away, climbing to the east and the coast into the rising sun. Once again I looked down on the breathtaking despoiled beauty through the wide-open loading doors. Now we were heading north; Nha Trang fell away behind and then Qui Nhon with all its memories. At Da Nang I could see the jets still and ceaselessly getting their bomb loads into the air. For another fifteen minutes we went north before putting down on the strip just south of Hue; the ground crew, in cowboy hats of their chosen red, were in action as the propellors were still windmilling, and off went the ammunition. What was this urgency for bullets and shells? Where was the battle – the only action I had heard of had come from the Buddhist students.

Until now the war had not touched Hue, or the villages and countryside for miles around. It was a beautiful, leisurely city, with its ornate pagodas rising among the brilliant red of the flame trees on both sides of the wide and exotically-named Perfumed River. On three sides of the gentle city of religious learning rose the thickly foliaged mountains and in them, somewhere, lived Vietcong. For years they had been there, but no one had bothered them and they had not bothered Hue. There was a strong suspicion that there had always been a tacit agreement between the Vietcong and the Buddhist stronghold, but never had a shot been heard. Perhaps they had found the perfect way of being at war but not being in it; certainly they did not want it and that was why everyone connected with Hue was refusing to fight now. 'A rebel city' it had been branded by the Saigon Government, but the people there were proud of the label if it meant that killing, maiming, burning and destruction did not come their way. Unfortunately, their rebellious attitude had clashed seriously with American plans and American decisions on who should be involved in the war and where; Hue and its surrounding countryside was definitely included and so was all that lay to its north. But Hue and its people were impeding the progress of the war, insisting on a continued peace; did they not realize that Vietnam was at war and Hue was part of Vietnam?

The extent of the American frustration I saw from the moment the jeep in which I was being lifted to the city turned on to the wide main road going north from the airstrip. For three miles huge American transports, tanks, gun carriers, troop carriers and all the movable implements of ground warfare were parked, nose to tail. GIs sat, lounged or stood around in their hundreds and this is how it had been – complete immobility, no possibility of turning back, and more continually adding to the useless column – since the morning before. At the head of the column trucks were parked at all angles where they had stopped after failing to negotiate the obstacles and get one more yard ahead. And the obstacles? As far as the eye could see along the middle of the perfectly straight road, and at regular intervals of ten yards, stood tiny Buddhist altars. Every house had one, if only a roughly made wooden table, a yard square or less, and from every house of every village between here and Hue, five miles away, the altars had come out at the word of the priests. Draped with colourful tassled cloths, each altar had its Buddha, whether in wood or metal or just a propped-up and framed picture; it had its candles and other tiny bits of mystic paraphernalia. To have touched one would have been sacreligious to an unthinkable degree, and the Buddhists had calculated correctly that the GIs would not dare; but, and just as an added precaution, a small boy or girl squatted beneath three or four out of every ten altars, and they were prepared to stay there in defiance of any tank. Our jeep was able to drive beside the altars but, as wide as the road was, it was utterly impassable for the military column. If the tanks and carriers had managed to reach Hue itself, they never could have passed through the city, for more altars stood in every street and the blockage was complete.

That first night I spent inside the compound which had been set up by military advisers, to advise whom I never really discovered. It was for my own safety, they insisted; the personnel from the Consulate were there and machine-gun posts were manned day and night. One wondered from whom any attack was expected; I found it all too much of a Hollywood melodrama, and by the morning I was prepared to take my chance in the dangerous outside world. Of all the places to discover in Hue, I found a bicycle hire establishment; I was mobile and moved over to the Sporting Club beside the river.

STORY UNUSED

The next few days were uncanny, to say the least, but they gave me time to see the museums, the intriguing libraries, the pagodas and the palaces which had once made Hue the religious capital of the whole of Vietnam. But hardly a soul did I meet in my wanderings; mine were the only footsteps which echoed hollowly through the great halls and corridors. The flower-lined avenues were deserted, and if troops were seen they were only singly or in pairs and carried no arms. Outwardly Hue was a city of ghosts, but behind its walls waited the living in their thousands, obeying the orders of Tri Quang. For what they waited they knew not, but it could not be long in coming; the tomb-like stillness could not continue. To the Sporting Club – where I lived in solitary state with a staff of one man and a boy – came an elderly French woman each day to swim from the pier below; she had lived in Hue all her life and was the only one of her countrymen or women to remain. On the fourth day she bade me farewell. 'I must try to leave,' she said. 'It is the end of Hue, the end of Vietnam – may God forgive them.'

From the moment the Saigon Buddhist leaders had agreed to compromise, Tri Quang had declared a hunger strike – 'until death or until the end of the Government and its American support'. A new and dangerous twist had come in the crisis which refused to end. Why he chose the hospital in which to fast I failed to see, for there were no doctors, drugs or, in fact, any other inhabitants, but that is where I found the rebel monk upon whom all attention was now focused. Cross legged, like Buddha himself, he sat on a bed in a single room; beside him on a chair sat his tiny but attractive, English-speaking nun 'secretary', and nearby were the radio and the telephone through which Tri Quang was still in constant touch with his faithful followers.

It was the fifth day of his fast and his broad face was becoming haggard; as far as he was concerned the official rumblings from Saigon were nothing if not sinister. Tri Quang had decided that his voice must be heard in the outside world for it may never be heard again. 'All we want is for the people of Vietnam to be left alone to work out their own destiny,' he said; 'but American actions and policy can only lead to a communist victory. They think only of the military aspects and their bombs kill too many civilians.' Buddhism had fared badly under the North Vietnamese administration and Tri Quang was not suggesting that it could co-exist with communism now. 'But we have not yet begun to fight the communists,' he said; 'we are still fighting our own people.'

It was a voice crying in the wilderness. Premier Ky was already moving his troops into position. 'We want peace most of all,' were Tri Quang's closing words to me. 'We don't want a Vietnam divided and destroyed, ravaged by war. We don't want foreign domination, whether it be communist or American.' Somewhere in Vietnam I had heard those words before.

Fourteen hours later and just before the first rays of sunshine were to bring back the vivid colour to Hue's flame trees, Government riot troops surrounded the hospital and carried Tri Quang away. Before his followers were aware that they no longer had a leader, the last voice of protest had been silenced and the monk was on board an American plane, bound for Saigon, forced feeding and house arrest. For the first time blood flowed in the city as students, monks and unarmed garrison troops were 'brought under control'. Systematically, Buddhist altars were moved from the roads and the American column passed through. The same evening I heard the heavy guns as they pounded the hills to the north and listened as the jet planes rained their bombs on what was to be virgin land no more.

Chapter 13

POLITICIANS, RIGHT AND LEFT

The Royal Air Force base at Labuan, just off the coast of North Borneo, was no more than fifteen minutes behind us when one of the Britannia's port engines stopped with a bang which shook the plane. In the cockpit the pilot hastily trimmed her to starboard, the dials of the three other engines were searchingly checked and the decision made to continue the flight. 'She's as safe as houses on three,' we were told.

That decision, on January 7, 1966, could have meant that Britain would never have had Edward Heath as its prime minister. For the plane was carrying him, Anthony Barber and Christopher Chattaway, half a dozen of Britain's best known diplomatic correspondents, two photographers and myself.

Half an hour later – and I almost crossed myself when I saw it was on the starboard wing – a second engine stopped. There was nothing between us and Singapore except 300 miles of the South China Sea.

With Labuan so close when the first engine failed nothing would have persuaded me to go on, but it was no business of mine and, no doubt, the pilot was bent on keeping to Heath's tight schedule. But now we were reduced in height and even more drastically reduced in speed; the Britannia would certainly fly on two motors but none of us were under the illusion that she would stay in the air on one.

For another hour and fifty minutes we sat in all the luxury of the V.I.P. chartered plane with hardly a word passing between us. I am sure some silent prayers were being offered up in the cockpit as well as among the passengers when the lights of Singapore came up on the horizon. And there were some very large sighs of relief as the wheels touched the airport runway. Appointments had been missed, but they were bothering nobody. We needed a stiff drink.

Edward Heath, as leader of the parliamentary opposition, was on a fact-finding tour of South-East Asia, his first visit to those parts. In Rawalpindi he had already had talks with the Pakistani President, Ayub Khan, who was to throw in the sponge long before Heath rose to high office. And he had called on India's Prime Minister, Shastri, who was to die deservedly a few days later at the end of peace talks with Ayub under the auspices of Russian Premier Kosygin at Tashkent.

Some sections of the British press were hopefully – but vainly – suggesting that Heath might be able to heal the breach between Singapore and Malaysia. But however much he may have wished to talk with Lee Kuan Yew and Tunku Abdul Rahman on Conservative policies regarding the defence and economic development of the region, it was to be a long time before Heath was in any position to implement them. Harold Wilson was about to outwit the Tories once again in an election and another four years were to pass before the British public finally tossed him aside.

Thinking back on the Edward Heath with whom I spent ten days or so in South-East Asia, I feel that he did not then have the stature, the knowledge, or the experience which were needed for a long tenure of Number 10 Downing Street. He needed time to overcome his natural shyness and apparent offhand manner. If mine had been a single meeting with him I could easily have been left with an impression which would automatically have pushed him into the ranks of political nonentities.

Before leaving London, Heath had asked if I could help with briefings on the varying aspects of a complicated area, and when I joined the entourage on its arrival in Singapore I soon realized that, unlike so many other politicians, he had not come out 'knowing' everything there was to know. Quite openly he said he had come to learn, that he knew nothing of South-East Asia. I remembered the heated parliamentary arguments over Singapore, Malaysia, Indonesia and Vietnam as Heath told me, 'There's hardly a soul at Westminster who knows a thing about this part of the world.' Not that this surprised me, for years I have writhed under the misinformed, uninformed and completely idiotic utterings of M.P.s and ministers alike. But here, at least, was a man honest enough to admit his shortcomings.

It was the intense shyness which could have misled me. Visits to the British troops defending Malaysia in Borneo were over and so were the talks with Lee Kuan Yew and the Tunku. Here we were in a Herald of the Malaysian air force – lent to us by the Tunku because Heath's replacement Britannia from England had gone out of action in Calcutta – winging our way towards Saigon from Kuala Lumpur. And Heath's request, as soon as we got airborne, was 'let's talk'.

Now he knew something about Malaysia and Singapore and, having interpreted some Labour government hints that Britain might pull out of the area after confrontation had ended, I believe I convinced Heath that, if ever he took the Tories into government, on no account should this be allowed to happen.

At that time, the one thing that worried me about Heath was that he found it difficult to look into one's eye when he was in conversation. Always it was a quick glance and then away – until he was more or less forced to look directly again.

From Malaysia, Singapore, British trade in the area, and her presence there, we switched to Vietnam, and then Heath said, 'Tell me the whole story; I know so little about it.' Did he want it really from the beginning, I asked, and Heath nodded. There was still an hour before we were due over Vietnam and a lot to tell. I began.

I had spoken for no more than thirty seconds when Edward Heath switched his gaze out through the plane window. Once or twice he glanced back as I continued talking, but within two minutes his head turned towards the window, never to return until I had stopped talking.

I certainly did not finish all I had to say; several times I had lectured on the subject and I could have talked until the flooded rice paddies of the Delta came into view. But what out-and-out rudeness! I began telling myself as I went on talking.

What a bloody rude man! Asks me to tell him about Vietnam and then cannot be bothered to listen!

I cannot imagine that the story of Vietnam has ever been told in so short a time, but I wrapped it up in fifteen minutes flat, inwardly fuming because not one sign came from Heath that he was hearing a word. I stopped. He continued to look out of the window for another full twenty seconds and then he turned to me. 'Fantastic,' he said. 'Amazing story with amazing detail.'

Edward Heath then asked me to expand on one aspect of the Vietnamese situation after another. He had listened to every word, every point – and absorbed each of one them.

If he had ever gone to Vietnam as Prime Minister, to enquire personally into the American involvement to which he gave such unfailing and blind support, Harold Wilson would, no doubt, have expected to meet the American C-in-C, General Westmoreland. But as nothing more than the leader of Her Majesty's parliamentary opposition, Heath had not expected such a meeting, and in fact the British Embassy in Saigon had not considered it as a possibility in the meagre programme they had planned.

So it came as more than a surprise to Heath, Barber and Chattaway to find that practically the first person to whom they were being introduced at Tan Son Nhut airport was the America C-in-C himself. The reception, so far as the British Embassy was concerned, was abysmal; not one of its officers was at the airport. True, our arrival was earlier than scheduled, but the British High Commission in Kuala Lumpur had sent a signal. Moreover, it was a Sunday morning.

It was left to me to arrange that our party should wait in the V.I.P. lounge. Not that it offered us any special comfort that particular morning, thirty or forty American officers had formed a farewell party for the departing defence secretary, McNamara; that harbinger of glad tidings was just taking off for Washington with another optimistic assessment, no doubt, of the situation for President Johnson.

At last someone from the Embassy appeared, a junior officer, the only one who could be raised by the telephone operator. His red face streaming with sweat, the appropriate apologies were attempted: the Ambassador himself was to have met Mr Heath but the message from Kuala Lumpur arrived too late. He collected our passports and disappeared to immigration.

It was as he went through the door that the unmistakable voice called, 'Hi, Art – where've you been all this time?' I turned as General Westmoreland walked towards me with his hand outstretched. It had been over six months since we had last met, since we had our weekly natter on the situation over drinks at the General's house. Westy had not been the only one to notice my complete disappearance, and I mumbled something about other things happening in my parish as Westy continued, 'Big things have been happening; I expected you, of all people, to be here.'

I had talked to Heath about him on the plane: no particular strategist, I had said, a tough paratroop commander who knew little more than the 'blast-them-with-everything' tactics. A good soldier in the American concept, at the same time humble, despite his rank; as a person, most likeable and, above all, obedient to his Pentagon masters. I had told Heath of the way in which the Vietnamese war was being run entirely from Washington and I had never wished for better confirmation. It had come from Westy himself on more than one occasion as he complained over a drink that he had been up for most of the previous night on the telephone to Washington.

One of the set pieces presented to every visiting US Senator, every visiting journalist or V.I.P. imagining he was being shown the real results of American intervention, was a 'peace' hamlet, twelve miles or so outside Saigon and off the road to the American air base of Bien Hoa. I had been dragged around it two or three times before and knew the routine: a briefing by South Vietnamese army officers and the uncovering of well-prepared maps showing the vast plan of pacified hamlets of which, it was suggested, this one was typical. Then came the tour of the hamlet, the village elders lined up to welcome the vistors and a row of young women, all of unmistakeable Vietnamese beauty, standing in front of a row of men – the village counsellors and teachers. All would be smiles and deep, oriental bows and the unfortunate vistor would be forced to tramp from this to that in the heat of morning until he was near to collapse and unlikely to ask to see more of the wonders which had been bestowed upon South Vietnam.

This was to be the main item on the itinerary of the second day of Heath's visit, with a possible meeting with Vietnamese 'politicians' to complete it. His first day had been little more than dinner with the British Ambassador, and I could see that he would learn little or nothing, while the only profit he could expect might be image-improving pictures published back in Britain of himself with beautiful Vietnamese women.

On the way out to the pacified hamlet I suggested to Heath that he should study the countryside around, and thus it was that he saw the South Vietnamese troops in camouflage uniform, hundreds of them, dotted everywhere to ensure that this was a peaceful day. At the briefing I mentioned that Heath might wish to see some of the other 'peace' hamlets we were told existed in abundance. His request was met with polite smiles and excuses that it was too difficult to reach them; Heath was hustled out of the briefing room. Nobody was going to allow him to interfere with a well-rehearsed routine.

But now the photographers were about to have their great moment of the tour. The Vietnamese women were lined up and Heath was to be led slowly past them and other members of the reception committee. It all seemed to be going well; Edward Heath dutifully paused and exchanged smiles and handshakes with the dignitaries. The photographers went on ahead and focused their cameras. Talking and smiling with the oriental beauties would make first class picture coverage.

Edward Heath was no more than two yards from the first of the women in line. At that moment he looked straight ahead and hurried past the women as though they had not been there. Even Tony Barber and Chris Chattaway made noises of dismay, but the opportunity had gone. They knew more of their chief's shyness than any of us present that day. But at least they had hoped, as we did, too. However, more important things had to be thought of and I told Heath flatly that he was merely being shown what America wished him to see and would know precious little of the real situation on his departure. Two days were not enough for a visit to Vietnam, I told him; at least four were needed even to scratch at the surface. He should request the British Ambassador to organize an extensive air trip around the country in the Air Attaché's plane. He should insist that the Military Attaché Colonel Charles Napier, accompany him and explain in detail what was happening in Vietnam.

And that is exactly what Heath did, without a trace of shyness. A surprised Ambassador learned that he had a house guest for four days instead of two and ordered the Air Attaché to jump into action.

It was not all that straightforward, however. That evening the Air Attaché arrived at the Ambassador's house, where we had gathered for cocktails, with his great flight plan for the morrow. Heath looked at it and to everyone's surprise said, 'I must ask Arthur what he thinks of this.' The next few moments were something more than tense and something short of explosion. I studied the flight plan before me; a trip north and lunch at an American base, from there another trip westwards to another base, and then return to Saigon well in time for early evening drinks.

If one liked flying, and especially in the Embassy's small Dove, I suppose it could have been a nice day out; but it would show nothing more than the might of arms at American bases, while briefings would be merely official. Heath was beside me as I observed: 'I would think that Mr Heath would rather see the effects of the war: the Delta area, for example, where it is almost entirely controlled by the Vietcong. Or perhaps Qui Nhon, where there are tens of thousands of refugees from American bombing.'

The air was electric. But Heath's voice came first. 'I rely on Arthur's judgment and those are the things I wish to see,' he said. And he did. Later he announced that the situation in Vietnam was more serious than he had ever realized.

From then on I was not numbered among the friends of certain officials. One of them said to me afterwards, 'If that's the leader of the Conservative party, I'll never vote for them *again*. And that goes for the whole Embassy. Bloody rude man. I spend the whole day trying to make sure he knows the truth of what goes on out here and he doesn't want to listen. Look's right past you, he does, and he does it with everyone.'

He could not understand why I grinned so broadly, until I

recounted my experience of the flight from Kuala Lumpur. 'Hope you're right,' he said at last. 'Must say I wondered why the Tories had picked someone like that.'

Thus the facts became known throughout the British gatherings in South-East Asia. 'Heath? Met him once – not a bad fellow, but very shy.'

What a totally different person was Denis Healey, Defence Secretary in Wilson's government. Like so many of his colleagues he was cocksure, often intentionally rude and, when he got the go-ahead, sailed ruthlessly into the task of abandoning all British commitments east of Suez.

Apart from Wilson himself, I doubt if any British minister has been so loathed over so wide an area. Leaders of British trade in the Far East, which more than paid for the cost of our Singapore and Malaysian bases, rapidly saw contracts slipping away from them to the Japanese, the Germans, the French and anyone else who cared to push their way in. It is not that I feel the British should have had no competition in those areas which, for so long, they had considered their own. It was the calamitous effect the announcement of the withdrawals had; overnight Britain became regarded as a third-rate nation and other countries lost no time in pointing this out. Why, it was asked, should British traders be given any type of priority when Britain was scuttling and foresaking her friends?

Naturally, as their minister, the top brass of the services showed complete respect to Healey, but several are those who, in confidence, termed him 'the wrecker' or other less complimentary things. Ministers and many other politicians in the areas which were to be affected by the British pull out acquired a distinct distaste for a man who so brashly pushed their arguments aside. And not least of them was Lee Kuan Yew of Singapore, a good socialist who regarded most of the British cabinet as personal friends and then realized that his 'friends' were badly, and perhaps dangerously, letting him down.

Healey had dropped the final bomb on Tunku Abdul Rahman in Kuala Lumpur and then flown to Singapore to deal similarly with Lee Kuan Yew. He was attacked by both for the anxiety caused locally and internationally by Britain's decision to pull out of the area but, in the true Healey style, all protests were brushed aside. Then Healey called a press conference to announce to the world how thoroughly he was doing the job.

The conference room at the C-in-C's headquarters at Phoenix Park in Singapore was packed on the afternoon of April 27th. Local press, world agencies, a few special correspondents and cameramen were all there in good time and the top brass had assembled and were in their seats. Admiral Sir Desmond Dryer, who had been Naval Commander in Singapore, had come out from London with Healey and we exchanged greetings; Air Marshal Sir John Grandy, C-in-C of the Far East Command, with whom I had dined only a couple of nights earlier, nodded across to me; Admiral Frank Twiss, Naval Commander at the time and one of the most natural and friendly of men, gave me a slight wave; and General Sir Michael Carver, the Army Commander, who sometimes water ski-ed with me, gave me a cheerful wink.

Florid and sweating profusely, the Defence Secretary arrived and promptly announced that the British forces would be cut by a further 10,000 in the following year. Reuters had an extremely keen and new man to the area and he opened the questioning: 'Could the Minister please give the reaction of the Prime Ministers of Malaysia and Singapore to the announcement?'

I have seldom seen anyone at a press conference bristle quite so much, but it was completely visible as Healey swung round on the questioner, his eyes glaring. 'Both governments fully realize Britain's financial reasons for doing this,' he rapped out.

'Will they be given any compensation by Britain for any possible effect on their economies?' was the next and quite legitimate question from the Reuter man.

Healey was looking daggers. 'Yes, I have promised them very large sums,' he snapped, and his face was definitely more florid.

The Reuter man persisted. 'How much?' he asked and seemed taken aback by the ferocity of the reply.

Healey was rattled. 'It is not for me to work out how this will be done,' he said, and his voice was slightly raised. 'That is for other members of the cabinet to arrange.'

It had never been my policy to raise salient questions at

press conferences for all and sundry to benefit from the answers. I preferred to see the Minister afterwards and ask the questions I regarded as most important. But the Reuter man was doing splendidly and, from the scribbling going on all around, everyone was enjoying his efforts.

'But doesn't your figure of 10,000 include local workers in the bases who will be sacked?' came the Reuter man's simple question.

Denis Healey was half out of his chair, his face puce, and he pointed a finger at the Reuter man. He was livid. 'I know you, Mr Cook,' he said, 'I know you very well. I know what you are trying to do and I refuse to answer any more of your questions.'

The Reuter man's mouth dropped open for a moment, but no sound came. I saw him scratch the back of his head as, with everyone else in the conference room, his head turned towards me. Mike Carver winked across and chuckled silently; John Grandy sat bolt upright, lips tightly pressed together to stifle a laugh as he caught my eye; Frank Twiss raised his eyebrows high and his face beamed across the room to where I was sitting – and Desmond Dryer hid most of his face with a large hand as he gave me the slightest of nods.

There came a few more questions and it seemed that the conference was breaking up as I rose from my seat. 'Excuse me, Mr Minister,' I said, 'my name is Cook. Could you please inform the press the time of your departure tonight for London?'

Complete confusion covered Healey's face and its colour went even deeper as he struggled for the words. 'Of course, Mr Cook,' he answered eventually, 'of course, we know each other so well. How could I have made such a stupid mistake?'

That was the end of the conference. Healey rose to leave, but not before he had had a few quiet words with Air Marshal Grandy beside him. There were still many amused grins as John said to me, 'The Minister asks if you would care to have a drink with him in my house in about half an hour.'

The explanation was simple. Flying down from Kuala Lumpur Denis Healey had asked 'Who's in Singapore from the London press, who should I beware of?' And got the reply 'There's only one man there at the moment who might give you some very awkward questioning. That's Arthur Cook.'

He had been given my description: tallish, dark and clean-shaven. Unfortunately that loose description fitted the Reuter man just as well as it fitted me.

Over drinks there were more apologies, especially as we had met on so many previous occasions. I could not remember a single earlier meeting, but did not bother to mention this fact. I led into the conversation with a question on the great compensation Britain would be paying Malta for discarding it as a base. 'Wouldn't it have been cheaper, after all, to hold on to it as a base?' I asked Denis Healey.

'As it's working out, that's perfectly right,' he replied, 'it would.'

'So if we have to pay out on the same scale here the same will apply,' I suggested, 'in the long run it would be cheaper to stay?'

'That's the situation,' said Healey, 'but we are committed to it now.'

'So surely,' I went on, 'the only certain way of cutting down on the expense of the British forces is to cut the overall strength and numbers of those forces.'

'Exactly,' said Denis Healey, 'and that's precisely what we intend to do. Have another drink.' Later that evening, as Healey winged his way back towards London, I wrote my article. I presented it as 'well informed' but, being as fair as possible to Denis Healey, I did not quote him in any way.

FORCES TO BE AXED? ran the headline in Britain the following morning and a streamer declared: 'Healey flies home with new plan to cut defence bill.' The article continued:

> 'The Defence Secretary flew home tonight convinced that the only way to cut defence expenditure is to make drastic cuts in all three services.
>
> 'He has been completely disillusioned by his six-day visit to Singapore and Malaysia, where he has discussed possible troop reductions with both governments.
>
> 'Mr Healey has come to realize that cuts in the number of troops in the Far East will save Britain almost nothing financially, etc., etc. . . .'

Naturally, it caused a storm in Britain: on the morning of April 28th, 1967, a horde of reporters, clutching my article, surrounded Healey as he landed at London Airport. 'Is this true?' they demanded. 'Is it the intention of the British Government to reduce the size of the forces?'

Healey read my article and spoke into the microphone as the reporters busily made their notes; 'This article is entirely untrue,' he said. 'I absolutely deny that the British Government has any intention of cutting the size of the British forces.'

Politicians are not the only ones who feel certain that it is their prerogative to make a statement one moment and deny it the next. The journalist can always be blamed for 'misreporting' or, as I have discovered, 'inventing'.

It was only a few months later that Denis Healey stood in the House of Commons, London, and announced the cuts in the British forces which had been decided by the government.

Epilogue

Home is where one makes it, and for a foreign correspondent possessions are divided between those which can easily be transported and those which can be disposed of at a moment's notice. There is little room for sentimentality, and when the instructions come to move on they are accepted with the same equanimity as a cabled request to interview the King of Nepal.

In 1967 the decision to close the Far East bureau was not unexpected. The newspaper was switching from a failed attempt to become a 'heavy' and was now trying to be accepted as a 'popular', with the accent on the pop. The editor had been changed, but that was no surprise; it happened with monotonous regularity. And nobody had to explain the finances. For the first time in my career I had become a boxing reporter at a world flyweight championship fight in Bangkok, because it was cheaper than sending the boxing expert from London.

Perhaps, so far as I was concerned, the change was timely; too long in tropical climes without sufficient break had left its marks and for some time the medicos had been advocating a rest and a change.

The car was sold and so were many other things which had been acquired over three and a half years, but had now served their purpose. The orchids passed to friends and there came the tearful farewell to Ah Keow, her sons, her daughter, her cousins and her aunts. In the cocktail lounge of the ship foregathered my closer friends – Chinese, Indians, Malays, British, a Vietnamese, Italians, Dutch and American – and to me there was no difference in the shade or colour or cut of their features. They were all the same and each with an equal claim to live on this earth, and I was one of them, no better, no worse.

In Jakarta, when the ship stopped there, friends came aboard for lunch – one Dutch, one Indonesian and two Argentine-born British. In Bombay my Parsee friends awaited me, and I dined ashore with Pakistanis in Karachi. At Djibouti I drank with my French friend and his Somali assistant, and then the ship was headed north and up the Red Sea, to Suez, the Mediterranean and Europe.

We were four hours at sea when the news came. It was June and my Arab friends were at war with my Israeli friends. The ship turned and headed for the east coast of Africa and the Cape. I was incarcerated, with no hope of leaving the ship before Mombasa, and by then it was too late.

As much as I hated war I wanted to be there. But that was one war I was to miss.

INDEX

Abdul Latiff, Dato Jamal bin, 247
Abhay, General Kouprasith, 125, 132
Ah Keow, 213, 239, 249, 308
Ah-Li, 85
Air America, 130–6, 140, 144–5
Ali, Pakistani taxi driver, 31, 32, 37, 41, 45–6, 49
All India Radio, propaganda of, 44
America, advisory capacity of in Saigon, 64–7; unofficial military rôle of in Vietnam, 68–75; misjudgment of situation in Vietnam, 66–7, 76, 164, 176–7; troops of in Vietnam, 84–5, 158–9, 190–208; inaccurate casualty reports of Vietnam war, 168–9, 182–3, 200, 206; aids Indonesia, 98, 99; fears China, 122–3; backs wrong army in Laos, 124–5, 128; troops of in Hong Kong, 275–6
American Aid programme, 178–9
American B52s, 207
American Boeing 720 airtankers, 284
American C123s, use of as 'flareships', 188–90, 291–2
American Marines, 159, 166–7, 207
American Military Assistance Command, MACVI, 159
American Sabre jets, use of in Indo-Pakistan war, 37, 49, 50; use of in Laos, 128
American Skyraiders, 74–5; use of in Vietnam war, 163, 181, 187, 189

American T–28 bombers, use of in Laos, 128, 138–9, 142
American Thirteenth Air Force Thunderchief and Phantom jets, 284
American tourists, 150–1
Ayub Khan, 26, 61, 297

Bacon, Squadron Leader Max, 211, 212
Bali, massacre in, 263–6; art in, 266–7; Monkey Dance, 267–8
Bandaranaike, Mrs Sirimavo, tyrannical rule of, 227–32; defeat of, 232; return to power, 234
Bangkok, Cook's stringer in, 134; contrasts in, 148–50; Americanization of, 151; peace talks in, 152–7
Barber, Anthony, 296, 299, 301
Batapur, battle at, 45–9
Beirut, Cook's base at, 58; he moves from, 78, 79, 82–3, 85, 88; he visits, 248–9
Bhutto, Zulfiquar Ali, 54
Bien Hoa, Canberras destroyed at, 201–2
Bottomley, Jim, 120
Bringle, Rear Admiral William Floyd, 180, 181
Britain, defends Malaya, 89, 209–24, 298; troops from in Laos, 129; supports American intervention in Vietnam, 164
British Canberra jet bombers, 197–202, 209

311

STORY UNUSED

British Hunter jets, 37, 38, 209, 210, 211, 212, 217
British Javelin jets, 209
British Marines, 209
Brown, Thomas, 281–2
Brunei, Sultan of, 59, 61
Buddhists, Diem's persecution of, 65, 75; opposition of to Diem, 76–82; demonstrations and suicides of, 78–81, 285–95
Bulwark, 214
Butler, 'Rab', 93, 121
Byrne, Corporal Archie, 219–21

Caravelle bar, 195
Carver, General Sir Michael, 304, 305
Catholic minority in Vietnam, 158
Central Treaty Organization, 54. See also SEATO
Ceylon, 225–38; miniskirts in, 225–6; oil company nationalization in, 227; neglect of agriculture in, 229; agricultural revival in, 233
Chabot, Captain, 199–200
Chattaway, Christopher, 296, 299, 301
China, attacks India, 29; friendship with Pakistan, 54–5; American fear of, 122; opposes American intervention in Laos, 128, 129; Chinese in Saigon, 193–4; Chinese in Singapore, 240–2; trades with Ceylon, 227; Chinese infiltrate into Hong Kong, 279; charters British ships, 280–2; Chinese superior to Malays, 59–60, 116
Cholon, 193–4
CIA, powers of in Vietnam, 65, 66, 75; disgrace of, 82; branch of in Laos, 130
Colombo, harbour at, 227; poverty in, 232; Savundra's home in, 235–6

Cook, Arthur, early life, 56–8; as Spitfire pilot, 18, 46, 49, 57–8; reaction to anti-cholera injection, 11–19; as correspondent in Pakistan, 21–55; in Singapore, 82, 83; as correspondent in Vietnam, 63–82, 158–208, 285–95; in Tokyo, 92–106; meets Sukarno, 97–9; meets Robert Kennedy, 105–6; in Manila, 106-14; in Kuala Lumpur, 115–20; in Vientiane, 125–34, 144–7; visits refugee camp and Kong Le, 134–44; at Bangkok peace talks, 152–7; at Da Nang, 167–9; at Qui Nhon, 169–74; joins river assault group, 185–8; on flareship, 188–9; in Canberra jet, 197–200; joins advance to Le Thanh, 204–5; joins British reprisals on Indonesians, 210–12; in Borneo jungle, 214–23; in Ceylon, 225–38; interviews Mrs Bandaranaike, 229–31; interviews Emil Savundra, 236; repercussions of interview, 237–8; attacked by Tunku Abdul Rahman, 242–3; visits Pontianak, 255–60; visits Bali, 264–8; interviews Sari Dewi, 271–4; joins Heath's entourage on SE Asia visit, 297–303; at Healey's press conference, 304–7; in Hong Kong, 275–82
Coomeraswamy, Punch, 83, 85
Co, Nguyen, 169–74
Cook, Anna, 207, 233, 239, 247
Cook, June, 20, 83, 85, 114–15, 207, 222, 239, 247, 249

Dalat, supplies from, 183–4
Da Nang, 180, 191, 207, 292; invasion film made in, 166–7; bridgehead, 167–8; revolt in, 285
da Silva, Jack, 153–6
Denpasar, 267, 268
Denson, John, 129

INDEX

De Puy, Lieutenant-General, 183
Dewi, Sari, Cook interviews, 271–4
Diem, President Ngo Dinh, private army of, 65–77, 78, 80–1; America supports, 66, 67, 75; overthrow of, 82, 83–4, 176
Dien Bien Phu, 67
Dong Hoi, 181
Dong Xoai, massacre at, 206
Donley, Bill, 216–22
Douglas-Home, Sir Alec, joins 'peace mission' talks, 93, 106
Dring, Simon, 126–7, 132, 133, 134, 144
Dryer, Admiral Sir Desmond, 304

Eagle, 214
Eden, Anthony, 67
Enterprise, 276
Erawan Hotel, 153–6
Eugster, Lieutenant Tim, 215–22

Far East bureau, creation of, 78; closed, 308
Ferguson, Flight Lieutenant 'Black', 211–12, 217
Fernando, Shelton, 228–9, 232, 234
Flashmans Hotel, 17–19, 27–32, 41–3, 50, 55
'Flying Bananas', unsuitable rôle of, 68–74
Foster Dulles, John, 66

Gall Face Hotel, 234–5
Geneva, agreement at on partition of Vietnam, 67, 176; 1962 conference at assures neutrality of Laos, 123, 128
Gilchrist, Sir Andrew, 62
Gopallawa, William, Governor General of Ceylon, 232
Grand Hotel, Vientiane, 126–7
Grandy, Air Marshal Sir John, 304, 305
Gurkhas, 209, 215

Haiphong, port of, 181
Hamilton, Major Gerald, 197–201
Hanoi, 164, 179
Harkins, General Paul D., 159
Harradine, Colonel, Director of Public Relations in Singapore, 89–92
Harris, Frank, 216–22
Harsono, Ganis, 94–7, 98, 99, 100
Healey, Dennis, proposes cuts in East of Suez commitments, 303–7
'Hearts and Minds', operation, 179. *See also* American Aid programme
Heath, Edward, tours South East Asia, 297–303; Cook interviews, 298–9; visits Vietnam, 300–3
Highway Four, 175, 184
Highway Nineteen, 172
Highway One, 169, 173
Highway Twenty, 183–4
Ho Chi Min, 164, 283
Hoffman, Leslie, 243
Holt, Estelle, 126–7, 146–7
Holt, Paul, 146–7
Hong Kong, 92; prosperity in, 275–82; Press Club, 277; British Week in, 278; Communist infiltration into, 279—80
Hotel Indonesia, Jakarta, 252
Hue, Buddhist revolt in, 285, 290–1; American occupation of, 292–5

Iban, one of, 218–21
India, war with Pakistan, 20–55, 248. *See also* New Delhi
Indian Centurion tanks, 52, 53, 54
Indonesia, 61–3, 119, 157; American Aid to, 98, 99; fight with Malaysia, 11, 209–24; decline of, 252–3; anti-Communist massacre in, 261–3; peace treaty with Malaysia, 270. *See also* Sukarno
Indonesian Borneo, Cook visits, 254–60
Indo-Pakistan borders, 247
Irish guards, platoon of, 214–23, 257

313

Jakarta, 62, 89, 93, 99, 100, 121, 254; battles in, 249–50; students riot in, 251–2; contrasts in, 252–3; press cables from, 260–1
Java, Communism in, 93
Johnson, President Lyndon B., 84, 299; interferes in Malaysian dispute, 92–3; sends 'peace mission', 93–4, 100; and Vietnam war, 163, 202; Buddhist plea to, 287
Johore, Indonesians attack, 211
Josey, Alex, 241

Kalimantan, garrison town at, 255, 256
Karachi, 21–2, 23–5, 43, 61
Kashmir, 247; clash over, 20, 32
Kennedy, John F., 75, 176; assassination of, 84, 92, 105–6
Kennedy, Robert, United States Attorney General, sent on 'peace mission' talks, 93–4, 98, 103, 104, 105–6, 113; in Manila, 114–15; in Kuala Lumpur, 119–20; in London, 121; quoted at Bangkok, 155–6
Khan, General, 159, 160, 163
Khoman Thanat, 154, 284
Kong Le, General of Laotian Neutralist Army, 124, 128, 134; headquarters at San Tong, 140–4
Kontum, 202, 206
Kosygin, Premier of Russia, 297
Kuala Lumpur, 115–20, 241, 242, 243, 246, 299, 300; airport at, 61; headquarters of Malaysian Security Forces, 89, 90; contrast in between Malays and Chinese, 115–16
Kuching, British headquarters at, 90, 214
Ky, General Nguyen Cao, 163, 295

Labuan, Royal Air Force base at, 296
Lahore, 32, 44, 45

Lanphouthacoul, General Siho, 125, 132
Laos, 123–47; Geneva agreement on, 123, 124. *See also* Vientiane, Pathet Lao, Kong Le
Lawrence, Tony, 154–6
Lee Kuan Yew, 59, 60, 85, 87, 297; joins Malaysian Federation, 60, 62; tension between Lee Kuan Yew and Tunku Abdul Rahman, 240–3; leaves Malaysian Federation, 243–6
Le Loi, 66, 77, 190
Le Thanh, Vietcong seize, 203–5
Lightbody, Jimmy, 216–22
Lodge, Henry Cabot, 160
Long An province, Veitcong administration of, 175–6, 177, 178
Lopez, Salvador, Cook interviews, 111–14
Los Angeles Times, 25

Macapagal, President of the Philippines, joins 'peace mission' talks, 93, 106; supports Indonesia, 111
Malaya, 59, 119; joins Malaysian Federation, 59, 119
Malays, laziness of, 115, 116
Malaysia, fight with Indonesia, 111, 209–24; British troops in, 156, 157, 209–24, 253; peace treaty with Indonesia, 270; possible troop reductions in, 303–7; elected monarchs in, 117–18; press attacks Lee and Cook, 242–3; Heath's knowledge of, 298
Malaysian Federation, creation of, 59–63, 82, 85; British commitments in, 89–92, 105; rift between Singapore and Malaya, 240
Malaysian Security Forces, 89–92
Malfilindo, Sukarno's concept of, 62, 119
Malik, Adam, foreign minister of Indonesia, 269–70

INDEX

Mandarin Hotel, Hong Kong, 276-7, 281
Manila, lawlessness of, 106-11; American tourists in, 109-10
Manila Times, The, 110
Mao Tse Tung, 276, 283
Margano, Captain, 257-9
Martin, John, 195-6
Maxwell Taylor, General, military ambassador to Vietnam, 160, 162, 165
Mekong river, 145, 185-8
Midway, United States aircraft carrier, 179-81
Minh, General Duong Van, 84
Moechsin, Lieutenant, 256, 257
Moore, General Joseph, 202
Morley, John, 165-6
Morrogh-Bernard, Major John, 217
Morris, Joe Alex, 25, 42-3
Musa, General Mohammed, 32
Muong Kheung, 142-3
McArthur, Tommy, 57

Napier, Sir Charles, views of on Vietnam war, 165, 183
Nasution, General, 250
Nehru, J., 61; death of, 145
New China News Agency Offices, Jakarta, burning of, 251
New Delhi, propaganda of, 25, 28, 29, 30, 50; Nehru's funeral in, 145, 146. *See also* All India Radio
Nha Trang, 180, 292
Nhu, Madame, 66, 81, 227
Nhu, Ngo Dinh, 66, 75, 76, 83-4
North Borneo, 58, 59, 61, 105, 257, 298; defence of, 89, 105, 106, 209-24; British killed in, 90-2; Lopez' claims to, 113. *See also* Sabah and Sarawak
North Korea, 281
North Vietnam, 158, 166, 283; American bombing raids on, 163-4, 179-81, 284; joins war, 203; British ships trading with, 280-2

Nosavan, General Phoumi, receives American aid, 124-5
O'Brien, Captain James, 180
O'Donaghue, Corporal Michael, 216-24
Oka, Balinese guide, 264-5

Pakistan, war with India, 20-55; financial crippling of, 54, 248
Pakistani Air Force Fighters, 49-50, 52
Pakistani Pattons, 53
Pan Malay Islamic Society, 213
papaya, 226
Pathans, 50-1
Pathet Lao, nature of movement, 124; advances southward, 125, 128, 131, 137; gains control of supply lines, 142; liquidates Kong Le's army, 141-4
Peking, policy of, 123, 125; Communism from infiltrates into Hong Kong, 279-80
Pentagon, The, policy in Vietnam, 76, 84, 163, 165, 180, 285; policy in Laos, 128
Philippines, The, 113, 119. *See also* Manila
Plain of Jars, Pathet Lao in, 128, 134, 138, 139
Pleiku, base at, 172, 205; Vietcong attack, 202-3
Polo Club, Singapore, 88; as source of information, 90-1
Pontianak, 255-60

Quang Ngai, 168, 169
Quat, Dr Phan Huy, President of South Vietnam, 164
Qui Nhon, 180, 292; Cook visits, 168-74; hospital in, 170; refugee camps in, 173-4, 179; American bombing raids on, 171-2, 302

Rawalpindi, 297; clinic at, 11-19, 248; Cook correspondent at, 25-32, 37, 50-1; bombing of, 41-3

315

Razak, Abdul, 241, 243, 246; in Bangkok peace talks, 153–7
refugee transit camp in Laotian mountains, Cook visits, 135–40; dumping of bombs on, 138–9
Restaurant Flottant, 195–7
rice ships from America, 184
river assault group, 184–8
Rozak, Lieutenant, 257–9
Russia, interest of in South East Asia, 122, 123, 177, 209; aids Indonesia, 255–6
Ryacudu, Brigadier General, 259–60

SEATO (South East Asia Treaty Organization), 151
Sabah, joins federation of Malaysia, 59, 62, 117, 119; Sukarno's ambitions for, 93
Saigon, French influence in, 63–4; American build up in, 64–7, 159; hamlets around, 75–6; Buddhist suicides in, 77–81, 285–91; student riots in, 160–2; evacuation of American families from, 163; American Marines in, 166; crisis in, 183–4; deterioration of, 190–7, 223; success of Chinese trade in, 193–4
'Saigon battledress', 194–5
Sandys, Duncan, initiates Malaysian Federation, 61, 62
Sarawak, 59, 62, 93; joins Malaysian Federation, 59, 62, 117, 119; Indonesian attacks upon, 259–60; Sukarno's plans for, 93
Sattahip, American airbase at, 283–4
Savundra, Emil, 235–8; Cook's interview with, 236; trial of, 238
Savundranayagam, Emil, see Savundra
Scots Guards, 214
scrip money, black market in, 192
Seaman, D., 31–2

Senanayake, Dudley, prime minister of Ceylon, 233
Shalabi, Ibrahim, 27, 28, 30
Sharkey, John, 79, 81
Shastri, B., 54, 297
Shienfoon, trades with North Vietnam, 281
Sialkot, Indian attack at, 44, 52, 53
Siam, Gulf of, 283
Sihanouk, Prince of Cambodia, 120, 130, 233
Singapore, 14–15, 209; Cook's home in, 20, 21, 55, 82, 83, 85, 114–15, 152, 223, 226, 239–40, 249, 276; character of, 58–9; prosperity of, 85–6; joins Malaysian Federation, 59–60, 117, 119; expulsion from Federation, 20, 243–6; tension with Malaya, 240–3; problem of Chinese in, 240–2; television in, 244–5; Communist infiltration into, 279; Heath's knowledge of, 298; Healey's press conference in, 304–7
Singapore Town Club, 86–7
Smith, Flight Lieutenant Dick, 210–12
Souphannouvong, Prince, leader of Pathet Lao, 124, 125
South Vietnam, 63–82, 123, 160–208; war in Delta area of, 67–74, 184–90, 302; collapse of communications in Delta, 175, 184; war weariness of, 158–9; America's mistaken rôle in, 177; Heath's interest in, 298–9, 300–3
South Vietnamese Rangers, 204–5
Souvanna Phouma, Prince, 124, 125, 131, 140
Stewart, Michael, 253–4
Straits Times, 242–3
Subandrio, foreign minister of Indonesia, 106, 111; at Bangkok 'peace talks', 154–7; arrest of, 251
Suez invasion, 1956, 67
Suharto, General, 270

INDEX

Sukarno, President of Indonesia, ambitions of, 61-2; 'confrontation' with Malaysia, 62, 91, 114, 120, 121, 154-7, 209-24, 253; routs Kennedy, 106, 121; organizes guerilla raids into North Borneo, 214; fear of, 111, 113; his women, 94, 99, 271-4; Cook interviews, 97-9, 103, 270; delayed overthrow of, 249-51, 270, 274
Sumatra, 262, 263
Surabaya, 262, 263

Tanglin Club, Singapore, 87-8
Tan Son Nhut airport, 63, 67, 79, 83, 180, 188, 191, 200, 285, 291, 299
Temple Trees, Colombo, 232
Tengah air base, 210-12
Thailand, 123; American bases in, 151, 283-4
Thai Phung, 191
'The Pentagon', Borneo, 215-23, 257
Thien Minh, grenade attack on, 290
Thieu, General, 163
Thieves Market, 194, 204
Thompson, Bob, 164-5
Thorneycroft, Peter, British Defence Minister, 91
Tokyo, 92-107; 'peace mission' talks at, 93; Press Club, 101-3; British Embassy in, 103-4
Tonkin, Gulf of, 158, 179-81
Tran Van Huong, General, 160, 161
Tri Quang, Buddhist leader, 286; strives for peace, 287, 290, 294-5
Tu Do, 63-4, 77, 190, 194, 196
Tunku Abdul Rahman, prime minister of Malaya, 59, 89-90, 209, 213, 246, 247, 297; joins Federation of Malaysia, 61, 62; initiates idea of Federation, 118-19; joins 'peace mission' talks, 93, 106, 113, 120; strained relationship with Lee Kuan Yew, 240-3; attacks Cook, 242-3; hatred of Chinese, 246

Twenty Squadron, Cook joins, 210-13
Twiss, Admiral Frank, 304, 305

Unger, Leonard, 131
United Malay National Organization, Youth Association of, 241
United States Information Services, 65, 67, 76, 159, 163, 188, 192
Untung, Lieutenant-Colonel, 249
USIS, *see* United States Information Services
Utapo, American harbour at, 283
U Thant, 52, 287
Utusan Melayu, 242

Vam Co Dong river, 189
Vatthana, King Savang, 125
Victoria, 214
Vien Hoa Dao pagoda, Saigon, Buddhist demonstrations in, 286-91
Vientiane, neutralist government in, 124; coup d'état in, 125; dirtiness of, 126-8; British, Russian and French embassies in, 129; North Vietnamese diplomatic mission in, 129; American embassy in, 130; uncaring attitude of generals in, 137; Cook returns to, 144-7
Vietcong, 64, 75; in Delta area, 69-73; growing strength of, 76, 84, 187-8; terrorism of, 159; use of guerila warfare, 167, 168; administration of Long An province, 175-6, 177, 178; estimated casualties of, 182-3; collect American dollars, 190-2; tax paid to, 193; sabotage Restaurant Flottant, 195-7; sabotage Canberras, 201-2; seize Le Thanh, 203-5
Vinh, North Vietnam, 181

Wakasa Bay, 280-2
war films, 38-41

317

Westmoreland, General, 299, 300
Whickham, Air Marshal Peter, 210
Wilson, Harold, 165, 297; supports America, 164; offers aid to Indonesia, 253–4
Wise, Don, 162, 196
Wong, Suzie, 275

GEORGE ALLEN & UNWIN LTD

Head Office:
40 Museum Street, London, W.C.1
Telephone: 01-405 8577

Sales, Distribution and Accounts Departments
Park Lane, Hemel Hempstead, Herts.
Telephone: 0442 3244

Athens: 7 Stadiou Street, Athens 125
Auckland: P.O. Box 36013, Auckland 9
Barbados: Rockley New Road, St. Lawrence 4
Bombay: 103/5 Fort Street, Bombay 1
Calcutta: 285J Bepin Behari Ganguli Street, Calcutta 12
Dacca: Alico Building, 18 Motijheel, Dacca 2
Ibadan: P.O. Box 62
Johannesburg: P.O. Box 23134, Joubert Park
Karachi: Karachi Chambers, McLeod Road, Karachi 2
Lahore: 22 Falettis' Hotel, Egerton Road
Madras: 2/18 Mount Road, Madras 2
Manila: P.O. Box 157, Quezon City, D-502
Mexico: Serapio Rendon 125, Mexico 4, D.F.
Nairobi: P.O. Box 30583
New Delhi: 4/21-22B Asaf Ali Road, New Delhi 1
Ontario, 2330 Midland Avenue, Agincourt
Rio de Janeiro: Caixa Postal 2537-ZC-00
Singapore: 248C-6 Orchard Road, Singapore 9
Sydney, N.S.W. 2000: Bradbury House, 55 York Street
Tokyo: C.P.O. Box 1728, Tokyo 100-91